❧ OTHER BOOKS BY MIRIAM UNGERER ❧

GOOD CHEAP FOOD

COME INTO MY PARLOR

COUNTRY FOOD

SUMMERTIME FOOD

SUMMERTIME F·O·O·D

MIRIAM UNGERER

RANDOM HOUSE ⌂ NEW YORK

Some of these recipes were originally published in
The Too Hot to Cook Book, published in 1966 by Walker Books.

Grateful acknowledgment is made to the following for permission to reprint previously published material:

BALLANTINE BOOKS: A recipe entitled "Fried Spaghetti" from *Nika Hazelton's Pasta Cookbook* by Nika Hazelton. Copyright © 1984 by Nika Hazelton. Reprinted by permission of Ballantine Books, a division of Random House, Inc.

CASA EDITRICE NERI POZZA: A recipe entitled "Italian Hebrew Soup" from *Il Gastronomo Educato* by Alberto Denti di Pirajno.

THE CROWN PUBLISHING GROUP: A recipe entitled "Cheese Pudding" from *Jewish Cookery* by Leah Leonard. Copyright 1949 by Leah Leonard. Copyright renewed 1977 by Violet Kanfer. Used by permission of Crown Publishers, Inc.

CUISINARTS: A recipe entitled "Lemon Tea Cake" that first appeared in a Cuisinarts pamphlet. Reprinted with permission of Cuisinarts, Inc.

VIKING PENGUIN, INC.: A professional technique used for roasting chicken from *American Charcuterie* by Victoria Wise. Copyright © 1986 by Victoria Wise. All rights reserved. Reprinted by permission of Viking Penguin Inc.

Library of Congress Cataloging-in-Publication Data

Ungerer, Miriam.
Summertime food.
Includes index.
1. Cookery.   I. Title.
TX652.U536   1989
641.5′64—dc19
ISBN 0-394-57535-0   88-26516

Manufactured in the United States of America
98765432
First Edition

Book design and contemporary illustrations by Lilly Langotsky

ACKNOWLEDGMENTS

MY MOST GRATEFUL THANKS TO REBECCA SALETAN
FOR HER CAREFUL, METICULOUS EDITING
AND FOR SHEPHERDING THIS BOOK THROUGH.

CONTENTS

INTRODUCTION

This book is for people who delight in rediscovering the remembered fragrance of last summer's strawberries, the salty tang of freshly dug clams, or half a summer's flavors cooked in a ratatouille. Even though the canner and freezer have made asparagus in December and brussels sprouts in July utterly commonplace, they do not replace fresh vegetables ripened at leisure and served in their own time and place.

Some of us will spend the summer at the shore or in the mountains; others will brave the city heat for all but a few weeks. There are dishes here for those with the time and inclination to indulge their food fancies, and there are recipes for people who enjoy eating but don't really wish to make a big production out of it.

To me, summer cooking does not mean that everything should be in aspic or turned out of a can at a moment's notice. It does mean taking advantage of the particular gastronomic pleasures of the season. Fresh vegetables and fish are rarely better than when uncluttered by a lot of time-consuming side dishes. The French and

Italian custom of serving new asparagus or baby string beans as separate courses makes a little event out of food that we usually treat in a routine manner.

Actually, fresh garden peas and unfrozen spring chicken may be nearing extinction. In the knowledge that we are possibly the last generation to know the true taste of foods that have not been mechanically tampered with, we should revel while we can in the fleeting flavors of summer.

Quite a number of rather fancy-sounding dishes can be made very quickly. Sauce Parisienne for poached or baked fish is an elegant touch; it is the base for a number of other sauces, and takes only about 10 minutes to produce. Flambéed Steak au Poivre takes about the same amount of time. Even the celebrated bouillabaisse with its rather frightening number of ingredients is only a fish stew with a lot of lovely flavors boiled rapidly together for about 30 minutes. Advocates of advance cooking are really safer with winter stews and cassoulets. But the informality of summer entertaining and the gregarious aspect of the hibachi and outdoor grill make last-minute cooking less of a chore.

Summer is the time of the clambake and the picnic, as simple or elaborate as you choose. One stop at a good Italian food shop can provision you with a spicy hard salami, some salty, thin sheets of prosciutto, a loaf of good bread and, in a few places, freshly made mozzarella, white and dripping with whey. You need only a bottle of wine and wheels to find a special place to enjoy your outdoor feast. For others, there is nothing like a good exhausting afternoon spent digging a pit for a clambake, starting the long-smoldering fire, scrubbing the clams, soaking the corn, and organizing the ritual feast.

Delicate chilled soups and airy mousses are elegant summer specialties to tempt the most jaded palate. But that is seldom a problem during vacation days. There are rather the monstrous appetites whetted by clean, fresh country air, and the relaxation that affords time to dwell on the pleasures of summer and of summer eating. I hope this book will add to both.

SUMMERTIME FOOD

STOCKING A SUMMER CUPBOARD

This chapter primarily concerns seashore or country vacation houses, since elsewhere you can just dash right out and get what you need, or forget the whole business and go out for dinner. A sophisticated array of foods and condiments in the grocery stores does not happen to be one of the charms of most resort villages and towns, although in the past couple of decades things have certainly changed in many places. Once clerks looked askance at a request for whole peppercorns, and totally blank at an inquiry about saffron in the seashore where we summered, now there are few delicacies, imported or domestic, that can't be found in the plethora of new, chic shops on the once quiet, bucolic South Fork of Long Island where I now live. Good cooking doesn't require a lot of exotic ingredients, but it is nice to be able to extend a last-minute invitation to dinner and to produce something a little more than routine.

With a couple of cans of kidney beans, some good olive oil, garlic, onions, and lemons you can produce a main course salad for eight almost immediately. Canned chicken and beef stock simplify the preparation of summer soups and risottos. A variety of pastas—cavatelli, fusilli, farfalle, or green noodles—in addition to the usual spaghetti and linguini, are all delicious with simple, quickly made sauces of fresh herbs and tomatoes, or just butter and garlic with some freshly grated cheese from your stores of Parmesan or Romano.

These are some other useful things to stock the vacation house cupboard with:

whole peppercorns (black, white, and green)

saffron

fine quality curry powder

cumin (ground)

cardamom (whole or ground)

olive oil, both light and fruity

peanut oil for deep-frying

canned tuna fish, anchovies, white kidney beans, red kidney beans, Italian plum tomatoes, tomato paste, liver pâté, garbanzo beans, nuts, tomato juice, dry oil-cured olives, ripe olives, pimentoes, artichoke hearts, hearts of palm, imported wild mushrooms such as those called *chanterelles* in French and *pfifferlinge* in German, smoked baby clams or oysters.

canned chicken and beef broths

capers

hot Dijon mustard and dry mustard

converted rice and wild rice

several kinds of dried pasta

piece of Romano or Parmesan cheese (refrigerated)

unflavored gelatin

smoked sausages and smoked slab bacon square (refrigerated)

red and white wine vinegar and tarragon vinegar

Madeira wine

dry sherry

an assortment of dry white wines and red wines for drinking and cooking cognac

Kirsch

bottled mineral waters

beer

unsweetened crackers in tin boxes

pie crust mix

jar of shelled, blanched almonds (in freezer)

semi-sweet chocolate

superfine granulated sugar (for fruit compotes)

Consider adding these items to your basic stores of sugar, flour, and so on—all are long-lasting if not absolutely nonperishable.

Besides *chanterelles,* imported cheeses, Kirsch, and Earl Grey tea, which one cannot expect to find in every village store, there are some other limitations to cooking in a vacation house. The equipment in a rented kitchen is often limited to a thin, battered tin skillet, a worn-out saucepan with a handle that turns, and a dime-store "stainless steel" knife with the tip broken off. This is not to mention the stove, which probably saw its finest hours during the Coolidge Administration.

If cooking and eating are any part at all of your summer enjoyment, do take along a few competent pieces of kitchen equipment and spare yourself needless frustration. In a cast-iron skillet with a cover, food can be sautéed, roasted, baked, broiled, boiled, or braised. One decent all-purpose steel knife for chopping and carving, a vegetable peeler, and the type of can opener you can operate safely will save a great deal of irritation, and maybe a finger. A wooden spoon, a wire whisk, and a food mill will enable you to make creamy sauces, pureed soups, or a superb mayonnaise. A cheap oven thermometer will help you to adjust to the crotchets of your stove and keep your hostessing gracious. And without a pot capacious enough for cooking corn, shellfish, and soups or pasta for at least eight people, you will suffer the annoyance of trying to cook these things in several batches. You can always use an 8-quart heavy aluminum pot to pack the other kitchen things in; it makes a rather striking piece of luggage.

HERBS

Dried herbs, no matter how fine the quality, can never compare with fresh. Summer's special gift to the cook is an array of fresh herbs. You can grow them in pots in a sunny city window, in a small country garden (even a weekend gardener can manage herbs), or buy them at farmers' markets or vegetable stands. Unfortunately, I have yet to see a supermarket, even at the height of season, that goes in for anything more exotic than parsley. But we may count that not too small a blessing, since parsley is probably the most versatile and useful herb there is.

Tarragon, sweet basil, bay leaf, thyme, marjoram, chives, summer savory, rosemary, and dill weed are, along with parsley, the most popular cooking herbs. (I have omitted sage from my list because I think its taste overwhelms almost any food, and oregano because I ate in too many cheap Italian restaurants many years ago.) Except for rosemary, which tends to drop dead if a draft hits it, all of them are easy to grow. You may purchase small plants from a nursery or order them by mail.

Fresh herbs will keep for a couple of weeks in the refrigerator if they are left unwashed and stored, loosely separated, in airtight plastic containers. Moisture and tight packing will rot the herbs.

Even if you set out only one of each herb you wish to grow, there will undoubtedly be a delightful surplus that you should by all means dry for winter use. If you do this very simple operation properly, your herbs will certainly surpass any commercially dried ones. Parsley and chives do not dry successfully, but fresh parsley is always available anyway, and frozen chives aren't too awful.

To dry herbs, leave the sprigs as intact as possible; the leaves will retain their flavor longer if dried on the stems. Using cotton string, tie the stem ends together in small bunches and hang upside down in a dark, dry closet. Or lay the herb sprigs in a single layer on newspapers, cover with cheesecloth and another sheet of newspaper, and dry them slowly in the oven at 140°F. or the lowest heat your oven can maintain. After about half an hour, turn off the oven and leave the herbs overnight. The leaves should be dry but not crumbling to powder. Store in labeled opaque or dark-colored glass jars with tight stoppers. Light deteriorates the flavor of herbs, which may be why commercial brands often taste as if they've been cremated rather than dried.

Hanging herbs to dry them may take a couple of weeks, but I think they are much more aromatic than artificially dried ones. When using dried herbs, remember that their concentrated taste requires only one fourth the amount of fresh herbs you would use. Of course, in the case of some commercial brands, you could use the whole jar without altering the character of the dish in the least. Always test any dried herb by crushing a tiny bit in the palm of your hand. If there is not an immediate pungent aroma, throw the bottle out and either omit the herb from your recipe or select a suitable alternate. Any dried herbs more than a year old should be thrown away.

HORS D'OEUVRE
AND/OR PARTY FOOD

H*ors d'oeuvre,* like *ennui,* is one of those French words that has entered the
language, possibly because we have no real equivalent: witness "appetizers" and "start-
ers." This whole category of food is shrouded in confusion. By hors d'oeuvre the
French mean a first course at the table, not the smattering of tasty bites served with
the aperitif. (When these bites are served gratis in a fancy restaurant with a name chef,
they're called *amuse gueule:* a tiny category.) We Americans take the term to mean
any food served with drinks—either before dinner or at a cocktail party where some
guests will make their evening meal on the so-called "hors d'oeuvres."

What one does about this ambiguous category—legitimate first courses eaten with
knife and fork at table are something else again—is largely up to prevailing custom
in your own social milieu. When I've spent a lot of time cooking a multi-course dinner
I often ruthlessly set out only peanuts and olives before the main event. This is not
a hit with some major grazers I know, but every cook-host has some eccentricities.

(There are people who apparently cannot bring themselves to offer red wine as well as white before dinner.)

Cocktail parties are the concourse of summer life—like native drumtalk—in my neck of the woods. And these occasions have come to require major outlays of food, though this was not expected until fairly recent times. This chapter deals, for the most part, with the savage requirements of cocktail party-giving. While caterers now almost outnumber plumbers on the South Fork of Long Island, their food is often mechanical and outrageously expensive. It's not so difficult to make most of the party food yourself and just hire someone else to serve it. A rotten time is usually had by all when the host tries to serve, talk, mix drinks, talk and introduce, and keep the food table pretty and the mess under control. One of the first rules of successful party-giving is *Get Help!* either from friends or hired hands (relying on the junior family members is risky business—launching a fourteen-year-old's bartending career is a dirty trick to play on guests).

Since tricky hot cocktail food demands a kitchen attendant, there is little of it here. There is much room temperature, cold, and made-in-advance, as well as simply "assembled" dishes. Though food fashion is retrogressing, no one seems ready yet for a return to the dull but simple days of the watercress and cucumber sandwiches, which have, alas, disappeared.

Merriment loves the company of food. Substantial platters of cold lamb, roast pork, or smoked fish with an array of breads, mustards, and butters are interesting alternatives to ham and/or turkey. Not that there's anything to denigrate about a good ham or a well-turned out turkey; people frequently prefer them to more exotic choices. A real country ham feeds the multitudes magnificently and is a snap to cook: It's the carving of it into paper-thin slivers that's tedious.

There's an oddity in eating patterns I've wondered about over the years: No matter how stunning the pâté, terrine, or *rillettes,* or how enthusiastic the guests, few will be bothered to spread their own bread or crackers. If you prepare these and pass a tray, all will be gratefully accepted—a point to remember if your lovingly made terrine is neglected. This guest-inertia can be a plus when one is invaded by the occasional gastronomic Green Berets who devastate buffet tables.

Raw or blanched vegetable assortments with a good dip of some sort—Tapenade (page 16), Sauce Aioli (page 82), or sour cream with herbs—never seem to flag in popularity, no matter that *crudités* have been on the American party circuit for two decades (albeit called "raw vegetables," because up until the sixties the French had never entertained the notion of raw veggies and the word meant "an off-color remark"). Whether because of guilt, diet, or vegetarianism, people polish off a good veggie tray, especially if it is revamped with especially young or exotic offerings.

Olives and peanuts can take you just so far, but there's always the old reliable cheese board for adamant non-cooks (who seem to read cookbooks with almost as much enthusiasm as dedicated cooks). The trick with this is to find interesting selections in their peak condition. Find a trustworthy cheese merchant to stick to for counsel.

While prepared "take-out" food seems to be having a great vogue, it does have one fatal flaw: Everyone else can buy the same food. The unmistakable imprint of the same caterer or specialty shop graven on party after party would not be so glaring if relieved by a few homemade treats.

The dinners and friendly barbecues of summer, aided by conveniences like the food processor and the electric dishwasher, are so much easier on the host than they used to be (except for people who had large staffs of servants). Dinners, balls, and huge cocktail parties used to be solely the life-style of the rich and famous, but no more. "Entertaining" is an entrenched part of middle-class life in the latter half of the twentieth century.

RAW SHELLFISH

A raw bar for clams and oysters makes a smashing centerpiece for a party. There are specialists for hire along the Atlantic seaboard who can handle a whole party single-handed. (Larry the Clam, who bears the slogan "Born to Shuck" on his professional T-shirt, is a legendary Long Island shucker.) Obviously, such an undertaking is not for the amateur, and it's the rare guest who can manage for himself.

Oysters are sold year-round nowadays (the "r" months still have the edge for quality, in my opinion) and clams, their proletarian brothers, are plentiful in summer and available all year round. Clam opening is an elusive trick I've struggled with for years—after a couple of dozen tries, you get the hang of it. My first encounters were guided by Stuart, a now-famous Amagansett fishmonger whose family still carries on the business. He cautioned that clams really do "clam up" if they're jiggled. Be calm and handle them quickly but gently. I find them to be more quiescent if they're ice cold from at least an overnight stay in the refrigerator. Freshly dug clams, a few hours out of the water, are just impossible to open. You can cheat by throwing them into a freezer for an hour to stun them. Wash them first so that you needn't upset them later.

Clam knives are essential (and useful for a lot of brute tasks in the kitchen). Their short, sturdy blade, with one thin edge to slip between the clam's "lips" at the top edge near the black hinge, cannot be matched by any other kind of knife. Hold the clam in one hand in a thick cooking mitt and insert the knife quickly near the hinge of the triangularly shaped shell. Slide the knife around the edge, prying up the shell as you go, holding the shellfish over a bowl to catch the juices. Cut the clam loose from its undershell and try to avoid mangling the clam in the process. (I've been served clams still attached to their half shell—an impossible thing to eat.) Pour the juice back over the clams when you have them all shucked and provide pepper mills and lemon wedges. I don't care for ketchup or any of its brethren, but many do. I prefer the simple sauce of mild red wine vinegar and coarse white pepper offered with oysters in French restaurants. Most oysters are, incidentally, much easier to open than clams. Get your fishmonger to show you how, or have him open them and arrange them on paper plates bedded with ice—they should be transported in a cooler and consumed within an hour. You will not perish from eating clams, oysters, or lobsters killed at the fish store, if they are carefully kept chilled and prepared at home not much later in the day.

SASHIMI

Sashimi, unlike sushi, which demands training and skill, is easily prepared wherever really freshly caught fish is obtainable. All skin, bones, and the dark meat, which runs along the center line of fish like salmon, should be removed and the very best center portions cut into a neat block. Slices are traditionally rather thick—about ⅛ to ¼ of an inch, so that too is a simple task. Always cut across, not with, the grain of the fish using a supersharp knife.

Wasabi, which is sold in tins and keeps forever, is powdered Japanese horseradish. It is mixed with just enough water to form a fiery green paste. A tiny blob is put on each plate to be mixed with soy sauce. Sometimes I squeeze a little lemon juice into the soy or add some toasted sesame seeds, neither of which are authentically Japanese. I use Kikkoman lite soy sauce, which has half the sodium of the regular and seems to lessen the raging thirst often occasioned by the excesses I often commit with sashimi and sushi.

Tuna is the preferred fish for sashimi by most Americans. But three or four kinds of fish (at least) should be offered. Consult with your fish dealer if you haven't caught your own, but almost any truly fresh fish makes great sashimi.

THE RAW VEGETABLE PLATTER,
A.K.A. *Les Crudités*

Boosted from the children's lunch box to the cocktail party staple by a new French name, *crudités* are served wherever people drink and diet—in other words, throughout this great land. This anomaly has made the almost obligatory raw veggie selection with a dip acceptable to everyone and cheap besides. At a village benefit party last year I heard one busy volunteer saying to another, "I say fill 'em up on crewdites, they're just gonna' goudge themselves anyway." Here, here!

While the French may be credited with name-glossing our native invention, I don't think raw vegetables have really ever been regarded as anything but an aberration by their chefs. But then, Francophile though I am in matters culinary, vegetables on French menus used to range from passable to awful. Nouvelle cooks seem to regard them as a garnish to be slivered and scattered around as color accents to plate compositions, painting them with sauces and other such silly practices.

When it comes to raw vegetables, however, marshal all the artistic skills available: Flower-arranging instincts should be fully employed, unusual or beautiful baskets and platters brought out. A few of my favorites are an old Japanese lacquer bento box (the first I'd ever seen, presented as a farewell gift by a Kyoto exchange student who lived with us), a tightly woven Geechee basket from the Carolina Low-country, a blue-and-white circular Chinese platter, some beauties from Bennington (Vermont) pottery, and assorted clear glass fantasies I've collected from Italy and France. I have some ice molds—a big polar bear and a seal—that were probably intended for caviar, but that I use in the center of chilled vegetables. This is an amusing presentation, but I'll have to admit it needs care. The ice sculpture must rest in a shallow pan concealed by greenery to prevent a rice paddy look almost instantly.

Large natural leaves arranged on boards or some simple flat baskets of various shapes and sizes are cheap, available everywhere, and make effective backgrounds for displays of fresh summer vegetables.

Sugar snap peas (a new hybrid), fresh Chinese snow peas, sliced fennel, young purple-top white turnips, daikon radishes, jicama (a Mexican root vegetable), small inner leaves of Belgian endive (a seasonless vegetable), ever-burgeoning varieties of pear-shaped tomatoes—both yellow and red (avoid the large ones that make clumsy two-bite eating), tender young green beans, omnipresent zucchini (blanched), little lemon cucumbers, small bumpy Kirby cukes (the pickling kind), and, of course, our new national obsession, sweet peppers from classic green to red to yellow to chocolate brown and some extraordinary ones with mixed colors—can all be refreshing alternatives to the carrots, celery sticks, and cucumber spears of the old-time veggie religion.

Not all vegetables are good raw—heresy to the vitamin-crazed but not to those who care about their taste. Broccoli, green beans, and asparagus are all tough and tasteless when raw. They only develop their flavor and unique crisp-tender textures via a boiling-water bath of three minutes or so, depending on their size and age. Zucchini is another frequent turn in the *crudités* routine that is virtually without taste raw but develops a delicate, intriguing flavor when blanched. However, I despair of convincing many people that blanching is worth the extra effort—it's a gospel I've been exhorting for many years with little public acceptance. One or two caterers I know have recently elected to make this effort to distinguish their own versions of the *crudités* platter (which remains ever-popular with their clients) from the run-of-the-season vegetable presentations.

It's a mistake to think that the dip will take the curse off carelessly chosen or ill-prepared vegetables. Imaginatively selected and presented, the vegetables are loved for themselves more than ever—many people appreciate them with only a Chinese "dip" of roasted salt and pepper. (Put three parts coarse kosher salt to one part freshly ground coarse black pepper, or a mixture of ground green, white, and pink peppercorns, in a cast-iron skillet and heat slowly, stirring constantly, until the salt just begins to color, a minute or two. This is best when used the same day it's made.) Blanching fresh vegetables, to set color and release flavor, will never seem dispensable once its magic is discovered. So far as food values are concerned, I think it highly unlikely that a brief plunge into boiling water and instant chilling could have any diminishing effect. Anyway, the most one hopes for in a *crudités* display is that it be pretty and harmless. Dips supply the thrills and strict dieters can stick to the roasted salt and pepper pot, which is a good idea no matter what other sauces are offered.

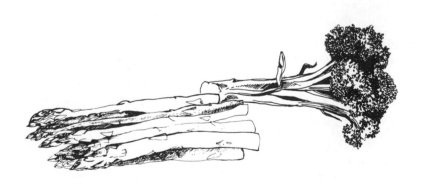

⚘ TAPENADE ⚘

Originally intended as a sauce for cold boiled beef or cold fish, this old Provençal sauce turns out to be a perfect salty and piquant accent for raw vegetables. The color is unprepossessing, but one taste and it wins instant fans.

Makes about 1 1/2 cups

1 tablespoon drained capers	*Juice of half a lemon*
1 2-ounce tin anchovy fillets	*1 clove garlic, pulverized*
1/2 cup olive oil	*2 teaspoons grated onion*
1 7-ounce can tuna fish	*Freshly ground pepper to taste*
8 stoned Greek olives	

Put all the ingredients into a blender or processor and mix to a not-too-fine puree—a few lumps here and there are the desired texture. Cover at once. Serve at room temperature.

⚘ ROUILLE ⚘

Rouille is a strongly spiced Provençal sauce like Aioli (page 82) that its creators (who never dreamed that human beings would eat raw vegetables) meant for cold fish, for cooked vegetables, or to be stirred into soups or stews. Bastardized versions of this red pepper sauce are beginning to bob up here and there, but before that gets too out of hand, here's the original idea.

Makes about 1 cup

1 large red sweet pepper	fresh white breadcrumbs
1 small fresh hot chili pepper	4 to 6 tablespoons olive oil
1 fat clove garlic	Salt and freshly ground pepper to
2 tablespoons (approximately)	taste

Roast the sweet pepper over a gas flame until it is well-blackened all over. Twist it in a paper towel and let it steam for about 5 minutes. Rub the skin off with more paper toweling. Discard the seeds, stem, and pith, chop the pepper. In a blender or processor, which already contains the hot chili pepper and garlic, pulverized, then add the bread crumbs. Spin to a thick puree, while adding the oil through the center hole or feed tube. Add salt and pepper to taste. This is a superb sauce to put on the table with all sorts of fish soups and stews—each person doctors his own portion to taste.

SMOKED FISH

Smoked Nova Scotia salmon, sturgeon, and whitefish are available in New York's fabulous delicatessens. Gourmet food departments of big stores provide these things in most cities. If your summer is spent on the shore, investigate the local smoked fish. On the eastern end of Long Island, smoked eel is relatively inexpensive and abundant in the summer; so is bluefish. Smoked butterfish is occasionally around. Smoked trout from England and salmon from Scotland are no bargains in price but are an incomparable way to splurge once in awhile.

Eel, butterfish, and trout must be skinned before serving and cut into pieces not more than 2 inches long. Slice some rye, pumpernickel, and white toast into pieces that match the size of the fish slices. Serve a small bowl of capers, some lemon wedges, and thin slices of onion, and provide a pepper mill.

Good smoked salmon is neither greasy nor particularly salty. It is rather dry and the slices tend to stick together. Since it is expensive and difficult to separate, it is the one thing that should be cut and arranged on thinly buttered slices of bread in advance. It may be covered with plastic wrap and refrigerated until serving time.

⚶ SHRIMP RAVIGOTE ⚶

Allow 1 1/2 pounds of shrimp for 4 people.

Cooking shrimp is so easy that it's ridiculous to pay the extra price for precooked shrimp of heaven knows what age and condition. However, cleaning shrimp is a great bore. Train your children early to do this job efficiently. Those pliers-like shrimp cleaners sold in hardware stores do not work.

Medium-sized shrimp are best for this dish. Rinse quickly and cook them, unshelled, in Court Bouillon (page 103). They are done when they turn pink; usually in 1 to 3 minutes. Drain them and clean as follows:

Pull off the legs all at once with your thumb, forefinger, and middle finger. Usually, the shell will slip off easily in one piece. *To devein:* Starting where the head was detached, grasp the tip of the back intestinal vein, and strip it down the back. It breaks sometimes and you will need a small paring knife to get out the bits of sand. On no account should you wash the shrimp after it is cooked; its flavor is elusive enough as it is.

Place the shrimp in an earthenware or china bowl and add some small, mild white onions sliced very thin. Pour on some Sauce Ravigote, cover, and refrigerate for several hours. Garnish with tomato wedges or little cherry tomatoes and serve as a first course or a main luncheon dish.

SAUCE RAVIGOTE

Few cookbooks agree on what this really is. Many recipes are almost identical to Sauce Rémoulade (page 82), but this version does not contain any mayonnaise. In any case, it is usually served on cold meats, fish, or vegetables, and is one of those thrifty French ways to dress up yesterday's dinner to make today's luncheon.

1 cup Sauce Vinaigrette (page 65)

2 to 3 tablespoons minced fresh
herbs such as parsley, chives,
chervil, tarragon, marjoram, or
thyme

2 teaspoons finely minced
scallions

1 teaspoon chopped capers

3 or 4 chopped anchovy fillets
(except when sauce will be
used with chicken)

Shake all ingredients together in a screw-top jar. Do not use a blender, as it destroys the individual textures and flavors.

✺ SHRIMP MARINATED WITH DILL ✺

Serves 6 as an hors d'oeuvre, with other appetizers, serves 12

2 pounds medium shrimp

Court Bouillon (page 103)

1 cup finely chopped fresh dill
weed

1/2 teaspoon salt

1 teaspoon dry mustard

1/2 cup dry white wine

1 cup olive oil

1/2 cup minced scallions

Poach the shrimp in the Court Bouillon.

In a narrow, deep, glass or china dish, alternate layers of shrimp and dill weed. The container should be filled to the top. Beat the salt, mustard, and white wine together, then slowly beat in the olive oil. Pour this dressing over the shrimp and dill, cover, and refrigerate for 8 hours. Stir the mixture twice during this time. At serving time, drain, sprinkle with chopped scallions, and mix lightly. The shrimp may be served on a small plate as a first course or on a large platter with toothpicks for spearing as an *hors d'oeuvre*.

⚶ SHRIMP WITH AIOLI ⚶

Allow 1 ¼ pounds of shrimp for 4 people.

Sauce Aioli (page 82) is a Provençal garlic mayonnaise, delicious on shrimp as well as on raw vegetables. Cook and clean the shrimp as for Shrimp Ravigote (page 18), then arrange the shrimp on a large round platter with a bowl of Sauce Aioli in the center.

Variations: Serve the shrimp with Sauce Rémoulade (page 82) or Green Mayonnaise (page 81) instead of Aioli.

⚶ SHRIMP BAGNA CAUDA ⚶

Bagna cauda means "hot bath" and is an Italian sauce usually served with raw vegetables as part of an antipasto. This sauce must be kept hot over a small flame while it is served.

Cook and clean shrimp as for Shrimp Ravigote (page 18), allowing 1 ¼ pounds per 4 persons. Refrigerate in a tightly closed plastic bag until serving time. Provide small skewers or toothpicks and serve with the hot sauce.

2 cloves garlic
¼ pound butter (1 stick)
5 anchovy fillets, minced
2 teaspoons chopped fresh basil

¾ cup olive oil
¼ teaspoon dried red pepper flakes or a few drops of Tabasco sauce

Mince the garlic and add it to the butter. Melt the butter, taking care that it does not brown at all. Beat in remaining ingredients with a wooden spoon. Serve very hot but not hot enough to fry the shrimp, as it is a sauce, not a cooking agent.

Variation: If you wish to augment the shrimp supply, add some sliced raw mushrooms or some slivers of green peppers.

🌿 CHINESE SHRIMP TOAST 🍃

This must be assembled quickly and at the last minute. It is so delicious that only a firm refusal to go on frying and frying will save you from missing your own party. Allow 2 pieces per person, although a lot of people will try to get three or four.

Serves 3

1/2 pound cleaned raw shrimp, minced

6 water chestnuts, chopped

1 teaspoon salt

Pinch of sugar

1 teaspoon minced fresh gingerroot or 1/2 teaspoon ground ginger

2 tablespoons chopped scallions

1 tablespoon sherry

1 egg, well beaten

Peanut or corn oil

1 tablespoon cornstarch

6 slices home-style white bread, 2 days old (or spread out to dry during the day)

Combine all ingredients except cornstarch and bread. Mix well. Stir in the cornstarch and allow the mixture to stand while you trim the crusts and cut each bread slice diagonally into two triangles. (The recipe may be prepared in advance up to this point.) Spread a heaping tablespoon of the shrimp mixture onto each triangle. Deep fry 3 or 4 pieces at a time face down in 1 inch of very hot peanut or corn oil, about 3 minutes, or until golden. (No matter how dubious the procedure sounds, the shrimp will not *fall* off the toast while frying.) Turn and fry briefly on the other side. Drain on absorbent paper and serve absolutely immediately.

🐟 MOULES MARINIÈRE 🐟

Mussels are still less appreciated by Americans than Europeans, and consequently are very cheap in the markets that carry them. They are one of the most succulent and easily prepared of all shellfish. The fact that you can gather all you want for nothing on Northeastern beaches outweighs the somewhat tiresome cleaning process. In some markets mussels are sold by the pound, in others by the quart. Allow at least 1 pint of mussels in the shell per person—more if your guests have decent appetites. Mussels must always be cooked prior to using them in any recipe. This recipe is the basic method of preparation.

Serves 2 as a main course

1 quart of large mussels (about 1 pound)
1 cup dry white wine
1 medium onion, chopped
1/2 bay leaf
6 to 8 peppercorns
1 clove garlic, split

2 sprigs parsley
Pinch chopped fresh parsley
Flour
1 tablespoon softened butter
Salt and freshly ground pepper to taste
French bread

Scrub the mussels under cold running water with a stiff brush until they are shining clean. Holding the mussel in your left hand, use an ordinary table knife to pry out the "beard"—the small, mossy growth it uses to cling to its rock bed. It isn't necessary to scrape off any barnacles except for aesthetic reasons. Put the wine, onion, bay leaf, peppercorns, garlic, and parsley into a large shallow kettle with a cover. Add the mussels, preferably not more than two deep. Bring to a boil, then lower heat and cover. After about 2 minutes of steaming, stir the top layer of mussels down to the bottom so that they all will cook evenly. Continue steaming until all the mussels are open. This should take no more than 5 minutes. *Do not overcook* or they will be rubbery, tasteless, and shrunken to near invisibility. Do not attempt to pry open any mussels that have not succumbed to the steaming. They are either full of mud or defective in some way and should be tossed out.

Using the lid to hold the mussels in the pot, pour out and strain the juices through a cheesecloth-lined strainer to catch the sand which the mussels have released. You should have three to four times as much liquid as you started with. Bring the wine and juices to a boil again. Work as much flour into the butter as it will absorb. Whisk it vigorously into the broth to thicken it a little. Taste for salt and pepper. Put about a dozen mussels in a shallow soup plate with a chunk of toasted French bread. Pour the soup over all, sprinkle with a bit of chopped parsley, and serve very hot.

Note: This dish is usually served as a main course; cooking directions given here should be followed in the following recipes

🌿 MOULES RÉMOULADE 🌿

Allow 6 mussels per guest. Steam the mussels as for Moules Marinière (page 22) but do not bother to thicken the soup. You may strain the liquid and save it to cook other fish or shellfish. Drain the mussels and remove the top shell, then loosen them from the bottom shell. Arrange them on a bed of romaine or other lettuce and squeeze a few drops of lemon juice on each one. Cover with plastic wrap and chill. When you are ready to serve, put about ½ teaspoon of Sauce Rémoulade (page 82), depending on the size of the mussel, on top of each.

🌿 MOULES VINAIGRETTE 🌿

Prepare as for Moules Rémoulade (page 22) substituting a well-flavored Sauce Vinaigrette (page 65). The mussels are often removed from their shells entirely and presented on a lettuce leaf. Forks should be provided, as this is a bit messy for finger eating.

🌿 SPICED CORNED BEEF 🌿

Corned brisket of beef may be bought in the meat department of almost any supermarket. It requires long, slow simmering but no finesse whatsoever. Buy a lean piece from the thin end, which has less fat and waste.

3 to 4 pounds corned brisket of
   beef (straight cut)
1 onion, stuck with 3 cloves
2 cloves garlic
1 tablespoon fresh thyme or ½
   teaspoon dried

1 bay leaf
1 teaspoon cracked black pepper
Water to cover

Wipe meat with paper toweling. Place in a heavy, covered pot and add all other ingredients. Add *no* salt. Slowly bring to a boil, skim, reduce heat to barely trembling, and let simmer for about 3 hours, with the lid slightly askew. Water level should be maintained at about 1 inch above the meat. Pierce with a fork to test for doneness. Don't cook it too long or it will fall to shreds when carved.

Allow the meat to cool in the broth. It will still be warm after 2 hours, and it absorbs more flavor during this time. Remove the meat from the broth, let rest on a carving board about 10 minutes, then slice it ⅛ inch thick. (If you weight and chill it, the brisket can be sliced even thinner. But, before slicing it should be returned to at least room temperature before serving.)

Ideally, the corned beef should be served tepid with a cold sauce made of sour cream or fresh whipped cream to which you have added freshly grated horseradish to taste. Serve with pumpernickel or ryo bread

𝕬 SMOKED TONGUE 𝕭

The growing sophistication of American eating habits may at last admit this once "ethnic" specialty to the popularity it deserves. Partisans of smoked tongue are loyal and they are always happy to see it on a buffet. So are people who don't know what it is. They think it's some kind of very smooth-textured corned beef.

Tongue is not the incredible bargain it once was, but still, a large smoked beef tongue goes a long way and can be successfully cooked by anyone able to lift a pot of water.

Smoked tongues weigh anywhere between 3 and 5 pounds. Most bear printed instructions and few require presoaking (as in earlier times when meat was smoked to preserve as well as flavor it). Rinse the tongue and place it in a pot with cold water to cover by 3 inches. Add 1 onion stuck with 2 cloves, 2 cloves garlic, bashed, 1 tablespoon of cracked black pepper, 1 bay leaf, and 1 teaspoon of crushed dried thyme. Bring slowly to a boil, reduce heat, and simmer for approximately 40 minutes per pound. Test with a sharp metal skewer after 2 hours. The meat should be very tender.

When the tongue is done, remove it from the pot and put it on a board. When it is cool enough to handle, peel the skin off, slitting it at the tip end with a small knife. (It will peel off easily.) Remove the tiny bones at the root end with your fingers, wrap the whole tongue in plastic wrap, lay it on its side, put a light weight on it, and refrigerate overnight. Take it back to your butcher and ask him to slice it *at an angle* (there are many modern butchers who have no idea of how to deal with it) about ⅛ inch thick—not transparently as they do boiled ham. If you are obliged to slice the tongue manually, lay the tongue on its side, keenly sharpen a thin carving knife, and begin slicing at an angle from the tip.

Smoked tongue does have one failing: If left exposed to air, the sliced meat turns from a bright cheerful pink to a dreary gray. Keep it closely covered with plastic wrap until serving time to avert this discoloring.

Thin slices of dark bread about 2 inches square are handy underpinnings for smoked tongue. Small presliced "party loaves" of rye are appropriate and convenient. Serve with good Dijon mustard or any exotic ones you fancy, or the following sauce.

✵ HORSERADISH CHANTILLY ✵

Whip 1 cup of heavy cream stiff. Stir in 2 tablespoons of very well drained, bottled white horseradish and season to taste with a little salt and white pepper. Black specks in the sauce look awful, so if you have no white peppercorns, omit the pepper altogether. The sauce should be light and mild so that it enhances but doesn't mask the tongue.

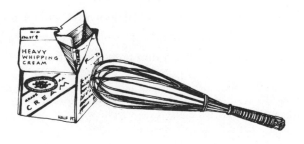

🌿 PEARL BALLS 🌿

Chinese cooking varies not only within the regions, but according to whether it is "home" or "restaurant" cooking. This is a dish I've found in several Chinese cookbooks but never listed on restaurant menus. Not that Chinese menus in English list half of what they've got listed in Chinese, but I've never even seen any Chinese customers eating these delicious little rice-studded meatballs. Perhaps they are served primarily in tea shops or dim sum parlors in China. At any rate, I've adopted them as an ideal cocktail-party dish. Pork chops, including a thin rim of fat for tenderness, are the best cut to use for these meatballs, which can be made in a food processor.

½ cup short grain white rice
1 pound ground pork (from chops)
2 tablespoons minced scallions
1 teaspoon grated fresh gingerroot.
1 teaspoon black (or Szechuan) pepper
1 tablespoon light soy sauce

1 tablespoon sherry or rice wine
1 tablespoon dark Chinese sesame oil
1 large egg, well beaten
Large pinch of monosodium glutamate, "M.S.G."* (optional, of course)
1 tablespoon cornstarch
1 tablespoon flour

Wash the rice well, cover it with fresh water, and soak it for 3 hours. Drain and dry the grains in a sieve, then spread them out on a tray. Mix together all the remaining ingredients except the cornstarch and flour, and beat the mixture with a spoon to fluff up the meat. Roll the meat into about 20 little balls, each a bit smaller than a walnut. (This part goes fast if you keep your palms cool and moistened with water.) Roll them

---

*Chinese Restaurant Syndrome, headache, and other disorders attributed to this entirely natural flavor enhancer are almost entirely imaginary according to recent studies reported in the *Tufts University Diet & Nutrition Letter.*

in rice—the balls do not have to be perfect, nor should they be too heavily coated, as the rice will expand. Lay damp cheesecloth in a steamer basket to prevent the rice from sticking, then steam the rice balls over boiling water for 40 minutes.

Serve with a dipping sauce of soy sauce flavored with Chinese sesame oil and a little grated gingerroot, or hotted up with a completely unorthodox dab of Chinese chili paste or Japanese wasabi paste (page 13). These should be served hot and could be speared with satay sticks for neatness (though they are usually snatched by eager fingers at my house—often before I can get them out of the kitchen and into circulation). Everything but the steaming can be done ahead, but if refrigerated—well wrapped to prevent the rice from dehydrating—the Pearl Balls should be returned to room temperature so that the cooking time will be dependable.

🌿 SIMPLE COUNTRY PÂTÉ 🌿

This becomes *your* "pâté maison" by whatever alterations you care to make to this basic recipe. Like meatloaf, almost no pâté—except for commercial ones—ever turns out exactly the same way twice, because the possibilities for experimentation are so tempting to every cook. Although pâtés do require some kitchen and oven time, they can be made in the peace of early morning and they keep (and improve) for at least a week. Actually, a pâté well sealed in its own fat and heavy foil will keep in the refrigerator for a month, but the flavor is best if it is eaten within a week.

Using the same basic technique, you can add strips of raw marinated chicken—breast or thighs—veal strips, small dice of ham or smoked tongue, various kinds of nuts or herbs, or dried wild mushrooms, to make several different kinds of pâté that can all be baked at once for a large party. This recalls a story (probably apocryphal) told about Princess Margaret in her entertaining youth: "Don't go to any trouble cook,

I'm having thirty or forty friends in after the theater tonight, but we can give them something cold."

Regrettably, some of the best cold summer food has to start out in a hot kitchen. But the work is considerably lessened with a food processor, and the return is well worth the bother. Just check the prices at any luxury food store.

1 pound boneless pork shoulder, ground

1 pound boneless lean veal, ground

1 pound fresh pork fat, sliced very thin or 1/2 pound fat plus sheets of caul fat

1 pound precooked ham steak

1/2 pound pork or calf liver

1 cup finely minced onion

6 cloves garlic, finely minced

1/4 cup cognac, gin, or dry red or white wine

1/2 cup heavy cream

2 eggs, beaten

1 tablespoon salt

2 teaspoons fresh coarse black pepper

1 tablespoon fresh thyme leaves, or 1 teaspoon dried

Big pinch of ground allspice

1 tablespoon juniper berries, ground (optional)

3 tablespoons minced fresh parsley

1/4 cup fresh breadcrumbs

Several small bay leaves

Have a butcher grind the pork and veal for you if possible; otherwise, remove any gristle or membrane and chop the meats semi-coarsely in a food processor. Line one 2-quart (or two smaller-sized) terrine with either thin slices of pork fat or sheets of caul fat. (Caul fat comes in thin, lacy sheets and should be carefully soaked in cold water first. It is the simplest kind of terrine lining and makes the most attractive finished surface. Most butchers will special order it for you and any excess can be frozen.)

Coarsely grind or hand chop the ham into small cubes. (Smoked pork chops, a specialty known as *Kassler Rippchen* in German pork shops, are fully cooked and a wonderful alternate to ham. Domestic *rippchen* is available in supermarkets.) Grind remaining pork fat (at least half a pound) with the liver and mix with all the remaining ingredients except the bay leaves. Beat the mixture until light with a wooden spoon; do not squeeze it with your hands as it makes the texture rubbery.

Pack the forcemeat into the terrine, bring the caul or pork fat up over the top to enclose it completely and lay a row of bay leaves the length of the terrine. (It is more work, but the top is much more attractive if covered with a lattice of thin pork strips.) Cover tightly with a double thickness of foil. Refrigerate overnight.

Set the terrine (or foil loaf pans) into a large roasting pan half filled with hot water. Bake the pâté in a 325°F. oven for about 2 hours or until the interior temperature is 165°F.—the pâté will cook even more as it cools. Remove the foil during the last 15 minutes so that the top can brown. Remove from the oven, replace the boiling water in the roasting pan with cold water, and set the terrine in it to cool. When cold, recover the terrine and refrigerate it overnight. Weighting can make a pâté too firm for my taste, but texture is one of the many variables in pâtés—chilled, most are hard enough to slice thin, or pâtés can be lightened with more bread crumbs and more liquids for a softer loaf to be cut thicker, or just left in the terrine for a rough spread. These are matters for experiment. The liver can be eliminated if you prefer or, for a very soft terrine, use mostly liver and reduce the amount of pork, veal, or ham. The ham isn't at all authentic in a French pâté, but the salt should be increased if it is lessened or eliminated. Duck breast in julienne strips and pale green chopped pistachios are dressy alterations to the basic pâté. With the availability of game in winter some very intricate combinations open up, but in summer pâtés should be kept on the lighter and simpler side. Garden spinach, shredded, blanched, and dried, is a particularly appealing addition for hot weather eating.

Note: Cooked pâtés tend to become rather wet and glassy after freezing, especially if there is a high liver content. But ordinary mostly ground-meat pâtés can be very successfully frozen raw, then defrosted and baked as the need arises. Keep in mind, ground meat of any description loses its flavor after more than one month in the freezer.

❧ BABA GANOOJH ❧

This was one of the delicious little unidentified dishes (the waiters never spoke any English) I used to eat in small Middle Eastern restaurants patronized by rug dealers in the West thirties of Manhattan. High rises have displaced them, but this "poor man's caviar" is a reminder of those happier times when Beirut was known as "the Paris of the Middle East." Baba Ganoojh is scooped up with triangles of pita bread and is wonderfully easy party food. Tahini can usually be found in health food stores as well as in neighborhoods with lots of rug dealers.

Makes about 3 cups

*2 medium-sized eggplants, about
    7 inches long*
Salt
2 cloves garlic
*2 tablespoons tahini (sesame
    paste)*
Juice of half a large lemon

1/4 cup olive oil
1 teaspoon ground cumin
Salt to taste
*1/8 teaspoon cayenne or 1 small
    fresh hot chili pepper, seeded
    and minced*
Minced fresh parsley

Split the eggplants lengthwise (the long, thinnish species have fewer seeds than the fat round ones) and slash the flesh in several places. Sprinkle them with salt. After half an hour, squeeze them gently and wipe the surfaces. Broil, skin side up, on an oiled rack under a top-flame broiler or skin side down on a charcoal grill until tender—about 5 minutes. The purple skins should blacken somewhat, which is what lends the puree its distinctive smoky flavor. Scrape out the flesh with a spoon and puree it with all the remaining ingredients except the parsley—if using a processor, puree the garlic first, then add the other ingredients. Taste carefully and don't go overboard on the lemon. Pile it into a shallow bowl and decorate the perimeter with a band of minced parsley.

ASSEMBLED THINGS

In addition to the smoked fish, excellent goose liver-style liverwurst, sausages, and cold cuts that are ready to serve when you get them home, there are some other ways to avoid the stove.

Fish Roes

Lumpfish roe looks something like caviar and is quite tasty even though it leaves you with a sooty smile. Red caviar is becoming more popular and is easily obtained in most localities. Serve it mixed with sour cream as a dip. Pressed caviar is relatively inexpensive (relative to fresh Beluga), but is unfamiliar except to connoisseurs. Serve it sliced on toast points with lemon juice.

Fresh fish roe, such as shad, is excellent poached, then mashed with lemon juice, raw onion juice, and a little olive oil. Beluga caviar is, of course, the ultimate solution for an hors d'oeuvre. Fresh American caviar is becoming more available and is delicious. Serve it in the jar on a bed of ice with lemon wedges and hot, buttered toast.

Sardines

Those lowly, plump, skinless and boneless sardines from Portugal served right in the can are one of my favorite snacks. But the silvery, tiny whole sardines from Norway are preferred by many. A selection of several kinds of sardines—a sardine tasting, so to speak—can be interesting. Arranged on a plate with some lemon wedges, thin slices of onion, and hot toast, they are a quite respectable offering at cocktail time. Sardines should always be part of an antipasto arrangement, along with the usual salami, artichoke hearts, pimentos, etc. Hard-cooked eggs and sardines seem to hit it off together, and a lusty sardine and onion sandwich on whole-grain bread is one of my favorite, if indelicate, combinations.

❧ INSTANT PÂTÉ DE FOIE ❧

Only one brand of liver pâté that I know of can be recommended for this delicious deception, and that is Sell's. The finished mixture should be packed into an attractive little terrine or soufflé dish.

4 tablespoons softened sweet	*¹/₂ small mild onion*
butter (¹/₂ stick)	*2 teaspoons cognac*
2 small cans Sell's liver pâté	*Black pepper, coarsely ground*

Cream the butter and liver pâté together with a wooden spoon. Grate the onion into the mixture, using the finest holes on the grater. Mix. Add cognac and pepper and mix thoroughly. Pack into a small mold, cover, and chill for at least 1 hour. Serve with hot toast or unsalted crackers. No one is going to think this is *foie gras,* but they won't know what it really is either.

❧ SALMON *RILLETTES* ❧

To my surprised delight, the publishing world's favorite restaurant, The Four Seasons, serves a very similar, but much more lavish version of this dish. The tiny, cheap red roe of Icelandic lumpfish is excellent and it doesn't get squashed or streak the *rillettes,* though it cannot be said that it approaches the thrill of big, translucent fresh salmon eggs that pop lusciously in the mouth. This is an easy food processor recipe that yields super dividends for the time invested. Serve with rice crackers and pale Canadian wheat crackers. You may use freshly poached salmon if you wish, but best-quality canned salmon has reliably excellent flavor. Nor is it necessary to use the finest Scottish salmon prodigally in this dish, but the best-quality smoked Nova Scotia salmon (not greasy "lox") is the least you can do for it.

Serves 18 to 20 with other hors d'oeuvre

1 8-ounce can red Alaska sockeye
    salmon
1 tablespoon roughly chopped
    scallion, white part only
1/4 pound sweet butter (1 stick)
1 teaspoon freshly milled coarse
    white pepper
1/4 to 1/3 pound good smoked

salmon, such as Nova, thickly
    sliced
1 tablespoon tarragon-flavored*
    or plain white wine
Few drops of lemon juice to taste
Melted clarified butter, optional
    (page 126)
1 4-ounce jar red salmon caviar

Pick over the salmon and remove skin and bones (no matter how much calcium they have—this dish is for tantalizing appetites, not nourishing the starved). Set aside. Put the scallion in the processor and finely mince. Add the butter and pepper and process until smooth.

Cut the smoked salmon into large pieces and add to the processor with the canned salmon and the wine. Run the processor in short pulses until the mixture is well blended, but not a fine puree. (Anything called *"rillettes"* should have a rather fibrous texture.) Season the *rillettes* with the merest hint of lemon juice to sharpen flavors; the taste of lemon should not be discernible. Pack lightly in a 2- to 3-cup crock and cover with a thin film of lukewarm melted butter. Chill until the butter sets, then seal tightly with foil.

You can make the *rillettes* up to 5 days in advance, but let it come to cool room temperature before scraping off the butter and serving. Or you can make it and serve it immediately, as I have many times, just piling it lightly into a stoneware mortar or some crocky-looking thing. Decorate with red caviar of your choice. You can also spread out the *rillettes* in a flat bowl and rim the perimeter with the entire jar of caviar. This is rather magnificent looking. But caviar, once opened, does not keep well. The salmon *rillettes,* however, does and can be saved if it isn't all eaten, and trotted out to other guests.

*Steep 1 heaping tablespoon minced fresh tarragon in a tablespoon or so of boiling white wine.

❧ SHELLY'S SMOKED BLUEFISH SALAD ❧

This concoction is a sort of fish *rillettes*—meant to be piled on crackers, too rich to eat as an actual salad. Buy small smoked bluefish fillets. Skin them and break the flesh into small pieces. Mix with finely chopped scallions and some lemon juice and olive oil. Pepper rather heavily. Use two forks to mix and tear the fish into shreds. Serve at room temperature with some plain crisp crackers.

❧ BIALY PIZZA ❧

Bialys aren't easy to come by where I live, but on occasion they show up at a South-ampton specialty food store I like. Even in New York City they are no longer easy to find. Bialys are round flat rolls, indented in the center and sprinkled with chopped onions before baking. They have a taste similar to pizza dough, though the big soft edges are deliciously chewy and not hard. These bialy pizzas are a good snack and can be assembled ahead, then baked, cut in four to six wedges and served with drinks.

1 bialy
1 or 2 Kalamata olives, stoned
4 small cubes fresh buffalo
   mozzarella
About 2 teaspoons olive oil

flavored with freshly pressed
   garlic
Coarse salt and freshly ground
   black pepper to taste

Slash the bialy diagonally around the edges so that you can insert the slivers of olive. Cut the olives lengthwise into about 6 crescents each. Insert these in the slits. Put the cheese cubes in the middle. Brush garlic oil over the bread and dribble a bit over the cheese. Sprinkle with salt and pepper. Lay on a foil-covered jelly roll pan in the upper part of a 450°F. oven and bake until the cheese melts. Serve at once, cut or whole. These can be habit forming.

OLIVES—QUICK EVER READY HORS D'OEUVRE

Glistening black, brown, purple, and green, olives are fine complements to most other foods commonly served with drinks. The great, juicy, brown-black Kalamata olives from Greece, the tiny, firm little footballs from Provence, the spicy green varieties from Spain, and the dry, wrinkled oil- and herb-cured black olives from Italy are among the many choices.

There is immense variety to be found among olives from different countries (except our own, of course; American olives are curiously bland—the green ones taste of salt and the black ones taste of nothing). So it is possible to keep on hand an interesting assortment to assemble on short notice. Olives, like cheeses, need a little time (but no work) to come to room temperature so that their distinctive flavors can assert themselves.

When you serve olives, remember to place a few dishes around so that people don't have to put the pits in their pockets. I've concluded that the pit problem is why olives aren't more enthusiastically eaten at parties. Things on sticks—satays and whatnot—present a similar dilemma and require disposal dishes.

CAVIARS

Caviars sealed in glass jars keep in the refrigerator for weeks, and it's nice to be able to come up with instant luxury.

Whether from the lowly lumpfish or the lordly sturgeon, caviars—black, gray, red, or golden—are a magnanimous treat. There may still be a few souls who think caviar tastes like fishy blackberry jam, but it's definitely a hit with most people. (I've noticed that fresh, first-quality mixed nuts also prove irresistible to nearly everyone, fashiona-ble or not.) Keep a few bottles of champagne or any good white sparkling wine on ice as well, for impulsive invitations to celebrate a sunset or whatever.

☆ CAVIAR WITH BUCKWHEAT PANCAKES ☆

When the Tsars were still around downing kilos of precious Beluga and Servuga caviar (transported from Iran at astronomical cost even then), it was served with blinis— tiny, silver dollar–sized buckwheat pancakes. You can make them quickly from a commercial mix. Almost any supermarket carries both red and black Icelandic lump-fish roe, and specialty food shops offer the expensive varieties (which are really appreciated best in the simplest presentation).

1 4-ounce jar caviar, well chilled
Small warm buckwheat
   pancakes (in a napkin)

Melted butter (with a brush)
Sour cream mixed with coarse
   pepper and minced scallions

The contrast of the warm pancakes and melted butter to the cold caviar and sour cream is wonderful. Having the sour cream premixed with the scallions and pepper facilitates service for the home cook as well as shortening the time it takes for guests to help themselves.

Arrange everything on a single tray and either brush the pancakes with melted butter and top them with sour cream and caviar, or encourage guests to build their own.

❧ CAVIAR PIE ❧

Both hen eggs and fish eggs are celebrated in this holiday "pie" composed of egg salad made with finely minced chives, celery, scallion, and a homemade lemon mayonnaise, and topped with red or black roe. An eight-inch pie is enough for about 20 people to spread on crisp wheat crackers or thin-sliced party rye. Four ounces of any kind of caviar may be used to cover the egg salad, which should be made with 4 or 5 hard-cooked eggs.

The egg salad ingredients should be finely chopped and the mayonnaise made fairly stiff so that the mixture holds together nicely. Don't salt the mayonnaise. Pat the egg salad into a small ring mold or a shallow soup plate and cover it with plastic wrap. Chill for several hours. Spread caviar over the top evenly, pat it down, and recover with plastic wrap until serving time. If using a spring mold, remove the rim and put the caviar pie on a serving plate; otherwise, serve the pie in the soup plate decorated with with very tiny lemon wedges. Use very small wheat crackers or halves of small loaves of party rye as underpinning for this rich dish.

❧ SMOKED EEL PÂTÉ ❦

Smoked eel is a local delicacy on eastern Long Island, and this pâté is an easy and elegant way to use it. As it has an intricate, rich flavor, a little goes a long way; it also keeps well, refrigerated, but must be brought to room temperature so that it spreads easily on crisp crackers.

1 whole smoked eel, about 1¼ pounds
¼ pound sweet butter (1 stick)
1 tablespoon grated white onion

1 teaspoon coarsely ground white pepper, or more
Few drops of lemon juice
Few sprigs of parsley

Cut off the eel head and set it aside (to decorate and identify the pâté). Skin and bone the eel. Cream the butter with the onion and pepper in a food processor, add the fish, process until smooth, then season to taste with lemon juice and more pepper if needed. No lemon flavor should be detectable in the finished dish. Spread the pâté into a small, shallow dish and place the eel head in the center, pushing the base down into the pâté. Circle it with minute parsley sprigs. The pâté can be made ahead of time, wrapped in plastic, and returned to room temperature before serving. Crisp crackers complement the creamy texture of the pâté better than bread does.

✄ MARINATED SCALLOPS ✄

Many clam and oyster fanciers are appalled at the thought of scallops in their natural state. But they are delicious raw, with the flesh made somewhat more firm-textured by a lime juice marinade.

Serves 4

1 pound sea or bay scallops   *Cucumbers*
Juice of 4 or 5 limes   *Sauce Vinaigrette (page 65)*
Lettuce

Rinse the scallops with cold water and drain them well. Sea scallops should be cut into halves or quarters so that the pieces are about 1 inch across. (Bay scallops aren't in season in the summer, but are sometimes offered frozen.) Put the scallops in a deep bowl with lime juice to cover. Marinate, covered, for 3 to 4 hours in the refrigerator. At serving time, drain the scallops and serve them on a bed of leaf lettuce and sliced cucumbers. Pass a bowl of Sauce Vinaigrette. This recipe serves 4 amply as a first course. Larger quantities are fine for parties and are convenient to eat with toothpicks.

❧ MELON OR AVOCADO WITH PROSCIUTTO ❧

Since melons and summer are made for each other, it's a fine time to take advantage of the local crop. Chilled cantaloupe and honeydew both present a luscious taste and texture contrast to thin, salty slices of Italian ham; the blandness of the avocado is an excellent foil for the ham's spiciness. Smithfield or Westphalian ham may be served this way as well.

For individual servings, slice the melon in wedges and drape each serving with 2 or 3 slices of prosciutto. For parties, cut the melon in small cubes; wrap each one in a thin strip of ham and fasten it with a toothpick. You will be amazed at how quickly these old-fangled treats disappear.

CHEESES

W hat a Friend We Have in Cheeses!" wrote anthologist William Cole in a poem celebrating one of man's most ancient foods. A friend it is indeed to the noncooking party giver. Despite the fact that we're not profoundly a cheese-eating nation in the sense that the French—who complete every meal with it—are, cheese consumption is on an amazing climb in this country. Whether we know anything about it or not, we know that we like it. The cheese array is a dependable attraction at any party. And it can be an effortless alternative to dessert, or served just before it.

Our white wine craze, perhaps beveling off now, was accompanied by an ever-widening cheese gourmandize. The "cheese board," a welcome fixture at summer festivities, is here to stay, whether or not the white wine fad bites the dust. Most of the best-known French cheeses are produced for sale from October through May, but the pasteurized versions sold in this country know no season.

In assembling a cheese tray for a cocktail party, it's probably not wise to get too precious. There are too few real connoisseurs to appreciate your finds, and besides, complicated aged cheeses deserve at least as much attention as a good wine. For instance, aged Parmigiano Reggiano is a compulsive nibble with a dinner's end glass of wine. But these magic crumbs must be contemplatively picked off with the point of a knife.

It is depressing to watch cocktail party guerillas vandalizing an expensive care-fully chosen cheese board. Good cheese manners demand that guests cut portions that leave any cheese as nearly as possible in its original conformation.

Choosing cheese is a tricky business. It requires a keen eye, a sharp nose, a probing finger and a lot of gall. If you don't know what you're supposed to be looking for, swat up with a good book such as *The Cheese Book* by Marquis and Haskell (recently republished by Simon & Schuster). For on-the-scene decisions, take along *The Simon and Schuster Pocket Guide to Cheese* by Sandy Carr. Regrettably, many fresh-faced cheese clerks, though supercilious as Gucci salesmen, know very little about their subject. A dead giveaway is "This will ripen when it warms up." Only if you are buying the whole, uncut cheese could this be true (and only under controlled conditions). Cheese is a living, breathing thing—like a pear or a peach—and once cut, is mortally wounded. It may rot, but it won't ripen further. What you see is what you get.

When you buy cheese, be sure the store has a fairly rapid turnover and a reputa-tion for reliability. Beware of the picturesque shops offering 101 varieties. They can't possibly maintain a stock in peak condition. When it comes to buying cheese, don't bargain hunt; go to the biggest and best seller. Some soft-ripened cheeses are in their prime for only three or four days. (Before that, they can be chalky in the center, since these cheeses ripen from the outside in. After these ideal *"à point"* days, such cheese—Brie and Camembert, for example—become sticky, ammoniated, and bitter.

Reputable dealers will not sell you a bad cheese, but if one slips through and you return it promptly, an exchange or refund should be offered without question. Depart-ment stores with gourmet shops are usually safe bets for cheese; only New York and a few other big cities have shops devoted primarily to the sale of cheese. While the public's enthusiasm has grown incredibly in the past two decades, general knowledge of cheese is still shaky. This is the most convincing reason for sticking to expert dealers

. . . if you can find them. There are few areas of food buying where the customers are so dependent on the knowledge (and honesty) of the retailer.

If you happen to spend your summers in a place where a wedge of Bel Paese is still the leading edge of cheese chic, it may be necessary to stick with domestics. *Chèvre,* which Americans now have the confidence to call "goat cheese," is made in the Pacific Northwest and New England, and has become as ubiquitous as all get-out. It may already be good strategy to offset its familiarity with a dribbling of fruity olive oil, some cracked pepper, or some chopped fresh herbs. (The passion with which the "goats" were embraced by nouvelle American cooks has swiftly pummeled the public into near *ennui* with this whole category.)

Liederkranz is native-born despite its Teutonic name, and there are American versions of both Brie and Camembert. Bierkäse is an innocuous-looking copy of a stinky German cheese (as is Limburger), meant to match its walloping flavor with onions and beer. American cheesemakers, though they've been copying European, especially French, cheeses for over a century, unfortunately seem on safe ground only with fresh, young cheeses such as cream cheese or cottage cheese. Vermont and New York State (Herkimer County) cheddars are the equal of any English ones I've tasted. Canadian versions are prized by cheddar lovers, who claim that they're the nearest to the *vrai* thing, if that's the kind of thing you're interested in. Personally, I've never seen much excitement in cheddar, with its nursery odor and peanut butter gumminess. But it's America's favorite cheese. (*Tomme de Savoie,* a mild but nutty French semi-hard cheese, is better than anybody's cheddar and is fairly easy to find.) Even our latest love, domestic goat cheese, is sold in infancy, at a mild-tasting few weeks old, and rather closely resembles a very soft, sour American cream cheese. You wouldn't find too many Americans eager to share space with the much-prized but evil-looking (and worse smelling) aged French *chèvres.* Mature goat cheese is a special taste, too acrid to be sprung on the unwary. In case you were wondering at the sudden fashion for olive oil–covered goat cheese in fancy food shops, it's because under a protective film of oil, young *chèvres* will *stay* young indefinitely. Even where a veil of blue mold has crept up, the cheese can be carefully scraped, then oiled and peppered and it's as good as ever—maybe better, since the taste is more pronounced.

The soft-ripened cheeses such as Brie and Camembert far outweigh the popularity of semi-hards such as Emmentaler (or its Norwegian imitator, Jarlsberg), Havarti, or Bel Paese, which were so often on cheese boards of a decade or so ago. (I suppose those Dutch bowling balls, Edams, in their bright red coats of wax, are still sold, but I haven't seen one in years.) *Morbier,* a French semi-hard cheese that is no longer obscure, gets ever more popular and available—even in supermarkets.

Dieters become amnesiac at the sight of the soft ivory double and triple cream cheeses. People who avoid butter on health grounds will dreamily scoop up endless quantities of creamy Explorateur, Reblochon, or Coulommiers. Sometimes it's best to pretend ignorance in exchange for bliss. Anyway, you might as well live a little because *all* cheese has lots of fat. But it's comforting to know that because of the high moisture content in the soft-ripened cheeses, they have no more fat than the concentrated—relatively dry—semi-hard and hard cheeses.

Chaumes is a mild-looking, little French, semi-soft cheese with a great deal more character than its appearance suggests. It's a family favorite, but it does have one drawback: it really needs about 24 hours at cool room temperature to bring out its charms. *Pont l'Evêque* is another of these pale but potent cheeses.

Unfortunately, it is impossible to know the true taste of what you're buying (in the state of New York, at least), no matter how generous the seller is with samples. By law, all cheeses—even a 5-year-old Parmesan—must be kept under refrigeration. Only the faintest ghost of the actual aroma, flavor, and texture can be determined in an icy cold cheese. When a cheese warms up, its character changes—often radically. The "refrigerator law" tends to make cheese buying hazardous and turns some of us into conservatives. I usually buy only a very small amount of unfamiliar cheese to try out at home under warm and properly aired eating conditions.

The veined, or "blue," cheeses are always a good addition to the board. Danish (Saga and Danablu) and American blues can be excellent and are available from Amarillo to Anchorage. Gorgonzola, the Italian entry, and a Bavarian blue, can be found in most localities. True Roquefort, that noble ewe's milk cheese, is rarer, though its name has been bandied around for eons to describe some ineffable bottled salad dressings. Nearly every country where dairying exists makes some kind of blue-veined cheese. Experiment with all of them.

All cheese should be served at room temperature. Most cheeses require 3 to 4 hours to breathe and warm up before they are served. This includes every category of cheese—even fresh cream or cottage cheese tastes remarkably better minus the deadening chill of refrigeration.

Cheese boards quickly become disheveled, and nothing is more disgusting than a collection of bashed, squashed, and battered cheeses. It's far better to distribute selections on three or four china platters (my favorite is round, flat, and dark blue, to show off the cheese colors) or in trays or baskets lined with dark leaves for the softer cheeses. A smallish marble circle or slab makes a nice presentation too. The giant cheese board, while photogenic at first, gets frowzy within minutes. Flowers aren't appropriate to decorate cheese boards or platters. If anything at all is to be added, a few tiny bouquets of fresh herbs tied with string or straw will do.

Finally, if there are significant amounts of salvageable ripe cheese left that no one wants to see for a week, freeze them. Connoisseurs may wince, but the alterations that occur in freezing are infinitely preferable to rot. The soft cheeses such as Brie freeze very successfully, unless they have been allowed to sit around running from their crusts for hours on end. This is another reason to make frequent fresh additions to a cheese board rather than serving it all at once. Semi-softs freeze fairly well too, but hard or cooking cheeses simply need tight fresh wrapping and refrigeration.

Generally, it isn't wise to buy so much cheese that you'll have to freeze some, but party appetites or fancies can't always be predicted. And if there's a sale at your favorite cheese store or you live in an area that has undependable supplies (where I live practically everything but rat cheese disappears from stores after the tourists leave for the winter), it can be comforting to have a supply of fine Parmesan, Gruyère, and Brie in the freezer.

Be certain to set out a varied selection of breads—white, dark, and medium dark, coarse, fine, and/or nutty or seeded—to go with the cheeses. Cut them in small (one- or two-bite) pieces. It's gilding the lily, but I am among the eccentric few who absolutely must have fresh unsalted butter to go with blue cheeses of all kinds. Crackers should be crisp but bland and very lightly salted if at all so that their flavor doesn't interfere with, or mask, the taste of the cheeses. Thin crisp-fried slices of bagel, called "bagel crisps," are sensational with soft creamy cheeses. But if they're not for sale in your cheese store—and they may simply be indigenous to New York—I would never attempt making them at home; plain, neatly trimmed toast triangles are excellent cheese companions and are easily made by anyone, anywhere.

Given the complaints of our dairy industry, it's hard to fathom why they can't make more decent and interesting cheeses with all that surplus milk. It takes roughly ten pounds of milk to make one pound of cheese! Meanwhile, we are importing and eating tons of Brie and Camembert, and the old chip-and-dip days linger only in nostalgia or high camp cookbooks (dried onion soup dip is probably due for a revival in the A.D. 2000).

We now import hundreds and hundreds of cheeses of all styles and flavors from all over the world, so the cheese advice in this little book is necessarily circumscribed. For the most part, I've limited myself to the cheeses most widely available. For the adventurous, new cheeses (new to us, anyway) seem to be appearing on the cheese counter every month, and the old favorites and "classics" are arriving and being sold in much better condition. As good cheese is not cheap, and cheese knowledge and sophistication is growing apace with wine, we can expect cheese merchants to make a little braver show for us. And we, in turn, can be a little more enterprising than to offer our guests twelve cheddar-clones with different names.

SOUPS

$\mathbf{S}$ummer soups used to be bounded on one side by jellied Madrilene and on the other by vichyssoise with the odd ethic excursion into borscht. But we brave Americans have journeyed far in the past couple of decades. Now, for every hot soup you can name (with the exception maybe of oxtail) there seems to be a chilled counterpart. And only a few short years ago I recall a waiter solemnly explaining to me what "the vichyswah" was.

But for all the new inventiveness along the soup line, it is still relatively rare to be given one of these lovely cold soups at summer dinner parties. Restaurants yes (after all, what could yield a higher profit?), but in private houses, for some mysterious reason, no soup, either summer or winter. I suppose this grave soup shortage must be owing to all this stand-up eating we do at summer bashes—that and the lack of a servant to remove the first course at sit-down dinners. Some very nice soups can be drunk out of a cup, though, and it would give me great pleasure if this admirable course were restored to its proper place in a dinner. What more appetizing starter can there be on a warm night than a chilled, chive-flecked cucumber soup? Or a lively, thin hot *soupe au poisson* full of Mediterranean flavor with almost no substance?

I should probably confess that I am a serious soup fan and will eat it even for breakfast during any season. Fortunately, I dwell in the region of clam chowder, so main course "soups" aren't unusual at relaxed dinners and luncheons. And, as the East End of Long Island has superb vegetables, there's nothing like brewing up a stunning mélange of them made headier still with the addition of Pistou (page 57), the basil-cheese sauce from Provence. Although we have pretty fine weather on the whole, this is not the Caribbean. There are within living memory of nearly everyone I know numerous damp summer weekends spent peering out at unremitting rain squalls. We used to start a chowder and get out the poker chips or cards (all summer houses should be equipped with these as well as Monopoly boards and Trivial Pursuit). So this chapter is by no means going to be devoted to cold soups.

EASY FISH CHOWDER

I used to make this with a base of Knorr's dried leek soup mix so that I could get something on the table after exhausting Friday trips from the city to the country. Two things have changed: Now I live in the country and don't make Friday trips, and the Knorr company changed ownership. This recipe is almost as quick as my old "commuter's chowder," though. With two people peeling and chopping efficiently, dinner can be on in under an hour.

Serves 4 to 6

4 strips thick bacon
2 medium onions, chopped
2 cloves garlic, minced
1 to 2 tablespoons butter
2 tablespoons flour
2 cups water
1 cup dry white wine or dry
  Vermouth
2 cups potatoes, peeled and diced

1 teaspoon dried thyme leaves,
  crushed
2 pounds whitefish fillets (cod,
  haddock, fluke, or blackfish are
  some possibilities)
1 cup heavy cream
Salt and freshly ground white
  pepper to taste
1/4 cup minced fresh parsley

Cut the bacon into matchstick-sized strips and fry them in a heavy soup kettle or Dutch oven over low flame. When fairly crisp, drain the bacon on paper toweling and reserve. Add enough butter to make 3 tablespoons of fat in the pan. Sauté the onions and garlic in this over low heat until transparent. Stir in the flour and cook, stirring over low heat so that the roux doesn't color.

Stir in the water and wine, then add the potatoes and thyme. Simmer, covered, until potatoes are almost falling apart, about 30 minutes. Stir several times to prevent scorching. Cut the fish into large chunks and add them to the chowder, stirring gently. Simmer about 5 minutes or just until fish is opaque. Then stir in the cream, heat, and taste for seasoning. Add salt and pepper (white is tastier and doesn't fleck the chowder with black specks). Dish up in hot chowder bowls with a little bacon and parsley on top of each serving. Corn bread and a simple salad round out this fine family meal that is perfectly okay for guests too.

⚝ CLAM CHOWDER ⚝

This is made in exactly the same way as fish chowder except that 3 or 4 cups of chopped quahogs (big chowder clams) are substituted for the fish. You can, of course, make the chowder opulent by using both. Clams can't be chopped in a blender; it turns them into a hideous goo. Use a knife if you haven't a food processor, which can do a wonderful job of clam chopping if you turn it on and off in short pulses. Do not add the clams until everything else is in the chowder. They need only seconds to cook or they turn into rubber bands.

⚝ MUSSEL SOUP ⚝

Alexandre Dumas was a noted gourmand and cook who devoted both his culinary skill and literary talent to his aphoristic *Le Grand Dictionnaire de Cuisine,* published post-humously in 1873. Like those of most good cooks, his methods were old-fashioned even in his time. But his knowledge of food and cookery was so sound that his methods are translatable into modern recipes in many instances. Dumas's soup required an eleven-in-the-morning start, but you may begin about an hour before dinnertime.

Serves 8 to 10

12 white onions
12 medium-sized tomatoes
2 quarts beef bouillon (canned
  bouillon will do)
5 pounds mussels (in the shell)

Salt and freshly ground
pepper to taste
2 cloves garlic
1 tablespoon olive oil
French or Italian bread

Chop the onions and tomatoes coarsely and simmer them in the beef bouillon for an hour. Extract the seeds and pulp by passing the soup through a food mill or by pureeing in a processor or blender. Put the mixture back into a pot and simmer, uncovered. Scrub and beard the mussels and put them in another pot with a few tablespoons of water to steam open, which should take about 5 minutes. Shell the mussels and strain their juice through cheesecloth. Add the juice to the tomato and onions. Crush the cloves of garlic and cook them lightly in the olive oil. Discard the garlic. Put in the shelled mussels and swirl them around in the garlicky olive oil, then pour them into the soup. Serve with plain French or Italian bread for sopping and mopping.

ꙮ GAZPACHO I ꙮ

This soup really should be the main course for two reasons: its flavors are so varied and interesting that people are willing to eat it in quantity, and it is a substantial cold soup, although low on dreaded calories. You can, of course, skip the avocado, but then you wouldn't be eating "The Best Gazpacho Ever"—which is what I consider this, my absolute final decision about how to make this great Spanish soup. (I've never had a very good version in Spain—chunks of ice and bread floated in it!)

Serve each person a small bowl of crisp croutons to be added a few at a time to the soup (they get too soggy if added all at once).

Makes approximately 2 quarts

2 cloves garlic, minced

1 medium-hot fresh chili pepper, seeded and minced

6 to 8 scallions, sliced thin

2 pounds large ripe tomatoes, skinned

2 hard, dark green 6- or 7-inch cucumbers, peeled and seeded

1 teaspoon ground cumin

1 cup watercress leaves

1 tablespoon lemon juice

2 tablespoons olive oil

1 quart cold water

Salt and freshly ground pepper to taste

2 small ripe avocados*

Small crisp croutons

This soup must be one of the reasons the Cuisinart food processor was invented. But it can certainly be made with only a knife and a bowl, or a blender, in several batches.

Mince the garlic, chili pepper, and scallions. Peel and quarter the tomatoes, and place the seedy pulp in the processor. Dice the rest of the tomatoes by hand and reserve. Finely dice one cucumber by hand and reserve; cut the other into chunks and

---

*The small, dark, very wrinkled California avocados are the best; they should be bought a few days ahead of time and ripened at room temperature away from the sun.

put it into the processor. Add cumin, watercress, lemon juice, and olive oil. Process in a couple of short pulses until the soup is thick and coarsely chopped. Transfer the gazpacho to a bowl and mix in the cold water; add salt and pepper to taste. Add the hand-diced tomatoes and cucumbers, stir, and chill, covered, for 4 hours or longer. Just before serving, peel and slice the avocados, arrange them in a pattern on the surface of each bowl, or simply roughly dice and put them in the soup. Serve a small bowl of croutons with each helping.

☙ GAZPACHO II ❧

This pureed version—totally unlike Gazpacho I (page 54)—was given me by a French chef who, of course, swore it was the only *true* gazpacho. He felt that using an electric blender deprived the soup of its delicate texture but, unless you have the galley staff of a Madrid hotel on hand, I think the small sacrifice in consistency is worth the savings in labor. The soup is delicious even though it veers far away from the Spanish original.

Serves 6 to 8

¹/₃ cup olive oil

1 cup tomato or V-8 juice

1 ¹/₂ cups water

10 sprigs watercress, large stems removed

Juice of 1 lemon

2 green bell peppers, seeded, chopped

Pinch of dried red pepper flakes or a few drops of Tabasco sauce

2 cloves garlic, split

1 small onion, chopped

2 cucumbers, peeled and seeded

Salt and freshly ground white pepper to taste

1 cup heavy cream

2 ripe tomatoes, skinned, seeded, and diced

8 scallions, very finely minced

Puree all ingredients except the cream, tomatoes, and scallions in a food processor or blender. (If good, fresh ripe tomatoes are unavailable, omit them.) Add salt and white pepper to taste and refrigerate for at least 2 hours. Just before serving, stir in the heavy cream with a wire whisk. Garnish the soup with the diced tomatoes and minced scallions and serve in chilled bowls.

𣏓 GARDEN SOUP 𣏓

There is no better moment to enjoy a garden-fresh vegetable soup than when the makings are at their peak of flavor. Unlike a rich, slow-simmered winter soup, hearty and filling with turnips and cabbage, a summer blend should be lightly cooked so that each vegetable retains its freshness, flavor, and texture. Prescribing what to put in a vegetable soup would be a bit like "painting" on a numbered canvas that the artist could never claim as his own. This is a rough outline to fill in with your own design.

Serves 8 to 10

2 quarts water
Salt
2 cups sliced, peeled baby carrots
2 cups diced, peeled new potatoes
2 cups diced, peeled ripe
*   tomatoes*
2 cups sliced scallions

1 cup fresh green lima beans
1 cup fresh tiny green beans, cut
*   in 1-inch lengths*
1 cup sliced fresh okra
1 cup fresh corn, scraped off the
*   cob*
1 1/2 cups cooked rice

Salt the water lightly and bring it to a boil. Add the carrots, potatoes, tomatoes, scallions, and lima beans, and boil gently for 30 minutes. Add the green beans, okra, and corn, and simmer for about 5 minutes after the water returns to the boil. Place a heaping spoonful of cooked white rice in the center of each soup plate and ladle some hot soup over it. Pass a bowl of the Provençal sauce—Pistou—for each diner to stir into his soup. (I used to pound up a somewhat rougher-textured Pistou in the traditional mortar and pestle, but the food processor does a smoother job in an eye-blink.)

PISTOU

4 cloves garlic
1/4 cup chopped fresh basil
2 tablespoons chopped fresh
   parsley

3 tablespoons tomato paste
1/2 cup freshly grated Romano or
   Parmesan cheese
1/2 cup olive oil

In a food processor, puree the garlic with the basil and parsley; add the tomato paste and cheese. Blend in the oil by droplets, then add 1 cup of hot soup. Pour the sauce into a small bowl and pass it around with the soup.

❧ ICED CHICKEN SOUP ☙

A first-rate brunch course, this light, delicate soup is soothing, healing, and simple to make.

Serves 6

3 cans clear chicken stock (the kind you do not dilute with water)
1 tablespoon minced fresh tarragon

¼ cup minced fresh parsley
1 cup heavy cream

Bring chicken stock to the boiling point and blanch tarragon and parsley. Remove from heat, stir in the cream thoroughly and chill for 2 hours. The soup should be quite thin and light textured. Serve it in large, chilled china or glass cups.

❧ ITALIAN HEBREW SOUP ☙

This borscht was eaten by an Italian food writer in the home of a Livornese Jewish family. He came away ecstatic and recommended it to all his friends, "baptized Christians, circumcised Moslems, idolaters or fire-worshippers." This is from *Il Gastronomo Educato* by Alberto Denti di Pirajno.

Serves 6

*¹/₂ pound cooked beets, fresh or
  canned*
1¹/₂ quarts salted water
1 tablespoon vinegar
3 eggs

*Salt and freshly ground pepper to
  taste*
*18 small new potatoes, unpeeled,
  boiled, and swirled in butter*

Simmer the beets in the salted water and vinegar for 20 minutes. Pass through a sieve (or puree in a blender). Beat the eggs briskly in a large bowl and pour the beet broth onto them, beating all the time. Season with salt and pepper to taste, and chill. Serve ice cold and give each guest a small bowl of tiny hot boiled potatoes that have been swirled in butter (goose fat is actually the traditional flavoring, but . . .). Eat a little potato with each spoonful of soup.

☘ SPRING PEA SOUP ☘

Every dish on the menu can't be a cold one without boring everyone to tears, no matter how warm the weather may be. This is a delicate hot soup that anticipates a refreshing chilled main course.

Serves 6

1 tablespoon butter
1 cup diced potatoes
3 cups chicken broth

1 cup freshly shelled green peas
1 tablespoon chopped chives

Melt the butter in a soup pot and swirl the potatoes around in it. Add the chicken broth and simmer until the potatoes are soft, about 20 minutes. Puree in a blender and return to the pot. Bring to a boil and put in the fresh green peas. Cook them until just tender (test by eating one) and stir in the chopped chives just before serving.

☆ SORREL SOUP ☆

This soup announces that summer has arrived in France. Sorrel, so frequently used in French cooking, is easier to find in the United States than it used to be. If you have difficulty locating it, try a European vegetable market—or grow it in your garden. Canned sorrel is available in food specialty shops, but it really isn't very good. This soup can also be made with Swiss chard, young spinach, or watercress, all of which taste different from sorrel, but are very good nevertheless.

Serves 4 to 6

¹/₄ pound fresh sorrel
2 tablespoons butter

1 egg yolk
1 cup heavy cream

Shred the sorrel and rinse it thoroughly. Wilt it in the butter in a medium saucepan over medium heat, put in the chicken broth, and heat to boiling. Beat the egg yolk with the cream and beat a little of the hot soup into the mixture. Then stir the egg-cream into the hot soup with a wire whisk. Reheat and serve hot, or cool in the refrigerator and serve well chilled.

🌿 CUCUMBER SOUP 🌿

The frequency with which this soup is served by anyone in possession of an electric blender has slightly blunted its considerable charm. It's an oldie but still goodie, and no summer soup chapter would be complete without at least one cucumber recipe. Cucumber soup is elegant, easy, and inexpensive to make for a large number of people. It even tastes good drunk out of paper cups at a picnic.

Serves 8

4 tablespoons butter (1/2 stick)
1/2 cup minced scallions
3 cups chopped, unpeeled
  cucumber
3/4 cup diced, peeled potatoes
1 quart chicken broth

1 cup watercress leaves
Salt and freshly ground black
  pepper to taste
1 cup heavy cream
1 cup milk
Minced chives or chervil

Heat the butter and wilt the scallions in it. Add the cucumber, potatoes, and chicken broth, and simmer together 15 minutes. During the last 5 minutes of cooking, add the watercress leaves. (They impart a sharp tang and pleasant green color to the soup.) Add salt and pepper to taste. Puree in a blender, then stir in the cream and milk. Chill for 2 hours in a nonmetallic container. Garnish the soup with minced chives or chervil, or a mixture of both herbs.

SALADS

Salads are the most abundant and appropriate mainstays of summer meal planning. However, no course was ever treated in a more monotonous manner up until very recently. Odd, since we Americans are generally thought by the rest of the world to be fanatic salad eaters.

Many otherwise competent cooks profess to be mystified by a plain oil and vinegar dressing. This is simple to master and easy to vary, especially with the recent influx of exotic exports such as walnut and hazelnut oil and a huge variety of cold-pressed olive oils from Italy and France. Then there are the High Priests of the salad bowl—usually men who have learned to officiate at a Caesar Salad (page 73). Somewhere between the two extremes lies the making of a simple, dewy fresh green salad, glistening in a light dressing, and fragrant with the season's herbs.

One ritual of no value at all is the anointing of the salad bowl with a sliver of garlic. Some garlic-hater must have thought up that effete practice. Another notion that must be dispelled is that all the preparation of an excellent, crisp salad must be done in a last-minute frenzy. It is, however, absolute Gospel that you cannot add other ingredients or dressing to the greens until the moment before serving. It is also preferable not to tear the greens until just before dressing them—and not to *cut* them at all (heinous!).

Those who have been resigned to serving a bowl of exhausted salad greens reclining listlessly in an acrid bath of oil and vinegar usually are victims of only two small, but fatal, mistakes: too much vinegar and too little drying of the greens. Therefore, we will start with basic training on that indispensable complement to a summer meal, Plain Green Salad.

PLAIN GREEN SALAD

It is best not to rinse salad greens in advance if you have to keep them more than two days. No matter how carefully they have been dried, even a little water starts to rot the leaves when they are stored in a plastic bag in the refrigerator. Generally, salad greens should be used as quickly as possible after purchase or picking.

Rinse the salad thoroughly, separating the leaves. Invert in a colander to drain. There is a well-made Swiss spin-dryer on the market (Zyss) or you can dry your greens the traditional way. Detach, shake, and pat the leaves dry between paper toweling. Store, rolled loosely in a dish towel, jelly-roll fashion, for up to 2 hours in the refrigerator. Some slightly wilted greens will crisp up nicely in an open plastic bag in the refrigerator.

Prepare a Sauce Vinaigrette, which is what French dressing really is. That pink-orange sticky banality we've all come to know and loathe as "French Dressing" is a purely American invention. The sheer density of it is enough to beat a tender little lettuce leaf into submission, to say nothing of smothering its delicate flavor.

⚘ SAUCE VINAIGRETTE ⚘

Measure into a small dry screw-top jar:

About ¹/₄ cup

3 tablespoons good olive oil
¹/₂ to 1 tablespoon wine vinegar
or 1 tablespoon lemon juice
¹/₈ teaspoon salt
Freshly ground black pepper to
taste

¹/₄ teaspoon dry mustard
(optional)
Mashed clove garlic (optional)
Minced herbs such as parsley,
tarragon, basil, or chives
(optional)

Shake all ingredients together well and leave at room temperature. (You may also beat the oil into the other ingredients in a a small bowl using a wire whisk.) This recipe makes enough dressing for 1 medium head of romaine or a large head of Boston lettuce. Unused dressing should be refrigerated.

Just before serving, stir in 1 to 2 tablespoons of minced green herbs such as parsley, tarragon, basil, or chives; use any one or a combination of up to three herbs. Or you may omit the herbs altogether and still have a basic vinaigrette. Try out different vinegars, such as raspberry and tarragon, but be frugal with all of them, especially Balsamic, which is very strong—a teaspoon is enough to start with.

Don't get carried away with too many of the various optional ingredients. Choose among them. Do experiment with the amount of vinegar that satisfies your taste, but keep in mind that salad dressing is primarily oil, *flavored* a little with other ingredients. I prefer only ¹/₂ tablespoon of vinegar or lemon juice to 3 tablespoons of oil, but the classic recipe calls for a ratio of three parts oil to one part vinegar.

It doesn't matter too much whether your salad bowl is glass, china, or wood, but it should be large enough to get both hands into it so that you can mix the salad thoroughly. Turn the greens gently at least six or seven times to be sure all the leaves are coated. The taste of the Sauce Vinaigrette should be judged on a salad leaf. Add dressing a little at a time, and when each leaf is glistening, stop! There should never be a well of dressing left in the bottom of the bowl after serving. Quantities of dressing should not be made up in advance because the oil quickly loses its freshness. In summer, all delicate oils should be refrigerated—especially those pressed from nuts.

Some people add sliced cucumbers or avocado, among other things, to a Plain Green Salad. A mixed green salad means a mixture of various types of greens—not a mixture of various green things. Like tomatoes, mixed vegetables are a very good salad in themselves, but adulterating a green salad with them is one national sin I wish we could abolish.

VARIOUS GREENS

Romaine: Available everywhere because of its travel hardiness, it suffers the drawback of having somewhat tough, fibrous outer leaves. The spine of the larger leaves should be ripped out. The paler inner leaves are tender and delicious. Its spicy brittleness is interesting mixed with other greens and it is excellent "bedding" for mayonnaise and meat or fish salads since its large, strong leaves do not wilt readily. It is essential in a Caesar Salad (page 73).

Chicory: Also called curly endive, chicory has the characteristic slightly bitter flavor of the endive family. Its leaves are sharply feathered and somewhat resemble Salad Bowl lettuce, but are much crisper. An entire salad of this green would be unpleasant to most people, but it adds a nice piquancy and texture to the softer greens.

Belgian Endive: Also called winter or French endive, it is a pale yellow to white, tight cluster of slender, pointed leaves, shaped something like a small banana. Its waxy, crisp texture and slightly acrid taste are best enhanced by a plain Sauce Vinaigrette (page 65) with a dash of mustard. Belgian endive, along with what we call Boston lettuce, are the greens most frequently served in France. It is mystifyingly expensive, since it ships well, but it is available the year round, although more plentiful in winter.

Watercress: It has real personality. Unlike any other green, its dark green, spicy, petal-shaped leaves have a distinctive pungent flavor that always seems to be best with a lemon and oil dressing and an extra dash of freshly ground black pepper. Watercress, which until lately shared the fate of parsley—chiefly to garnish steaks and chops—makes a delicious salad all by itself or in combination with other milder-flavored salad greens.

Escarole (with its tough, leathery leaves) and **Iceberg Lettuce:** These are last resorts; I would rather eat coleslaw.

Spinach: This green makes an unusual addition to a mixed green salad. Only the small, dark, glossy leaves of very young spinach will do for salad. It is really supreme in counterpoint to freshly sliced, raw white mushrooms.

Calves Tongues (also called field salad and in French, *mâche*), **Dandelion Greens** (alias Pissenlits), **fiddlehead ferns,** and **nasturtium leaves:** These greens are for esoteric tastes and likely to stay so since they are so difficult to obtain. They are quite good for one-upping food snobs if you really want to go out of your way. New York restaurants, though, have done in the cachet of *mâche* by serving it incessantly, just as California restaurants have dimmed whatever appeal, aside from color, radicchio may once have had.

Arugula: This is an Italian salad plant with a wild and weedy flavor. It has dark green, long slender leaves and is usually sold in clumps with the roots attached. It is deservedly becoming better known outside its ethnic beginnings by many names: rucola, rugula, roquette, and just plain rocket (as it was known in Elizabethan manuals).

⚘ RICE SALAD ⚘

Rice salad—sort of like Chinese fried rice, but better—is suitable as both a main dish and as part of a buffet. It can be as elaborate or as simple as the pocket permits. Rice blends well and provides a substantial background for an enormous number of other things: vegetables, meats, poultry, and seafood. A properly made rice salad has grace and elegance, and you can go on changing it about *ad infinitum.*

There is but one problem, and it's a lulu: even given Uncle Ben's best effort, converted white rice with all its vitamins intact, many cooks are (for mysterious reasons of their own) unable to cook a pot of simple, firm-grained, but dry and tender rice. (See directions on rice cooking on page 186.) Other ingredients of the salad may have to be kept cold until the last minute, but never chill the rice.

Serves 8

5 cups tepid cooked white rice
1/2 cup light olive oil
1 ripe California avocado*
1/4 cup fresh lemon juice
1 medium-sized Belgian endive, sliced in rings
1 red Italian onion, finely diced
1 tablespoon minced fresh coriander (optional)
2 tablespoons minced fresh dill
2 tablespoons minced fresh parsley

1 tablespoon hot fresh chili pepper, seeded and minced
1/2 cup stoned ripe olives, sliced (use Moroccan, Greek, or Italian cured olives)
Coarse salt and cracked white pepper to taste
2 cups leftover or freshly cooked chicken, fish, or shellfish, shredded, flaked, or diced

Turn the cooked rice into a large colander. Toss it up and down to cool it quickly, then dump it into a large bowl and mix in the oil. Peel the avocado, dice it with a stainless steel knife (to avoid discoloring the delicate flesh) and toss it in some of the lemon juice to keep its nice pale green color from turning black. Add the remaining juice to the rice. Add all the remaining ingredients, then season to taste with salt and pepper.

*Florida avocados are very large, with pale, thin skins and watery flesh. This regrettable quality makes them unsuitable to mix with rice.

(Hands are the best instruments for mixing rice, as it should be handled delicately.) Last of all fold in the diced avocado.

If you want to make this a vegetarian dish, in place of the chicken or fish, put 3 hard-cooked eggs, cut in wedges, around the perimeter of the finished salad. You can also substitute heart of celery for the endive, or add various other vegetables you fancy—nothing wet or juicy, though. Odd as it may sound, fresh young white turnips (the kind with purple shoulders) furnish a crisp, spicy accent—just a small handful, cut in very thin julienne strips. Cilantro (the Spanish name for coriander leaves) is becoming fairly well known as it is ever more present in the New American cookery; however, it has a curious flavor that some people dislike, so add this herb in moderation or omit it altogether if you wish. The other fresh herbs are all-important to this rice salad; dried ones will not do at all.

✷ TOMATO SALAD ✸

Red, ripe, juicy tomatoes are one of the most keenly anticipated joys of summer. Their rich, sweet taste should be savored with just the mildest of dressings, or, sometimes, just salt. Never buy those pink, hard tomatoes encased in cellophane, wait for summer's blessed field-ripened tomatoes.

Note: Never refrigerate tomatoes; their flavor will evaporate in a matter of hours. If you must have chilled tomatoes, cool them quickly by dropping them into a pot filled with ice cubes and cold water. If you are stuck with a few under-ripe tomatoes, let them ripen at room temperature but never in direct sunlight. Fairly ripe tomatoes will keep quite well at room temperature in a brown paper bag, for 4 or 5 days.

Serves 4

4 medium tomatoes
1 tablespoon chopped fresh
  parsley

3 to 4 minced scallions (optional)
Sauce Vinaigrette (page 65)

Slice the tomatoes from top to bottom with a sharp knife, using a light, sawing motion. (This way of cutting them seems to hold the flesh and juices together better than cross-cutting.) Cut out any green stem with the point of the knife. Arrange in overlapping slices and sprinkle with parsley and scallions. Drizzle Sauce Vinaigrette over all and serve at room temperature. Or dress them simply with a drizzle of best-quality cold-pressed olive oil and a sprinkling of salt and pepper.

Variation: Alternate slices of tomato with thin slices of smoked mozzarella. Drizzle with olive oil. Sprinkle with shredded basil leaves.

🌿 SPINACH AND MUSHROOM SALAD 🍃

A pound looks like a lot of spinach, but a good many of the outer leaves must be discarded. Only small, fresh, tender leaves should be used. The best spinach is available in the spring and early fall.

Serves 4

1 pound fresh young spinach
1/2 pound fresh white
*   mushrooms*

1/4 cup Sauce Vinaigrette (page
*   65) made with lemon juice*
Freshly ground pepper to taste

Snip off the coarse stems and rinse the spinach through three waters. Rinse the mushrooms with cold water and dry them in paper towels. Break off the stems and discard. Slice the caps in 1/8-inch slices. The spinach may be prepared ahead of time as for any green salad, but the mushrooms will darken if prepared in advance. Sprinkle the mushroom slices with a few drops of lemon juice and toss together with the spinach, Sauce Vinaigrette, and pepper to taste just before serving.

✿ MIXED BUFFET SALAD ✿

For a large number of people this is an excellent choice since it gets the hostess off the hook and allows guests to indulge their own salad idiosyncrasies. This way, both the purists and the mad scientists of the salad bowl can be happy.

Arrange three or four bowls of different kinds of salad greens with diverse flavors and textures on the table. Surround them with smaller bowls of sliced raw mushrooms, diced cucumbers, canned artichoke hearts, toasted croutons, Greek olives, tiny whole cherry tomatoes, crumbled Gorgonzola or goat cheese, hearts of palm, diced avocado turned in lemon juice, minced scallions, fresh chopped herbs, minced hard-cooked eggs, and anything else you especially fancy. You need not have all of these; three or four extra tidbits are enough. I envision these creative efforts as large green salads with the other additions as condiments more or less arranged around, not in, the greens. However, if people want a messy mixed salad, there is nothing you can do to restrain them.

Just before serving time, mix each bowl of salad greens separately with a vinaigrette dressing and leave some extra dressing in a bowl or bottle on the table.

This is a good first-course salad because it leaves you free for last-minute kitchen duties while the guests are wandering among the salad choices.

✒ CAESAR SALAD ✒

This is the Crêpe Suzette of salads and should be tossed with great style and grace at the table. Accordingly, it must be served as a separate course, usually first.

Serves 10

1 ½ cups crisp fried croutons

2 tablespoons garlic-flavored oil

1 clove garlic

½ cup olive oil

1 large head of romaine, rinsed
   and dried

Salt and freshly ground black

pepper to taste

2 1-minute eggs

Juice of a large lemon

8 to 10 anchovy fillets, chopped

½ cup freshly grated Parmesan
   or Romano cheese

Fry the croutons, either packaged or fresh ones made from stale French bread, in a little garlic-flavored oil until crisp. Drain on paper towels. Puree garlic and mix with the olive oil. Tear salad greens into a large bowl. Add salt and pepper to taste. Pour on oil and toss thoroughly. Pause eloquently, then break the eggs into the salad and, with a sweeping gesture, squeeze the lemon juice over it, and toss madly again. Add chopped anchovies, croutons and cheese, and toss very lightly.

❧ CUCUMBER SALAD ❧

The French cut out all the seeds, but if you can get young, small, dark green cucumbers, this should not be necessary. (Kirbys, normally used for pickling, are delicious in vinaigrette, and they need only scrubbing, no peeling.) Europeans serve the cucumbers wilted, while we usually go to great lengths to keep them crisp. I like them both ways, but the wilted cucumbers absorb more dressing and have more flavor.

Serves 4 to 6

3 or 4 small, dark-green cucumbers
½ cup Sauce Vinaigrette (page 65)

Salt and freshly ground pepper to taste

Peel and thinly slice the cucumbers. Mix thoroughly with the Sauce Vinaigrette and season with salt and pepper to taste. Store covered in a small, deep bowl in the refrigerator if you prefer the wilted version. Otherwise soak the peeled, but unsliced cucumbers in ice water for an hour and make the salad just prior to serving.

❧ CUCUMBERS IN DILL ❧

This has vaguely Scandinavian overtones and is very complementary to boiled or broiled fish. It is also a cooling side dish to serve with highly spiced or curried foods.

Serves 4 to 6

3 medium cucumbers

3 tablespoons chopped fresh dill weed

¹/₄ teaspoon salt

1 cup sour cream

Peel and slice the cucumbers, sprinkle with dill and salt, and place in a covered bowl in the refrigerator for at least ¹/₂ hour. Remove and drain off the water which the salt has extracted from the cucumbers. Arrange on a platter and cover with sour cream.

⚘ STRING BEAN SALAD ⚘

My grandmother concocted this then bizarre combination in an effort to teach me to like green beans without really noticing it. Since those days long gone, Americans have become quite accustomed to the notion of cold green beans. In Escabeche from Mexican cookery, Salade Niçoise from French cookery, and green beans vinaigrette, they have become positively commonplace in restaurants. Nevertheless, this is an early food conversion in my life, so I'll pass it on to cure other bean-haters.

Serves 4

¹/₂ pound tiny, young, fresh green beans

8 small cherry tomatoes, halved

4 medium scallions, sliced

¹/₂ cup Sauce Vinaigrette (page 65)

Salt and freshly ground black pepper to taste

Top and tail the beans, which should be as small as possible; pick them out one by one if necessary. Throw them into a pot of rapidly boiling salted water and when they turn dark green and lose their starchy taste—usually about 3 minutes—drain, and plunge them into cold water. Drain again and dry lightly on paper towels.

Put them into a bowl with all remaining ingredients and toss lightly, adding salt and pepper to taste.

🌿 ZUCCHINI SALAD 🌿

Young, raw zucchini has a slightly spicy flavor and a lovely texture. This salad is a bit like an uncooked ratatouille. It goes well with grilled steak, lamb chops, or Italian sausages.

Serves 6 to 8

6 small, firm zucchini
1 green Italian cooking pepper
3 small, ripe tomatoes
3 scallions, thinly sliced
¹/₂ teaspoon salt

Freshly ground black pepper to taste
¹/₂ cup olive oil
1 to 2 tablespoons wine vinegar
1 tablespoon shredded fresh basil

Rinse zucchini, using a soft brush or cloth under cold running water to remove sand. Do not peel, but thinly slice them. Cut the green pepper in thin julienne strips. Blanch the tomatoes in boiling water for 10 seconds to loosen the skins, then plunge them into cold water. Peel and chop the tomatoes. Put all ingredients, except the basil, in a bowl. Toss lightly, cover, and let stand for about 1 hour, adding the basil just before serving.

🌿 SNACK SALADS 🌿

In Strasbourg, eating is a regional pastime. Unlike other parts of France, there are *brasseries* and little *stubes* that serve between-meal tidbits at all hours of the day and night. After a creamy, rich wedge of Quiche Lorraine, a Strasbourgeois might pass the time with an order of wurst or cheese salad before he goes on to some *Pâté en Croûte*, more *Zwicker* (Alsatian white *vin ordinaire*), and perhaps a taste of the day's *tarte à l'oignon.* These cheese and sausage or cold cut salads don't fit into a menu really, but are lovely for midday or evening snacks in the summer.

> Leftover roast beef, lamb, pork, or veal
> Knockwurst, bologna, mortadella, or soft salami
> Gruyère or Swiss cheese
> Sliced red Italian onions
> Sauce Vinaigrette (page 65)

Choose *one* of the above meats or cheeses and cut it into julienne strips. Add the thinly sliced onions. Pour on some dressing and toss with a fork. Marinate for about 1 hour (in the fridge if the day is extremely hot) before serving with white wine or beer and hard rolls.

紊 COMPOSED SALADS 糸

Composed salads made of vegetables, meat or fish, and mayonnaise or other dressings are particularly compatible with hot weather and weekend guests. There are several excellent brands of mayonnaise on the market, but homemade mayonnaise is richer and fresher flavored. Once the technique is mastered, it really isn't too difficult or time-consuming. I use an electric mixer and finish with a wire whisk. This method is also good for Hollandaise and its derivative sauces.

Blender mayonnaise is absolutely painless to make and is somewhat lighter in texture, since it will not absorb as as much oil as a hand- or mixer-made mayonnaise. Commercial brands are improved by beating some air and a few drops of lemon juice into them with a wire whisk.

⚘ MAYONNAISE ⚘

This recipe is for hand-beaten, electric mixer, or food processor mayonnaise. All ingredients and equipment should be at room temperature. Rinse the bowl in hot water and dry it to ensure that the egg yolks are warmed. Oil may be heated to tepid. Light olive oil is best, but plain unflavored vegetable oil may be used for half the volume of oil if preferred. The bowl must be glass, ceramic, or stainless steel, of about 3-quart capacity even though you are making only 2 cups of sauce.

About 2 cups

3 large egg yolks
1/2 teaspoon Dijon mustard
1/2 teaspoon salt
1 1/2 cups olive oil or equal parts
  salad and olive oil
1 tablespoon white wine vinegar
  or lemon juice

2 tablespoons boiling water
  (optional)
Additional salt, pepper, or lemon
  juice to taste

Beat the egg yolks a couple of minutes until very thick and sticky. If using an electric mixer, beat on medium-high speed and keep scraping the egg yolks into the beaters with a rubber spatula.

If using a food processor, blend egg yolks, mustard, salt, and 1 tablespoon oil at high speed 30 seconds. Add oil in driblets until half is incorporated; then add the rest in a fine stream. Add the vinegar or lemon juice, salt, and mustard and beat a few seconds longer.

If using a wire whisk, prepare for prodigious and uninterrupted beating. You will have to figure out your own best way of keeping the bowl tilted, either between your knees or steadied in a larger pot with a dish towel stuffed under one side. One hand must beat and the other control the droplets of oil to be slowly incorporated into the yolks. Watch the oil constantly, not the sauce. Beating need not be too rapid, but it must be constant.

Drop by drop, beat in about ½ cup of the oil. It should thicken to a heavy cream consistency before you rest. Then begin adding the oil in a thin stream or in 1-tablespoon quantities, blending thoroughly after each one. If the sauce becomes too stiff, thin it out with a few drops of lemon juice or vinegar. Beat the boiling water in to improve the mayonnaise's keeping quality. Adjust seasoning. There! It's all over and should have taken about 10 minutes.

If somehow you wind up with a curdled blob at some point in the preparation, you can bring it back this way:

SAVING THE MAYONNAISE

To a warm, dry bowl, add 1 teaspoon of Dijon mustard and 1 tablespoon of the turned sauce. Beat with a mixer or wire whisk for a few minutes until the ingredients coagulate. Thoroughly incorporate the rest of the sauce, bit by bit.

🌿 BLENDER MAYONNAISE 🌿

As with the handmade sauce, ingredients should be at room temperature. This is a lighter, paler sauce than classic mayonnaise because a blender clogs with egg yolks only. It is excellent for use in composed salads such as egg or tuna.

About 1 1/4 cups

1 large whole egg	*1 tablespoon lemon juice or*
1/4 teaspoon dry mustard	*vinegar*
1/2 teaspoon salt	*1 cup olive or salad oil*

Put the egg, mustard, and salt into the blender, cover, and blend at high speed for about 40 seconds. Turn off motor and add lemon juice or vinegar. Blend a few seconds. With the blender at high speed, pour the oil through the cover opening by droplets directly into the center of the whirling mixture. If the sauce thickens too quickly, add a few drops of lemon juice or vinegar. Taste for final seasonings.

Despite the grave warnings in old cookbooks, homemade mayonnaise keeps perfectly well, tightly covered and refrigerated, for at least a week. Never leave it sitting about in a warm kitchen, however.

Variation: For a spicy dressing, begin with 1/8 teaspoon of cayenne and add more to suit your palate. I sometimes put a roasted, skinned, seeded, and chopped jalapeño chili into the blender along with the egg.

❧ GREEN MAYONNAISE ❧

Delicious on fish and shellfish (an unexpected delight on a shrimp cocktail), this lovely green herbal sauce lifts even a few prosaic hard-cooked eggs into a thoroughly presentable main-course salad.

About 2 cups

6 young spinach leaves	*¼ cup watercress leaves*
2 tablespoons chopped scallions	*1 tablespoon fresh tarragon*
⅓ cup parsley leaves	*1½ cups Mayonnaise (page 78)*

Blanch the spinach and scallions in a small amount of boiling water for 1 minute. Add remaining herbs and boil another minute. Drain, rinse with cold water, and dry. If you are making mayonnaise by hand, puree the greens in a mortar or finely chop them and force through a sieve before adding to the finished mayonnaise; or add the whole greens to blender or processor mayonnaise before you run in the oil. Mix the pureed herbs into the 1½ cups of finished mayonnaise.

⚶ SAUCE RÉMOULADE ⚶

Another sauce that lost nearly everything in the translation to American "restaurant-ese," this has come to mean anything from horseradish-flavored bottled chili sauce to even less definable orangy mixtures. Actually, it is a salty, herbal mayonnaise used chiefly to garnish fish and shellfish.

About 2 cups

*1 teaspoon or more chopped
  capers
1 ½ cups Mayonnaise (page 78)
1 tablespoon each minced chives,*

*parsley, and tarragon
1 hard-cooked egg, minced
3 or 4 mashed anchovy fillets,
  drained*

Rinse the capers before you chop them if they are the large, salt-preserved type. Stir together all ingredients. Try this with any chilled, cooked shellfish.

⚶ SAUCE AIOLI ⚶

Although this thick garlic mayonnaise is normally used as dressing for hot poached fish or boiled potatoes, it is also a welcome change from the sour cream dips so monotonously offered at summer parties. Serve Aioli surrounded by a selection of fresh, raw summer vegetables cut into convenient pieces and this will obviate the salad course as well as the *hors d'oeuvre*. Aioli can be approximated by pounding the garlic to a smooth paste and adding it to 1 ½ cups of store-bought mayonnaise, but it will not be remotely as fine.

About 1 1/2 cups

1 crustless slice of day-old white
   bread
3 tablespoons wine vinegar
4 to 6 cloves garlic, roughly
   chopped
1 large egg yolk

Pinch of salt
1 to 1 1/2 cups tepid olive oil
2 tablespoons lemon juice,
   approximately
Boiling water

Soak the bread in the vinegar about 10 minutes. Remove and squeeze dry. Put the garlic and bread into a mortar and pound with a pestle until it is a smooth paste. Beat in the egg yolk and salt. When the mixture is thick and sticky, start adding the oil by droplets; when about one third of it is incorporated you may pour a little faster and use a wire whisk to complete the beating in. Add some lemon juice when the mixture becomes very heavy. Thin with a bit of boiling water if necessary. Aioli should be about the consistency of commercial sour cream. If it curdles, the sauce may be reconstituted in the same manner as regular mayonnaise. (See page 78.)

❧ GREEN GODDESS SALAD ❧

Considered a "classic" of old California cuisine, this luncheon salad was created in honor of George Arliss, who was appearing in a play called *The Green Goddess* in 1915 in San Francisco. Since it almost qualifies as a regional dish, there are numerous versions; you can work out your own and add another theory to the din.

Serves 6

*1/4 cup minced fresh parsley, plus
  additional for garnish*
*2 tablespoons minced fresh
  tarragon*
1/4 cup minced chives
6 to 8 anchovy fillets
2 cups Mayonnaise (page 78)

*3/4 cup Sauce Vinaigrette with
  garlic (page 65)*
1 large head romaine
*1 1/2 pounds cooked scallops,
  lobster, shrimp, or crabmeat,
  or a mixture*

Mix together the parsley, tarragon, chives, and anchovies. Beat them into the mayonnaise with a fork along with about 1/4 cup of the Sauce Vinaigrette. (Don't use an electric mixer because all the herbs will cling to the beaters.) Tear the romaine into rather large pieces and toss with the remaining Sauce Vinaigrette. Arrange the salad greens on six individual chilled plates. Working quickly, mix the cooked seafood with the green mayonnaise and pile lightly onto the romaine. Garnish with additional minced parsley. You may also simply heap the seafood onto the salad greens and spoon the dressing over the top.

🌿 TONGUE AND CHICKEN SALAD 🌿

I have eaten everything from pineapple to walnuts in chicken salads but rarely anything as complementary as tongue. The temptation to make a sandwich and forget the salad must be resisted because the salad is unforgettable.

Serves 6

12 large slices of cooked smoked
   tongue, ⅛ inch thick
2 cups cubed, cooked chicken
1 tablespoon minced celery
2 tablespoons minced parsley

1 small white onion
1 cup Mayonnaise (page 78)
¼ teaspoon dry mustard
Watercress
3 hard-cooked eggs

Cut the tongue into julienne strips about 1½ inches long. Add it to the cubed chicken, celery, and parsley. Grate the onion into the mayonnaise; blend in the mustard. Fold into the meat mixture. Serve each portion on a bed of watercress and garnish with half a hard-cooked egg.

Variation: Add a pair of calf's sweetbreads, prepared in the following manner and cut into small pieces.

BASIC PREPARATION OF SWEETBREADS

Buy very fresh calf sweetbreads from the heart and use them the same day. Plunge them in salted ice water for 1 hour. Remove and place in a small pan with cold water to cover. Add a small onion stuck with 2 cloves, a piece of bay leaf, ¼ teaspoon salt, and the juice of a lemon. Bring them slowly to the simmer and poach them for about 15 minutes. Plunge again into ice water for 5 minutes, then remove the tubes and membranes. This procedure must be followed prior to using sweetbreads in any recipe.

泰 FRENCH POTATO SALAD 袋

This is a classic French version of the salad so dear to the heart of every Southerner. Dixie-Style Potato Salad (page 88) is usually filled with eggs, olives, pimentoes, pickles, onions, and lavishly bound with a rich mayonnaise. Although I remember it fondly, I have grown to prefer this more subtly flavored French-style potato salad. It may be an accompaniment to wafer-thin slices of Smithfield ham, hot or cold fried chicken, charcoal grilled meats and sausages, or when elaborately garnished in the Alsatian style, it may serve as the main course.

About 6 cups

8 to 10 medium all-purpose potatoes (do not use Idahoes or Russets as they crumble when sliced)
4 to 5 tablespoons dry white wine, heated
2 tablespoons wine vinegar

½ teaspoon salt
1 teaspoon dry mustard
7 tablespoons olive oil
Salt and freshly ground pepper to taste
6 scallions, minced
½ cup minced fresh parsley

Scrub the potatoes and boil them in their jackets in salted water until just tender when pierced with a very sharp kitchen fork. Drain and shake over low heat to dry thoroughly. Peel them as hot as you can handle them; the potatoes should still be warm when the dressing is added. Slice them in ⅛-inch rounds and place in a large mixing bowl. As you put in each layer of potatoes, sprinkle with some of the wine.

Next beat the vinegar, salt, and dry mustard together in a small bowl with a wire whisk or electric mixer. Beat in the oil slowly until you have a creamy emulsion. Taste for salt and pepper. Then taste the potatoes for saltiness before adding any more to the dressing. Sprinkle the potatoes with the minced scallions and parsley. Pour on the dressing and mix lightly with your hands, taking care not to break the potatoes any more than necessary. If the salad is not to be served at once, cover it with plastic wrap and leave it at room temperature, then turn out onto a lettuce-lined platter and garnish with all or any of the following: sliced hard-cooked eggs, skinless and boneless sardines, anchovy fillets, half-circles of hard salami, kosher dill gherkins, radish roses, ripe or green olives, drained tuna fish, or smoked eel.

This gloriously decorated platter takes a while to make but it is well worth the effort. Naturally, if the potato salad is to be served as a side dish, eggs and pickles are quite enough garnish.

🖎 EASY FRENCH POTATO SALAD 🖎

Steam 2 pounds of well-scrubbed tiny new potatoes (Red Bliss is the best variety if you cannot get the small brown potatoes that are called "gleaners" on Eastern Long Island) until *just* tender when pierced with a sharp fork. Drain well but *do not peel* the potatoes. Cut in halves if tiny or quarters if larger than 1½ inches in diameter. Mix with the dressing as above and add plenty of chopped parsley and a little minced chive.

🔺 DIXIE-STYLE POTATO SALAD 🔻

There may not be as many disagreements about what goes into this rococo production as there are about Brunswick Stew, but I doubt it. This salad was served on witheringly hot summer Sundays with enormous platters of fried chicken, pitchers of iced tea, and hot biscuits straight from the inferno of the kitchen. The whole heavy, rich, splendid midday gluttony ended with dishes of soft peach ice cream cranked to smoothness under the shade of a chinaberry tree.

*10 medium-large all-purpose or
  "boiling" potatoes
1 cup chopped scallions
3 hard-cooked eggs, chopped
1 green pepper, finely chopped
1/2 cup coarsely chopped sweet
  pickles*

*1/4 cup minced celery
2 tablespoons chopped
  pimento-stuffed olives
1 to 1 1/2 cups Mayonnaise
  (page 78)
Salt and freshly ground black
  pepper to taste*

Boil the potatoes in their jackets in salted water until just tender, about 30 minutes. Peel and slice or dice them. Blend in all ingredients, except the salt and pepper, and enough mayonnaise to bind the salad together. Use a wooden fork and spoon, lifting and folding the potatoes as gently as possible. Taste for seasoning and add salt or pepper if required. Turn into a large shallow bowl or platter and decorate with any of the garnishes listed. Garnish: Sliced hard-cooked eggs, dill or sweet gherkins, strips of canned pimento, sliced cucumbers, stuffed green olives, or (my preference) black Italian olives.

⚛ TUNA SALAD MY WAY ⚛

It seems absurd to include a recipe for this popular dish we all tasted at one time along with our first peanut butter sandwiches. However, because tuna is so much used and so dreadfully abused, I insist upon offering my version of this American favorite. It is a quickie, serving two as a main course.

Serves 2

*1 7-ounce can white, solid-pack
  tuna fish in oil*
*3 scallions with some green,
  minced*
1 tablespoon capers, drained

½ cup Mayonnaise (page 78)
2 hard-cooked eggs, chopped
Romaine
Kalamata black olives

Drain the tuna and break it into small chunks with a fork. Mix it with the scallions, capers, and mayonnaise, then carefully fold in the hard-cooked eggs. Pile lightly on washed and dried romaine leaves, and garnish generously with the black olives. Of course you can always make sandwiches with it too, but use freshly toasted bread and serve right away.

EGG SALAD ADVICE

Please leave off, cease, and desist with the chopped celery, or at least reduce the amount to a small crunchy accent. Instead, add chopped fresh tarragon, parsley, and chives to the mayonnaise.

Throw in a few capers or leave out the tarragon and add some curry powder to the mayonnaise about ½ hour before combining it with the hard-cooked eggs.

Chop up some ripe olives and add them.

Garnish the salad with crossed anchovy fillets or a dollop of red or black caviar.

Serve it on a bed of crisp salad greens and decorate with chunks of drained tuna or some strips of ham or salami.

🌿 CANNELLINI WITH TUNA 🌿

Cannellini are white kidney beans. I first ate them in Rome served cold, with oil and lemon. I made my version of this dish for some Roman friends who gave it their seal of approval. Italian food distributors have made cannellini available in most supermarkets. It is much better, however, if you cook dried Great Northern beans from scratch, because canned beans are nearly always overcooked.

Serves 6

1 1/2 cups cooked cannellini, canned or dried

2 scallions, minced

1/4 cup olive oil

Salt and freshly ground pepper to taste

1 tablespoon chopped fresh parsley

1 7-ounce can white chunk-style tuna packed in oil

1 lemon, cut in wedges

Drain the beans and rinse under cold water. Drain well. Combine beans with the minced scallions and olive oil. Arrange individual portions on small plates and sprinkle with salt and pepper to taste, and parsley. Garnish with drained chunks of tuna and lemon wedges. This is best served as a first course at an otherwise light luncheon or supper.

🌿 KIDNEY BEAN SALAD 🌿

I think this mishmash of flavors is Pennsylvania Dutch in origin. It is my analysis of what I ate many times in western Pennsylvania with a few alterations I prefer to the more authentic sweet-sour version. In Pennsylvania they use sweet pickles and a boiled salad dressing; I prefer dill pickles and mayonnaise. It sounds ghastly but even those who cast a wary eye on the salad end up fighting over the last bean. Since the ingredients are usually on hand it's a lifesaver for quick lunches.

Serves 4

2 cups cooked red kidney beans,* canned or dried

1/2 cups minced scallions or red Italian onion

2 tablespoons chopped kosher dill pickles

1 hard-cooked egg, chopped

3/4 cup Mayonnaise (page 78)

Drain the kidney beans and rinse lightly under cold running water. Drain thoroughly. Combine all ingredients and mix gently. Chill for at least 1 hour. This is good served with a variety of sliced cold sausages and beer.

*Although canned beans are a perfectly acceptable way of cutting down kitchen time, home-cooked dried beans are preferable. As dried legumes freeze exceptionally well after cooling, it's good to cook double the quantity needed for a recipe and freeze the remainder for another dish.

❧ ANOTHER KIDNEY BEAN SALAD ❧

The combination of ingredients in this version is somewhat less alarming and may be adapted to almost any kind of cooked dried beans. One might substitute pinto, marrow, or soldier beans, chick peas, or lentils.

Serves 4

2 cups cooked red kidney beans, canned or dried

1 Bermuda or red Italian onion

¹⁄₄ teaspoon salt

¹⁄₄ teaspoon dry mustard

¹⁄₈ teaspoon (or less) curry powder (optional)

1 tablespoon white wine vinegar

1 tablespoon olive oil

1 clove garlic, pulverized

Drain the beans thoroughly and place in a small, deep bowl. Halve the onion and very thinly slice it. Add it to the beans. Mix the salt, mustard, and curry powder with the vinegar, then add the oil and garlic. Stir briskly and pour over the beans. Mix gently with your hands and do not mash the beans. Cover tightly and store overnight, or at least 12 hours, at room temperature. The various flavors will not ripen properly in the refrigerator.

⚘ CRABMEAT SALAD ⚘

Most "fresh" crabmeat, all picked out, is actually pasteurized and frozen down in Louisiana somewhere and sealed in cans, which are opened and thawed out by retail fish dealers. Backfin is cheaper than chunk crabmeat, just as tasty, but not as attractive. Frozen crabmeat is quite delicious. I just object to being told constantly that it is "fresh." There are a few fish dealers (I have a great one) who can supply real, fresh crabmeat from Maryland. Processed canned crabmeat is not worth discussing; have chicken instead. Allow about ¼ pound of crabmeat per person. Pick over the crabmeat carefully with your fingers so that you can feel any little bits of shell or fin that may be hiding. Heap it on individual romaine beds, ladle on some Sauce Rémoulade (page 82), and garnish with lemon slices. This is simple, elegant, and outrageously expensive.

⚘ CRACKED CRAB ⚘

Live crabs used to be totally unavailable unless you caught them yourself. But I now find them in Long Island fish markets. If you manage to get some, boil them in salted water seasoned with chilis, bay leaf, onion, and cumin seed until they turn bright red. To prevent them from "throwing" their claws, put them in a sinkful of fresh cold water for 15 minutes before cooking them. Cooking time varies with the size of the crabs, but even the largest Atlantic blue crab should not take more than 10 minutes. For local varieties, ask the fish dealer's advice. Picking out the succulent meat is a labor of love, so each crab lover should do it for himself. Just crack the claws, pull off the back, and remove the spongy substance under it, then replace the back shell. Turn the crab on its back and pull off the underside apron. Discard the stomach, intestine, and gills. All else is edible. Provide knives, little forks, and picks and let each guest fend for himself. Pass a bowl of Mayonnaise (page 78) or Sauce Rémoulade (page 82).

❧ LOBSTER SALAD ❧

Always buy live lobsters and cook them yourself. Often precooked lobsters are dried out and of dubious freshness. I saw one fish dealer actually wash the cooked meat under running water. He got rid of the roe, the tomalley (green liver), and the flavor in one fell swoop. *Never* wash seafood after it is cooked.

Various humane ways of cooking live lobster have been proposed. But since there are no living witnesses to vouch for any of them, I suppose this is as good a method as any. Prepare the following Court Bouillon:

Serves 6

2 cups dry white wine
4 quarts boiling water
2 tablespoons salt
Bay leaf, thyme, and dried red
    pepper flakes to taste
1 peeled onion stuck with 2
    cloves

1 3-pound live lobster
Mayonnaise (page 78)
Rinsed, dried, and chilled salad
    greens
Garnish: hard-cooked eggs and
    minced fresh parsley, chives,
    and chervil

Mix together the ingredients, simmer for 20 minutes, then plunge the live lobster into it. Lobster should be cooked 5 minutes for the first pound and 3 minutes for each additional pound. (If you cook shellfish or fish often, you can strain this broth and freeze it for use another time.)

Lay the lobster on its back. Clip open the tail shell with heavy kitchen shears. Cut through the body with a large heavy knife. If the lobster is large you may need a cleaver for the body. (Incidentally, 3 pounders are a good buy for salad as they are cheaper and just as juicy if you don't overcook them.) Remove the sac near the head. Reserve the roe or coral, and eat the green tomalley (cook's dividend) on a piece of toast.

Pick out the meat from the body cavity, especially at the joints where the small legs are connected. Remove the claw meat and tail meat in one piece if possible. Slice the tail meat into rounds. Chill the claw, tail, and body meat in airtight plastic bags, separately.

Rub the red coral through a sieve and beat it into a good mayonnaise. Arrange some of each kind of lobster meat on each plate on a bed of chilled greens. Put a spoonful of sauce in the center. Garnish with hard-cooked eggs, a sprinkle of chopped mixed green herbs (parsley, chives, and chervil), and pass additional sauce at the table. One 3-pound lobster will yield enough meat for salad for six. If serving individual lobsters, allow half a 1½-pound lobster per person.

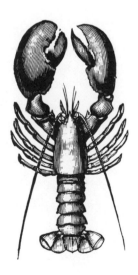

🌿 SUNDAY LUNCH CHICKEN SALAD 🌿

This American favorite has as many versions as there are families—from the sublime to the revolting—and made with care it can be a triumph. Roast chicken makes a tastier salad than poached chicken, but there is more danger of drying out the flesh. In hot weather, however, it is more sensible to poach the chicken in a good broth rather than firing up the oven. The foundation of a good chicken salad is homemade mayonnaise, which, surprisingly, is still not the norm in average households that have had blenders and food processors for at least 30 years. (I've known a person so accustomed to commercial dressings that she actually prefers them to homemade. But she's an odd duck, I hope.) The flavoring of the mayonnaise can change the character of the chicken salad from heartland picnic to a luxurious dinner entrée with Oriental overtones. Curry, garlic, herbs, lemon or orange zest, almonds, and currants are but a few of the various accents possible.

Serves 6

1 3 1/2-pound chicken

POACHING INGREDIENTS:

*1 quart chicken broth plus
    enough water to cover chicken
    by 1 inch*
1 onion stuck with 2 cloves
1 branch celery
Half a small carrot
Couple of sprigs of parsley

1 cup Mayonnaise (page 78)

Few drops lemon juice and water
*1/2 cup drained, chopped water
    chestnuts*
1 cup finely sliced celery
1/4 cup minced scallions
*2 tablespoons minced fresh
    parsley*
Romaine leaves
1 tablespoon grated lemon zest

Put the whole chicken and all the giblets (but not the liver) into a deep, narrow stock pot. Cover with the cold chicken broth and add water if needed to cover the chicken by an inch. Add the onion, celery stalk, carrot, and parsley sprigs. Bring to the simmer and poach, at just under the boiling point, for about 35 minutes—until the leg moves easily in its socket. Remove from the heat and let the chicken cool in the broth for half an hour; you now have excellent double-strength broth for use in another dish or a light summer soup.

Pull the skin off with your fingers, then pull the chicken meat from the carcass. You may have to dice some of it with a knife. Discard the skin and bones and all traces of fat or gristle. Thin the mayonnaise with just enough lemon juice to give it a slight edge—it should not be sour or blatantly lemony—and enough water, usually about a tablespoon, to loosen the texture somewhat. Otherwise the salad will be heavy and sticky. Fold the thinned mayonnaise into the chicken and add the water chestnuts, celery, scallions, and parsley. Pile this into the center of a round platter lined with rinsed and dried romaine leaves extended to show off their delicate gradation from dark green to pale yellow. Sprinkle the lemon zest over the chicken salad. This dish is at its ultimate personal best when freshly made and at room temperature. Of course that's a counsel of perfection, but please do not make it too far ahead or serve it refrigerator cold.

Variation: If you've a mind to try roast chicken salad, which is entirely feasible unless you're living in a torrid climate, here's a quick method. It is a professional technique I found in the excellent *American Charcuterie* by Victoria Wise. Ms. Wise ran a charcuterie called Pig-By-The-Tail in Berkeley, California, and she is one of the conscientious young chefs who studied and trained in her demanding craft. Her book is written for home cooks and is unique among contemporary cookbooks.

In a tight-fitting pan, roast the chicken, untrussed, stuffed with an onion and some herbs, and well-rubbed with butter. (Ms. Wise suggests using a bread pan, which did not work for me—either my chicken was too big or my bread pans too narrow. Stuff it into the smallest pan you can.) Roast the chicken at 475°F., breast up for 10 minutes, then breast down for 50 minutes. Remove and cool to warm. Remove the skin and bones with your fingers, then pull or cut the chicken into bite-sized pieces and proceed with the recipe for Chicken Salad.

Variations:

Chicken Salad Vindaloo: Heat a tablespoon of vindaloo (hot) curry powder in a small skillet over a low flame until it perfumes the kitchen. Add this to the homemade mayonnaise. Omit the water chestnuts or the celery and add instead a couple of tablespoons of dried currants and some chopped red onion. Garnish with a few more currants instead of the lemon zest.

Chicken Salad Caribe: I've never actually had any decent chicken salad in the West Indies but my fantasy here does employ tropical flavors. Thin the mayonnaise with orange juice instead of lemon juice and water. Slice a ripe avocado and turn it in the orange juice, which will keep it from darkening as well as lend an unexpected taste. Garnish the salad with the avocado and sprinkle the top with grated orange zest. Eccentric though it may sound, this version is even more wonderful with a sprinkling of crisp bits of freshly cooked bacon. Another strange idea that worked wonders: chopped macadamia nuts, lightly toasted and sprinkled over the finished salad. Although rarely found in good condition beyond their native grounds, ripe papayas and persimmons are delectable sweet-tart counterpoints for chicken salad.

As you can see, a basically good chicken salad is open to a lot of interpretation.

🏮 CHICKEN SALAD CHEZ MA TANTE 🏮

This is a "salad" only in the "nouvelliest" sense of the word, but that's what the chef at a favorite Greenwich Village bistro calls his dish. This is my interpretation of his idea; it's a marvelous luncheon dish, with lots of flavor and texture if a bit on the ephemeral side. Serve lots of good, fresh crusty bread and a mound of herbed butter with it.

Serves 4

4 chicken cutlets (2 whole
    breasts, halved, skinned, and
    boned)
Flour
Salt and freshly ground pepper to
    taste
1 egg, beaten with 1 tablespoon
    water
2 cups fresh bread crumbs

2 tablespoons finely grated fresh
    Parmesan
Plain salad oil
Approximately 1 quart of mixed
    summer greens, including a
    little arugula or Upland cress
    for bite
½ cup Sauce Vinaigrette with
    garlic (page 65)

Rinse and dry the chicken cutlets, and pound them to flatten. Dredge them lightly in flour mixed with salt and pepper, and shake them free of the excess. Dip each cutlet lightly in the beaten egg, then roll in the breadcrumbs, which have been mixed with the Parmesan, pressing this mixture into the cutlets. Lay the cutlets on a rack, uncovered, and refrigerate for half an hour or more.

Heat the salad oil in a wide skillet and sauté the chicken cutlets over medium heat until brown on both sides and just cooked through, a total of about 7 minutes. Drain on paper toweling. This can be done an hour or so in advance, but do not refrigerate the sautéed cutlets or they will be soggy.

Wash and dry the greens and toss them well with a good vinaigrette made with fine, cold-pressed olive oil. Arrange the greens on four plates. Slice each chicken cutlet into long strips and lift it (still whole-looking) onto the greens.

FISH AND SHELLFISH

Traditionally, fish was served as a third or even a fourth course at formal dinners. But that overwrought gilded era of dining has long since disappeared, and now fish is served as a dignified main course. In our running, jumping, and dieting age, the popularity of low-calorie seafood has skyrocketed. (Unfortunately, so has its price.) A whole baked fish is simple to prepare and makes a dramatic presentation. Served hot or cold, the delicacy and lightness of fish is especially appropriate during the summer months.

There are endless ways to deal with the immense variety of fish from American waters. Fish are divided into either the "fat" or "lean" class. *Any fish may be substituted for another in the same class for almost any recipe.* Shellfish are all lean. Any good fish dealer will be able to tell you into which class the fish you select falls. When buying whole fish, allow ½ pound per person.

BUYING FISH

Fresh fish should not smell "fishy." Its eyes should be bright and bulgy—not flat and opaque. Gills should be bright red, the skin glistening, and the flesh firm to the touch. Filleted fish should be almost odorless or, at most, smell faintly of sea water. Frozen fish *should* be odorless if it has indeed been hurtled from the boat to the freezer as is generally claimed. But it generally isn't. Probably the lack of freshness is the fault of the grocer rather than the processor, since frozen fish does not keep well indefinitely. Except for gifts from fishing friends, I've never had any satisfactory frozen fish. Occasionally I'm tempted by the vivid memory of "truite au bleu" enjoyed in Switzerland, and take a disappointing flyer on rainbow trout. Since I live on the seacoast, I have plenty of fresh fish to amuse myself with.

COOKING FISH

Whether you are poaching, broiling, baking, or frying fish, you should keep in mind that it cooks very quickly. There is no remedy for overdone fish; it simply falls to bits when it is served. Handle the fish as little as possible while you are cooking it to avoid breaking it. It it difficult to give precise times for cooking fish because the size of the fish and the amount of heat vary. I find the Canadian Fisheries edict of cooking fish 10 minutes for each inch of thickness to be a fairly reliable guide. Testing with a fork or toothpick until the fish is opaque will determine when it is done. As a further precaution, make a small incision with a small knife in the thickest part (near the backbone in whole fish) of the fish to be certain it is cooked through. Although I'm mad for sushi and sashimi, the fad for rare-cooked fish leaves me cold.

FISH SAUCES

Saucing adds variety to the bland flavor of many fish. The base of nearly all fish sauces is Court Bouillon, which is then reduced, enriched, and thickened with egg yolks, cream, and butter.

⚘ COURT BOUILLON ⚘

2 cups dry white wine
1 quart water
Fish trimmings (heads and
   bones)
1 medium onion, peeled and
   sliced
1 small carrot, peeled and sliced

1/2 bay leaf
1 teaspoon salt
1 teaspoon freshly ground white
   pepper
3 to 4 sprigs of parsley
Sprig of fresh thyme or pinch of
   dried thyme

Put all ingredients in a soup kettle and bring to the boil. Simmer for at least 20 minutes with the lid askew. Strain, then proceed with your recipe.

Variation: When you don't have ingredients or time for this, Knorr (Swiss soup manufacturer) makes an excellent fish bouillon cube that yields 1 pint of broth.

⚘ SAUCE PARISIENNE ⚘

This is a simple sauce that takes only about 10 minutes to make but it will lift even a plain flounder fillet into the realm of *la grande cuisine.*

2 cups of sauce

2 tablespoons butter
2 tablespoons flour
1 1/2 cups boiling, concentrated
   Court Bouillon (above)
2 egg yolks

1/2 cup heavy cream
Salt and freshly ground pepper to
   taste
Lemon juice

Melt the butter in a heavy-bottomed saucepan and stir in the flour. Cook on low heat, stirring constantly, for 2 minutes. Do not let the mixture brown. You now have a white roux. Pour in the Court Bouillon all at once and stir vigorously with a wire whisk. Continue stirring and boiling over high heat for about 2 minutes. Set aside. Beat the egg yolks and stir in the heavy cream. Add a little of the hot sauce to the egg and cream mixture, beating with a wooden spoon. Gradually beat in the rest of the sauce, then return it to the saucepan, stirring for a few seconds just until it thickens. Do not let it come to a boil or the yolks will curdle. Add salt and pepper and a few drops of lemon juice. You may add more cream if you prefer the sauce thinner and more butter if you wish a richer sauce.

DERIVATIVE SAUCES

Sauces that are heavily butter-enriched tend to separate if left standing, although they can be held briefly in a double-boiler over warm (not simmering) water. If not to be used immediately, the sauce should be covered with a thin film of cream. Reheat over medium heat, beating rapidly with a wire whisk or wooden spoon. Although these sauces aren't for dieters, they *seem* light and a little goes a long way toward gussying up an otherwise boring fish fillet.

Sauce Mornay: Add about 4 tablespoons grated Gruyère or Swiss cheese to the basic sauce.

Sauce Aurore: Add 2 tablespoons tomato paste and 2 tablespoons mixed minced basil and parsley to the basic sauce.

Tarragon Sauce: Combine 1 cup white wine with ¼ cup fresh, minced tarragon and reduce the mixture to 3 tablespoons over high heat. Add it to the Sauce Parisienne along with 1 tablespoon butter and 2 tablespoons chopped parsley.

Mustard Sauce: Add 2 tablespoons very strong prepared Dijon mustard and 3 or 4 tablespoons butter to the basic sauce.

Caper Sauce: Add 3 tablespoons small drained capers to the basic sauce and beat in 2 or 3 tablespoons softened sweet butter.

POACHED WHOLE FISH

Almost any fish is suitable for gentle simmering in an aromatic Court Bouillon (page 103).* Poached fish is generally served with one of the preceding fish sauces, but the flavor of most good fresh fish can get by with as little adornment as melted butter, parsley, and lemon. Allow ½ pound per person.

Rinse the fish under cold running water and wrap it in a double thickness of cheesecloth with long ends if you do not have a special fish kettle. (A fish kettle has its own rack and is useful for steaming shellfish and cooking corn, among other things.) Using the ends of the cloth as handles, lower the fish into the simmering Court Bouillon, letting the ends of the cloth hang out over the edges of the pan, which should be long and deep enough to hold the fish plus an inch of liquid. Simmer the fish 10 minutes to the inch at its thickest section. Test for doneness by inserting a toothpick near the backbone. Remove the fish and drain it on a dish towel.

A large whole poached fish is easier to serve at the table if the body has first been skinned; but, leave the head and tail intact. Peel the skin off one side with your fingers, then roll the fish gently over onto a heated platter and skin the other side. Often the skin will cling to the dish towel, removing the skin for you. Cover the eye with a lemon slice. Pour butter or sauce over the whole fish, and warm it or brown it lightly under the broiler before serving. Pass extra sauce in a pitcher or sauce boat at the table.

*Exception: Bluefish, one of the commonest on my coast, doesn't respond well to poaching. It should be baked, broiled, or sautéed. Blues are especially suited to charcoal grilling.

☙ POACHED FISH FILLETS ❧

When buying fillets, be sure to ask the fish dealer for some trimmings; otherwise your Court Bouillon (page 103) will be insipid. Very thin fillets, such as flounder, are easier to handle if they are first rolled and tied with soft white string. The fish will hold its cylindrical shape after cooking even though you remove the string before serving.

Fillets of flounder, fluke, or lemon or gray sole will be cooked in about 5 minutes if arranged flat; they will take from 8 to 12 minutes if rolled. The Court Bouillon must be maintained just under the boiling point or you will have a pan of fish flakes for your trouble. When the fish tests tender with a toothpick or fork, remove it to a cloth dish towel, then roll it gently onto a heated flameproof platter. Fillets should be sauced or buttered, then run under the broiler for a quick heating up.

☙ POACHED FRESH SALMON ❧

Salmon is nearly always cut into steaks and it is invariably expensive, but there is very little waste. A whole poached salmon of about 8 pounds makes a magnificent buffet centerpiece, but the service needs a practiced hand.

Have salmon steaks cut about 1 inch thick. Allow 1 per person. Ask for some extra trimmings. Make the Court Bouillon (page 103), and simmer the salmon steaks for about 10 minutes. Start testing after 7 minutes to be certain you don't overcook them. Salmon, like swordfish, is a fat fish, but its large flakes easily become dry and unpalatable. (When broiling salmon and swordfish steaks, frequent basting with melted butter is necessary.)

When they are done, drain the steaks on a dish towel, then transfer to a platter and serve hot or chilled with Hollandaise Sauce. A mayonnaise to which you have added a few tablespoons of finely diced, seeded cucumber and some chopped tarragon, is a particularly appropriate summer sauce for cold fish.

🌿 BROILED SALMON TAILS 🌿

Flat fillets cut from the tails of smallish salmon are often listed as *paillardes*—a recent coinage on restaurant menus. (My French dictionary says the word means "ribald." It does not appear in *Larousse* or any French cookbooks so it must be a little joke from some contemporary French chef.) Anyway, whatever the salmon tails are called, I prefer them to steaks, which have to be pinned into shape.

Serves 2

2 filleted salmon tails, about 1/2 pound each	pepper to taste
Salt and freshly ground	1/4 cup Crème Fraîche (page 123)
	Minced fresh dill (optional)

Lay the fish, skin side down, on a piece of buttered foil laid on a small baking pan. Preheat the broiler. Salt and pepper the fillets and spread equal amounts of *crème fraîche* over them. Slide them under the broiler about 5 inches from the flame, lower the heat, and watch constantly, as these fillets may cook in less than 5 minutes. No turning is required; the fish cooks through. Avoid overcooking, as these fragile fillets will continue to cook a bit when you remove them to hot plates. Strew a little fresh dill, or minced parsley or tarragon (fresh only), over the salmon. Steamed new potatoes and buttered peas make up the classic Independence Day meal in Maine—it beats hotdogs all hollow.

衤 FILLETS OF SOLE MARGUERY 衤

Named for the famous chef and owner of the Restaurant Marguery in Paris, this dish is an elegant classic. Wine, butter, cream, and eggs are blended into a buttery sauce glazing a platter of poached sole, oysters, and shrimp. Mussels can take the place of oysters. (Although oysters are now sold year-round, I think we should give them a break during spawning season.)

Serves 4

Softened butter for pan
Salt
8 small fillets of gray or lemon
* sole, or flounder*
3/4 cup dry white wine
Juice of 1 lemon
2 tablespoons melted butter
16 medium-sized shrimp

16 medium-sized mussels
2 egg yolks
1 cup thick white sauce
* (Bechamel)*
4 tablespoons softened butter (1/2
* stick)*
1/4 cup minced fresh parsley

Preheat oven to 400°F. Butter a large rectangular pan and lay the fish fillets in it. Salt the fish lightly and pour the wine and lemon juice around the fish. Spoon a bit of melted butter over each fillet. Bake for 15 minutes, basting once.

While the fillets are baking, poach the shrimp, shell and devein them (see page 18). Steam the mussels open in a little water over high heat and set aside to keep warm.

Carefully lift out the fillets and arrange them on a hot, heatproof platter. Reserve pan juices. Garnish with the shelled shrimp and mussels. Over high heat reduce the pan juices to 3/4 cup. Beat the egg yolks into the white sauce, then add the fish liquid, stirring with a whisk. Beat in the softened butter and pour the sauce over the fish platter. Glaze briefly under the broiler, sprinkle with parsley, and serve immediately.

☙ BAKED FISH FILLETS ❧

When in doubt, this is a safe method of preparation for any fish fillet. Even though you do have to use the oven, fillets bake in a few minutes and make a quick, easy dinner. Any type of flounder, or fillets of bluefish, shad, perch, bass, or red snapper are some possibilities.

Serves 4

4 large fish fillets
1/2 cup dry white wine
4 tablespoons butter (1/2 stick)
Salt

Freshly ground pepper to taste or
  hot Hungarian rose paprika
Minced fresh parsley

Preheat the oven to 400°F. Lay the fillets (skin side down, if any) in a buttered oblong pan just large enough to hold them. In a small saucepan, reduce the white wine over high heat to 1/4 cup. Add the butter to the wine and when it is melted, spoon a little of the mixture over each fillet. Sprinkle lightly with salt and pepper or a bit of hot Hungarian rose paprika. Bake 10 minutes, basting frequently with the remaining wine and butter, and pan juices. There is no need to turn the fillets. Test for doneness and remove to a heated platter. Sprinkle with parsley and pour on a bit more melted butter. Serve at once with plain boiled new potatoes and a green salad or a salad of field-ripened red tomatoes dressed simply with fine olive oil.

🌿 SEA BASS BÉARNAISE 🌿

Have the fish cleaned but left whole. You may have the head removed if you just can't bear the reproach in its eyes, but it won't look as good.

Serves 4

1 3-pound sea bass (dressed
   weight)
1 quart Court Bouillon (page 103)

Slice of lime
1 cup Sauce Béarnaise (page 156)
Cherry tomatoes

Poach the bass in the Court Bouillon for about 30 minutes. (Test for doneness by inserting the point of a small knife near the backbone.) Remove to a towel, peel off the skin between the head and tail, then gently roll the fish over onto a preheated platter. Peel the skin off the other side. Cover the eye with a slice of lime. Pour the Sauce Bearnaise over the fish and garnish the platter with little cherry tomatoes. Serve with boiled, parslied new potatoes and fresh young asparagus.

🌿 RED SNAPPER ISLE DES SAINTES 🌿

I have no idea if snappers even exist in the Caribbean waters surrounding the Isle des Saintes, a tiny Breton fishermen's community off the coast of Guadeloupe. In this remote place with no hotels, plumbing, or restaurants, "Madame in the blue house" cooks superbly on a charcoal burner for the occasional yachtsmen who come ashore. Snapper serves well to reproduce Madame's peppery fish.

Serves 4

1 3-pound red snapper   ¹/₄ pound butter (¹/₂ stick)
3 tiny red-hot fresh chili peppers,   Juice of 1 lemon
   seeded and minced   Lemon slices

Have the snapper cleaned, boned, and split. Ideally, the snapper should be charcoal broiled, but if this is impossible, remove the broiling rack and turn the broiler to its highest setting. Oil the rack thoroughly. Dry the fish on paper towels and grease both sides liberally with melted butter. Lay the fish, flesh side down, on a double thickness of aluminum foil. Mix the peppers with the butter and lemon juice. Spoon a little of the mixture over the fish. Broil, skin side up, 3 inches from the heat, for about 5 minutes. When the skin is nicely browned, roll the fish over onto the oiled rack and discard the foil. Spoon more of the peppery butter over the flesh side. Broil 5 minutes longer, basting once or twice. Begin testing, and when the fish is done transfer it to a hot platter. Heat the remaining butter and lemon juice to foaming and pour it over the fish. Garnish with thin rounds of lemon. Serve with an inexpensive, icy cold, dry white wine. This is only for guests known to possess courage and a love of hot food.

⚜ TROUT IN BROWN BUTTER ⚜

If you are lucky enough to have a source of fresh trout or live near a hatchery, this is a splendid recipe. All the frozen trout I have ever tried have been disappointing. Try some other small, whole fish instead.

Serves 4

*4 small, whole trout, about 1 1/4
    pounds ea.*
1 quart Court Bouillon (page 103)

4 tablespoons butter (1/2 stick)
4 lemon wedges

Lay the trout in a shallow pan and cover with the boiling Court Bouillon. Hold at the simmering point 10 to 15 minutes, depending on the thickness of the trout. When they are tender but still firm, drain them on a dish towel and remove to a hot platter. Heat the butter in a small heavy saucepan until it turns a rich, light brown. Pour over the trout and garnish with lemon wedges. Plain boiled potatoes are the only thing to serve with this purist's delight.

⚜ COLD TROUT WITH GREEN MAYONNAISE ⚜

On a really hot day, nothing could be more pleasant for lunch or dinner than this delicate fish. Allow one small trout per person. Sea bass may also be prepared in this way.

Serves 4

4 small trout, about 1 pound
   each
1 quart boiling Court Bouillon
   (page 103)

4 eggs, hard-cooked
Parsley sprigs
Green Mayonnaise (page 81)

Poach the trout in the Court Bouillon 10 to 15 minutes. Drain, peel, and chill the fish, well-covered with plastic wrap. Garnish each plate with sliced hard-cooked eggs and a few sprigs of parsley. Serve with a bowl of Green Mayonnaise.

☀ SEA SQUAB PROVENÇAL ☀

Sea squab is the euphemism created by sensitive fish dealers for the lowly blowfish. Once the least expensive fish on the Northeast coast, and probably still the ugliest, it is no longer plentiful or cheap but is nevertheless delicious. It is always sold cleaned, skinned, and beheaded so that it resembles a very large shrimp with a backbone. Overcooking these morsels turns them into little rubber balls. I use certain elements typical of southern French cooking—hence the name for my purely Long Island invention.

Serves 4

Salt and freshly ground pepper to
   taste
1½ pounds blowfish or jumbo
   shrimp
Flour
⅓ cup olive oil
1 pound ripe red tomatoes or
   1-pound can whole Italian
   plum tomatoes

1 onion, chopped
2 cloves garlic, minced
½ cup dry white wine
Sprig of fresh thyme or pinch of
   dried thyme
½ bay leaf
Minced fresh parsley

Salt and pepper the blowfish and dust them lightly with flour. Sauté them in the olive oil in a heavy skillet until golden. Remove fish and set aside while you make the sauce. Peel and chop the fresh tomatoes in a bowl so as not to lose the juice. Add the onion to the skillet along with the garlic and cook until soft, adding a bit more olive oil if necessary. Add the tomatoes, white wine, thyme, and bay leaf, and simmer uncovered for 30 minutes. (Recipe may be prepared in advance up to this point.) Return the blowfish to the skillet and let them simmer in the sauce for 5 minutes to heat through. Serve sprinkled with parsley. Rice is good with this.

涿 BAKED BASS WITH POTATOES 岺

Years ago, when I lived a few miles east in Amagansett, I made a practice of taking a stroll on the beach when the haulseiners were pulling in their nets. Huge striped bass by the ton were landed then, and the smaller ones—anywhere from 3 to 6 pounds— could be bought on the beach for a dollar or two. This most prized North Atlantic fish is now outlawed by the State because of high PCB levels in this fish that spawns in the Hudson River. Though nothing really can replace striped bass, a fresh firm cod in early summer or, later on, a large fluke or sea bass, may be substituted.

Serves 8

*1 whole white-fleshed lean fish,
  about 6 pounds.*
3 large onions
3/4 cup butter (1 1/2 sticks)
4 large Russett (baking) potatoes
*Salt and coarsely ground pepper
  to taste*

*6 sprigs fresh thyme or 1/4
  teaspoon dried thyme leaves*
*2 to 3 tablespoons minced fresh
  parsley*

Have a fishmonger clean and fillet the fish so that you have two large matching pieces. (Ask for the head and carcass, out of which you can make an excellent spicy "soupe au poisson"). I used to make this with a whole fish; it made a stunning presentation but was very hell to serve with skin, bone, potatoes, and onions all tangled up.

Butter a heavy ceramic or Crueset-type oval baking dish that can go from oven to table. Peel and thinly slice the onions, and very slowly sauté them in 4 tablespoons butter. Peel, slice medium thin, and blanch the potato slices in boiling water for 5 minutes. Drain and pat dry. Spread them evenly in the baking dish and salt and pepper them to taste. Melt 4 more tablespoons of butter and pour over the potatoes. Lay one half the fish on top of the potatoes, then the sautéed onions, add more salt and pepper to taste, and add the thyme sprigs. Cover with the matching half of the bass. Cover tightly with a double thickness of foil and bake in the center of a preheated 400°F. oven for about 40 minutes. Uncover, test for doneness (the bottom fillet is unlikely to be quite cooked through), and continue to bake, uncovered after basting with the pan juices, for another 5 to 10 minutes. Melt the remaining 4 tablespoons butter. Remove the fish from the oven, peel off top skin, pour on the melted butter, and sprinkle with parsley. Serve in the baking dish. This is a simple, but very elegant (and quite expensive) dinner party entrée. It deserves the best white wine you can afford. I wouldn't say no to a Corton-Charlemagne.

🎋 DEEP-FRIED WHITEBAIT 🎋

These silvery little fish, hardly larger than minnows, are a delicious summer treat—passed by, more often than not, because many people are uncertain what to do with them. They are best deep-fried. Because they're so tiny, they need no gutting or beheading—the entire fish is eaten. Simple rinse and dry them well, put them in a plastic bag with a little seasoned flour, dump the whole thing into a colander, and shake well to rid the little fish of excess flour. Heat at least 2 inches of salad oil to 400°F., then add the floured whitebait, a small handful at a time. Do not crowd the fish. Lift them out with a wire strainer after a few minutes, when they are brown and crispy. Drain on paper towels briefly and serve very hot, sprinkled with coarse salt. These are more of a summer afternoon snack, or what the French call an *amuse-gueule*, to make for a few friends who don't mind hanging out in the kitchen.

🌿 DEEP-FRIED SOFT CLAMS 🌿

Steamers, or soft-shell clams (which are not actually soft, but have thin, smooth, white shells), are increasingly rare in restaurants—undoubtedly because they must be washed and soaked in water for several hours with a handful of cornmeal to rid them of sand, and even then, eating them is a practiced technique. However, "fryers" are frequently found in fish stores, if not on menus. These are shucked, de-sanded soft clams with plump bellies and a rather messy rim attached. Don't be put off. Fried soft clams are one of the most succulent (and difficult to find) feasts of the Atlantic northeast.

Try to avoid giants, as they can be just too much of a mouthful—like overgrown raw oysters. Do not rinse the clams, but dry them as best you can on paper towels, then shake them in a bag with flour seasoned with salt and pepper. Cook them as in the recipe for Deep-Fried Whitebait (page 115).

⚜ SPICY MARINATED SQUID ⚜

Until quite recently, Americans were content to leave the world supply of squid to the Italians and the Japanese. But with our warm embrace of Oriental delights in the past decade, you can find fresh squid now at almost any good fishmonger's. What follows is a hybrid Japanese-Italian appetizer I worked out a few years ago. Though a trifle messy to eat (toothpicks or fingers), this was enthusiastically received with pre-dinner drinks. It is neither very filling nor fattening.

Serves about 8 with other appetizers

8 medium-small squid, about 2 pounds
3 to 4 tablespoons peanut oil
2 tablespoons sesame seeds
A few drops dark sesame oil

3 tablespoons Japanese soy sauce
1 tablespoon lemon juice
1 clove garlic, pulverized
¼ teaspoon dried red pepper flakes

How to Clean Squid: The filmy, veil-like, dotted lavender skin of the squid is easy to remove, and though the beast looks formidable, it is quickly cleaned. Throw the squid into a basin of cold water and proceed as follows: Lay a squid on a board near running water. Cut off the tentacles, push out and discard the little hard button in the center of them, and reserve (these are choice). Pull out and discard the gelatinous innards and transparent quill. Rinse with cold running water. Cut off the "wings" and discard. With a paper towel, rub off the skin. The squid is now pearly white, and totally unthreatening to all but the most conservative eaters. Slice the squid into ¼-inch rings and dry these and the tentacles very thoroughly, or they will spit at you furiously when they hit the hot oil.

Necklace a fairly large wok with the peanut oil and roll the wok about to coat it well. In a separate heavy skillet, lightly toast the sesame seeds. When the wok is near smoking, throw in half the squid rings (all of them would cool the pan too much and they would cook too slowly) and stir-fry them rapidly over the highest heat for about 30 seconds. Remove with a slotted spoon to a cold platter to halt the cooking. Fry the remaining squid and tentacles, adding a bit more oil if necessary. Remove and cool.

Mix the toasted sesame seeds with the sesame oil, soy, lemon juice, garlic, and pepper flakes. Turn the squid in this mixture to coat well and let rest at room temperature about an hour before serving. (If the kitchen temperature is above about 70°F., refrigerate the squid, covered, until about 15 minutes before serving. It should not be served cold.)

Variation: This becomes a main course luncheon dish with a few additions: half a pound of medium-small shrimp, poached in their shells for 1 minute, then cooled, shelled, and deveined; about a quarter pound of fresh crabmeat or the Japanese fake crabmeat called surimi; or, some leftover cold white fish broken into small chunks, some finely minced scallions, celery, and crisp, red bell pepper bits, the whole bound in the sauce described above and served on large leaves of romaine with a few ripe olives for garnish.

☞ SHRIMP PERLOO ☜

You would be justified in thinking the word *perloo* had been lifted out of the great Walt Kelly's famous Pogo comic strip. But you would be wrong. It means pilaf, or pilau, or however this rice dish is spelled, and in the Carolina low-Country it was pronounced "perlow" or "perloo" and eaten at least once a week. Shrimp were so cheap and common they were used for bait, so the dish was nothing special. Now that shrimp cost the moon, our old "perloo" can be proudly served to any gathering.

Serves 4

1 pound small shrimp (about 28
   to the pound)

2 tablespoons kosher salt

2 cups Court Bouillon (page 103)

1 small bay leaf

A few grinds of white pepper

2 strips thick bacon, cut in
   matchstick-sized strips

2 cloves fresh garlic, minced

1 medium-sized onion, finely
   chopped

1 cup peeled tomatoes, drained
   and coarsely chopped (canned
   or very ripe fresh ones)

1 1/4 cups long grain converted
   rice

1 teaspoon dried red pepper
   flakes

Tomato juice (optional)

1 tablespoon cornstarch

2 tablespoons olive oil or clarified
   butter (page 126)

1/2 teaspoon dried red pepper
   flakes or Chinese hot chili paste

Salt to taste

2 tablespoons minced fresh
   parsley

Rinse, peel, and clean the shrimp, reserving the shells. Put the shrimp in a bowl with half the kosher salt and whip them around with a pair of chopsticks until they froth up. Rinse them with fresh cold water, add another tablespoon of kosher salt and cold water to cover. Cover with plastic wrap and refrigerate. This is a Chinese technique I've adopted for all shrimp dishes, because it gives them a wonderful crisp texture. It can be done several hours ahead. (Ninety percent of the shrimp bought outside Louisiana and South Carolina have been frozen; if you have miraculously got hold of some truly fresh—not "fresh-frozen," whatever that means—shrimp, the salt treatment isn't necessary—but it can't hurt.)

Put the shrimp shells in a small saucepan with 2 cups of light court bouillon and weight them down with a slightly smaller pot containing an inch of water. (This keeps the shells submerged so that you get full-flavor value from them.) Simmer them for half an hour with the bay leaf and pepper.

Try out the bacon slowly in a heavy saucepan with a tight lid capable of holding all the ingredients. When the fat has run sufficiently, add the garlic and onion, and sauté slowly until transparent. Add the tomatoes, rice, and 1 teaspoon of red pepper flakes. Strain the bouillon and, if necessary, add enough tomato juice to measure 2 cups. Pour this into the rice and stir. Bring to a boil, lower heat, cover, and simmer for 15 minutes. Turn off heat and leave the pot undisturbed to steam for a further 15 minutes.

Meanwhile, rinse and dry the shrimp. Dust them with cornstarch and sauté them for about 2 minutes in olive oil or clarified butter. Season with more red pepper flakes or some Chinese hot chili paste and, when the rice is tender and dry, mix in the shrimp. Sprinkle with minced parsley and serve. A pot of black-eyed peas is the Charleston thing to serve with this, but in New Orleans it would be red beans. Chopped fresh hot chili peppers are another Charleston touch, but this may be a bit much for the non-native born.

🎣 LA COTRIADE 🎣

From Brittany, this regional French fish stew is the probable forerunner of New England (white) clam and fish chowders.

La Cotriade is a fisherman's stew that summons up a place like our own Montauk: gorse-carpeted dunes, rocky beaches, and oilskin-dressed men who wrest a living from the sea. French food critic Robert Courtine, reminiscing about this, one of his favorite dishes, writes about the farmhouse restaurant where as he eats "a gust of wind blows in through the open door bearing a whiff of seaweed and cider." "Kenavo" is the old Breton greeting as you wait, sipping a draught of hard cider, for this triumph of fish stews.

Serves 4

2 medium onions

4 tablespoons butter (½ stick)

1 pound Russet or Idaho potatoes
   (approximately 3)

¾ cup dry hard French cider or
   white wine

2 cups fish fumet

4 white fish steaks (cod, haddock,
   halibut, bass)

2 live small 1-pound lobsters

¼ cup heavy cream

Homemade Fried Croutons,
   recipe follows

Shallot-Vinaigrette Sauce
   (optional), recipe follows

Slowly cook the onions in the butter, covered, in a heavy stew pan. Peel and slice the potatoes in thick rounds; add to the onions, turning to coat them with butter. Make a fumet using a dry white wine if dry hard French cider is unavailable—no American cider is dry enough and you may prefer wine anyway. The Bretons have no native wine; they drink hard cider and Calvados and I can think of worse hardships.

Arrange the fish steaks on the potatoes along with the lobsters cut in half lengthwise. If you're not up to cutting through live lobsters, have your fish dealer do this and keep the lobsters on a bed of ice until you cook them—which should be promptly. Pour the heavy cream over everything, cover the pan, and steam the fish and lobster about 10 minutes, basting them with the pan juices several times. Serve in heated bowls with Fried Croutons to mop up the juices. The Shallot-Vinaigrette Sauce gives this stew an added flavor jump, though it doesn't really need it.

Fried Croutons: Cube some ½-inch slices of French bread (or any good bread you happen to have) and fry them in a little hot olive oil until they are crisp and golden brown on both sides. Drain on paper towels and serve hot.

Shallot-Vinaigrette Sauce: Finely mince 1 whole shallot and add it to a basic vinaigrette made of 1 part white wine vinegar to 4 parts olive oil flavored with a little salt and pepper. Spoon a bit of this on the fish, not in the soup.

杰 BAKED MONKFISH WITH OYSTERS 秦

Monkfish, a.k.a. anglerfish (on French menus, *lotte*) was a trash fish locally. I haven't saved any whales, but two fish I have saved by hauling them into respectability are blowfish and monkfish. I've tried to promote each in my column in the *East Hampton Star.*

Monkfish is not the finest creature in the sea, but it is bland and harmless and does absorb the flavor of its betters—such as lobster or oysters. Only the tails of monkfish are sold retail; buy the thickest part and be sure it is cleanly skinned. It can be tough and stringy so care must be exercised to see that it's tender before adding other ingredients, such as fragile oysters.

Serves 4

1 pound cut of monkfish
16 to 20 stewing oysters, shucked,
   with juices
1/4 cup clarified butter (page 126)
10 scallions (approximately),
   cleaned and cut into 1/2-inch

lengths including only the
   tender part of the green
Salt and white pepper to taste
White wine (optional)
1/2 cup Crème Fraîche (page 123)
   or reduced heavy cream

Cut the monkfish into 2-inch chunks and dry well. Drain the oysters and reserve the liquid. Sauté the monkfish in the butter until golden, then add the scallions. Add the oyster liquor, a little salt and pepper, a little white wine or water if the oysters don't yield much liquid, cover, and stew on low heat for about 10 minutes. Stir the fish around, test for tenderness, and simmer further if necessary.

Add the *crème fraîche* or some reduced heavy cream, reduce it a few minutes, then correct the seasoning. Other herbs conflict with oysters so don't get fancy at their expense. *They* are the expense. If very large, cut the oysters in half before adding them to the pan. Simmer, uncovered, just until the edges curl. Serve this on a bed of rice with some plain chopped parsley. Or you could serve it on toast points if you prefer.

⚹ BROILED FISH *CRÈME FRAÎCHE* ⚹

Some years ago (many!) I hit upon the idea of broiling bluefish fillets under a layer of mayonnaise, which would both flavor and moisten the fish. Though bluefish is a so-called "fat" fish, there is *no* fish that can be broiled without some kind of lubrication. *Crème fraîche,* an item known to few American kitchens until quite recently, has a wonderful effect on all sorts of fish and no system could be easier.

For skinless fillets, such as flounder, gray sole, fluke, etc., simply butter a metal platter, lay on the fillets, grind on pepper, and slather on the *crème fraîche* (do not use salt, which draws out the juices, until after cooking). Cover and refrigerate or let sit at room temperature for not more than 30 minutes. Broil 6 inches from a medium flame—you cannot charcoal grill these fish fillets—about 5 minutes or just until they are firm and lose their translucence. [Some food critics are strong advocates of rare fish; I think it's awful and prefer mine raw, as in sushi, or merely perfectly cooked, which is just cooked through.] Add a sprinkling of sea salt and some minced parsley, chives, or tarragon, or some combination of these.

CRÈME FRAÎCHE:

Heat 2 cups of heavy cream to 110°F. Stir in 2 teaspoons of buttermilk. Pour into a thermos and let stand, covered, for 8 hours or until thickened. Scrape it into a glass jar and refrigerate; it will keep well for 2 weeks. If you don't use it often, store it in two smaller well-sealed jars.

🎋 BROILED SHAD 🎋

Commonly thought to be a spring fish, shad is in fact an Atlantic deep-sea fish available most of the year. (Though shad aren't recommended in winter, when they take their mud baths.) When the rivers are warm in spring, the shad swim in from the sea to spawn, and it is then that the greatly prized shad roe is in season. The fish itself is also a great delicacy and, because it is "fat," it broils well. Whole buck shad is cheap. But because the shad contains an aggravating number of fine bones, it must be filleted and it takes a real master to do it. I've read of a method of baking a shad until its bones dissolve—but so would its texture.

Serves 4

1 3-pound shad, boned and cut   *Capers*
  into serving pieces   *Lemon slices*
½ cup melted butter (1 stick)
Salt and freshly ground pepper
  to taste

Oil and preheat the broiler. Lay the shad pieces on the broiler rack and brush with melted butter. Sprinkle with salt and pepper. Broil about 3 inches from the heat for about 8 minutes. Baste frequently with the melted butter and resign yourself to watching the fish during almost the entire broiling time to be certain that it does not dry out or overcook. Do not turn the fish. (The preheated broiler will cook the underside, although it won't brown it.) When the fish tests done with a toothpick, lift it onto a heated platter or, preferably, the heated dinner plates—the less handling any fish receives, the more likely it will be to reach the table in an attractive, unbroken condition. Pour a little melted butter on each portion, scatter with a few capers, and garnish with lemon slices.

Small bluefish, called "snappers" are also excellent prepared in this way. Thin fillets, such as flounder, are not suitable for broiling. A stir-fried mélange of fresh vegetables goes well with broiled fish.

🌿 SMALL WHOLE BROILED FISH 🌿

Flounder and porgy, fresh mackerel, whiting, butterfish, mullet, perch, lemon sole, sunfish, and weakfish are all good choices for broiling when they weigh less than 1½ pounds. Get the very freshest small local fish you can buy and have them gutted but left whole. Allow one whole fish per person. Rinse and dry them, then rub them inside and out with the cut side of half a lemon. Salt them inside and out and massage well with softened butter.

Do *not* preheat the broiler since you will want to turn the fish to brown on both sides, and preheating would overcook it. The fish should be laid directly on a well-oiled broiler rack, not on aluminum foil. (The juices would collect in the foil and spoil the lovely brown crustiness of the skin.)

Broil the fish under medium heat, about 3 inches from the flame, for about 5 minutes. Brush the fish with melted butter and turn carefully, using 2 spatulas to roll the fish gently over. Brush the uncooked side with melted butter and broil for another 5 minutes. Test for doneness with a toothpick; broiling time will vary enormously, depending on whether you are cooking a flat flounder or a plump trout. Thus, a long, thin fish weighing 1½ pounds will cook much more quickly than a short, thick one weighing less. Serve them with butter—heated in a small heavy skillet until it turns a rich, light brown—poured over and garnish with thin lemon wedges.

❧ PANNED WHITING ❧

Whiting is also known as silver hake in different localities. Its flesh is very delicate, white, and lean; it is particularly suited to this rich, buttery cooking method. Flounder fillets cooked in this way are what you usually get when you order *Filet de Sole à la Meuniere.* If the whiting isn't strictly fresh, take flounder or something else that weighs from ¾ to 1 pound. Have the fish cleaned but the head and tail left intact. (It's hard to get a flounder that hasn't been filleted, but if you can, "flounder-on-the-bone" (minus skin) is delicious.

Serves 4

4 whiting, about 1 pound each
Salt and freshly ground pepper to
 taste
Juice of ½ lemon
½ cup flour

½ to ¾ cup clarified butter*
¼ pound sweet butter (1 stick)
Chopped fresh parsley and
 tarragon (optional)

Rinse and dry the fish. Rub the cavities with a little salt and pepper and lemon juice. Dust them with flour and brown them in the clarified butter for about 4 minutes on each side. Transfer the fish to a hot platter and season with additional salt, pepper, and lemon juice.

While you are frying the fish, let the ¼ pound of sweet butter brown slightly in a small pan. Stir it from time to time and take care that it doesn't burn. Sprinkle the fish with the herbs and pour the foaming brown butter over all.

*Clarified butter is made by melting sweet butter, letting the milky sediment settle, and carefully pouring off the clear butterfat. It will not smoke or burn as easily as ordinary butter. The flavor of good butter is of paramount importance to this dish and you cannot substitute any other frying medium.

❦ SCALLOPED SCALLOPS, SHRIMP, ❦ AND FLOUNDER

This is a dish I devised to cope with those evenings when I don't quite know how many guests are coming, or when. It can be made in the morning, refrigerated, then reheated at serving time. Since the dish requires no knife and the casserole keeps it warm, it is practical for a buffet.

Serves 12

1 1/2 pounds sea scallops
Court Bouillon (page 103)
2 pounds small shrimp
12 flounder fillets, each about 6
  inches long
4 cups Sauce Parisienne (page
  103)

1 pound mushrooms, sliced
3 tablespoons butter
2 tablespoons chopped fresh
  parsley or tarragon, or both

Cut the scallops across the grain, if large, into bite-sized pieces. Put them in a strainer, wire basket, or cheesecloth bag and cook them in the barely bubbling Court Bouillon for 1 minute. Remove and drain. Rinse the shrimp and cook them for 2 minutes in the same Court Bouillon. Shell and devein them. Roll up the flounder fillets and fasten them with a toothpick. Put them in the Court Bouillon for about 5 minutes. Drain them and save the fish stock to make your Sauce Parisienne.

Sauté the mushrooms for a few minutes in the butter, until they are rather dry and add them to the Sauce Parisienne. Butter an ovenproof casserole and stand the rolled fish fillets (toothpicks removed) inside its perimeter. Fill the center with the scallops and and shrimp. (Recipe may be made in advance up to this point. The Sauce Parisienne will have to be gently reheated and beaten with a wire whisk before continuing.) Pour the Sauce Parisienne over all. Bake in a 450°F. oven about 5 minutes or until hot through. Strew with the chopped herbs and serve.

❧ AMAGANSETT BOUILLABAISSE ❧

My bouillabaisse has little in common with the famous soup of Marseilles, which is always full of eels and never contains lobster. You may put fresh eels in, along with any firm-fleshed fish, preferably of varying sizes and textures. I loathe boiled eel, so I have omitted that and added all the fish and shellfish I do like. This is a splendid summer Sunday brunch dish. Always provide debris bowls for all the shells.

Serves 12 to 14

2 3-pound sea bass or blackfish
3 pounds porgies or fresh
  mackerel (or both, mixed)
2 1 1/2-pound live lobsters each
2 quarts mussels (about 2
  pounds)
1 pound Little Neck clams
1 1/2 quarts dry white wine
3 quarts lightly salted water
1 bay leaf, 2 sprigs thyme, and 10
  peppercorns, tied in a
  cheesecloth bag

3 medium onions, sliced
3 large cloves garlic, minced
Olive oil
1 large can Italian peeled
  tomatoes, crushed, or 1 1/2
  pounds ripe fresh tomatoes,
  peeled and crushed
1/2 teaspoon saffron
1 pound shrimp, rinsed
Flour
1 tablespoon butter
Several loaves of French bread

Get all the trimmings left over from your fish after the dealer prepares it this way: Have the sea bass split and boned; the porgies and mackerel cleaned and boned. Some fish dealers don't like to spend any time with cheap fish like porgies and mackerel. If they won't bone it for you, take the fish home and bone it after you boil it. (Traditional bouillabaisse is an obstacle course of bones, but I think there are really very few people who enjoy this kind of authenticity.) The lobsters should be alive and lively, the shellfish tightly closed.

At home, cut the bass into large slices about 1-inch thick. If they are boned, cut each porgy or mackerel into 3 or 4 pieces. Wash and scrub the mussels with a wire brush, then remove the beards. Lobsters and mussels are quite safe to buy the day before. They can live several days in the refrigerator, but it's best to cook them as quickly as possible after you get them home.

Boil up all the fish trimmings with the wine, water, bay leaf, thyme, and peppercorns, and simmer it for 30 minutes. Meanwhile, sauté the onions and garlic in olive oil in a heavy skillet. Add the tomatoes to the skillet. Strain the fish stock and return it to a large pot along with the onions, garlic, and tomatoes. Add saffron, bring to the boil, and simmer on medium heat for 10 minutes while you prepare the lobsters.

Kill the lobsters by plunging a knife into the thorax and splitting the lobster lengthwise. Discard the small sac near the head and cut up each lobster into about 6 pieces. Detach the claws from the second joints and crack them. Add to the soup. Next add the sea bass and simmer for 10 minutes. Add the porgies and/or mackerel and shrimp (in their shells, legs detached); simmer 5 minutes. During this last 5 minutes, steam the mussels open in a little water in a separate saucepan over high heat. Work as much flour into a tablespoon of butter as it will absorb. Thicken the soup slightly with this by stirring it in vigorously.

Put a chunk of French bread into each large, flat soup plate. Ladle some hot soup and fish into the plates and decorate each with several clams and mussels. Be sure to have 4 or 5 loaves of French bread and pass extra baskets of it around with the soup. Serve a dry white wine and provide some fruit and a selection of cheeses for dessert.

Despite the terrifying length of the directions, this bouillabaisse takes only about 45 minutes to prepare. It's a gorgeous "one-pot" meal for a large number of guests.

🌿 SHRIMP GUMBO 🌿

Fresh okra is in season during the summer and increasingly available, though once hardly known outside the South; however, you may have to use the frozen product. Traditional gumbo recipes call for long cooking, but the flavor and texture of both shrimp and okra is much nicer with brief cooking.

Serves 4

1 medium onion, sliced
1/2 green pepper, sliced
2 cups peeled and chopped ripe
  tomatoes
1 bay leaf
1 sprig thyme
Salt and freshly ground pepper to
  taste

1 pound fresh okra or 1 10-ounce
  package frozen okra
1 pound shrimp
1 teaspoon dried red pepper
  flakes

Sauté the onion and green pepper in a little olive oil. Add the tomatoes, herbs, and salt and pepper to taste, and simmer, uncovered, for 15 minutes. Slice the okra in 1/4-inch rounds and cook it for about 5 minutes in the tomato sauce. Peel and clean the raw shrimp, cut them in pieces if they are large, and add to the pan. Simmer for 5 minutes. Serve with a bowl of white rice.

⚘ STEAMER CLAMS ⚘

Any clams can be steamed but the best variety are known as "steamers" along the coast. They are smooth, thin-shelled clams that plump up to a tender juiciness, rather like poached oysters. Unfortunately, they tend to be rather sandy. Soaking them a couple of hours in cold water into which you have thrown a large handful of cornmeal seems to help them disgorge some of the sand. Steamers should be well scrubbed with a medium stiff brush before cooking, since their broth is served along with them. People who like steamers will eat so many they will eat nothing else, so I always serve them as the main course. Allow 1 quart of steamers per guest—remember, they're not getting anything else—unless you want to steam up some fresh summer corn on the cob to go with them and have a real eating orgy.

Serves 4

4 quarts steamer clams   *½ pound butter, melted (2 sticks)*

Put an inch of cold water in the bottom of a large heavy pot or clam steamer. Distribute the clams evenly in the pot, turn the flame to high and cook, covered, stirring them up from time to time. All should be open in less than 10 minutes. (A clam steamer takes longer to open the clams and I can see no particular virtue in using one except that it's a great-looking pot with a spout on it for pouring off the juice.) Lift out the clams with a slotted spoon (or you may tie them in cheesecloth serving bundles before cooking) onto hot soup plates. Carefully pour the broth through a cheesecloth-lined strainer. Serve individual cups of broth and melted butter to each guest. Medieval manners prevail, so provide plenty of napkins.

❧ HUSH PUPPIES ❧

How this deep-fried fritter received its inscrutable name has several explanations. One I cling to is that fishermen sitting around their campfire frying the day's catch tossed these fish-flavored bits to their dogs with the admonition "Hush, puppy." They are nearly always served at Southern fish fries cooked in the fat the fish were fried in. But they can be fried in plain salad oil, too.

Serves 6

1 cup cornmeal	*1 egg, beaten*
3/4 teaspoon salt	*2 tablespoons bacon fat or*
1/4 teaspoon pepper	* melted butter*
2 teaspoons baking powder	*1 medium onion, minced*
3/4 cup milk	*Fat for deep frying.*

Mix the dry ingredients together, then blend in the milk, egg, bacon fat, and onion. Do not overmix. Drop by rounded teaspoons into deep hot fat (about 375°F.) and fry until golden, 3 to 5 minutes. Drain on absorbent paper and serve very hot.

Variation: Not traditional but wonderful; stir 2 tablespoons parsley and chives, minced together into the batter.

MEATS AND POULTRY
& OUTDOOR COOKING

W hat a phenomenal change! Just twenty years ago, when I first wrote about outdoor cooking, backyard chefs were few. And their usual fare was steak or hamburger, blackened in an inferno of smoke and flame."—James Beard, 1960

The odyssey of the backyard barbecue continues—from quintessential Saturday night gamboling on suburban lawns to chic restaurants where mesquite-fired open grills are center stage. Once the object of scorn by sophisticated gastronomes (especially Europeans), the barbecue grill is today the cynosure of all fashionable eyes. From *barbe* (beard) to *queue* (tail), insist some Francophiles, but I accept the oracular Larousse's verdict that the Spanish word *barbacoa*—"a raised frame" is the origin of the term "barbecue," as used to mean anything grilled over a wood fire.* Whatever the origins, barbecuing is universally regarded as an American specialty.

*The noun "barbecue" is an altogether different matter: pit-roasted pig, shredded and saucily spiced, is the subject widely discussed by experts from Cape Hatteras to Waco and all points in between. There are thousands of opinions, each as immutable as the Rosetta stone.

Charcoal grilling is a companionable and fairly low-calorie way of cooking for family as well as guests, so its popularity is entrenched even though the trendy restaurants may abandon their "open kitchen" floorshows. It's worth taking the time to learn about fires, fuels, timing, and grill distance rather than bumbling through endless summers of hit-or-miss grill skirmishes.

It's unclear to me why people who normally wouldn't essay a simple roast chicken *inside* the house, attempt Flying Wallenda stunts at the barbecue grill—amazing bravura, when one considers how capricious a charcoal fire is compared with the stolid performance of the kitchen range. (Outdoor cooking as a faintly risible spectator sport is a quaint attitude, though it needn't be replaced with fanatic solemnity either.) Learning to build a proper fire and then to *wait* for it may be the most difficult—maybe the only difficult—thing about successful outdoor cooking. It assuredly is the element of greatest disagreement.

FIRE AND SMOKE

Where there's smoke, there's sometimes just smoke. But starting up those summer-damp lumps of charcoal has become less of a challenge with the more widespread distribution of a commercially made "firestarter" can, which requires only a sheet of newspaper beneath the coals to get a good foundation fire going. No more need for marinating good oak charcoal in lighter fluid. This gadget also simplifies replenishing coals for long, slow covered-grill jobs—formerly a tedious process of double fire building. Left alone, the chemical aura burns away from charcoal in good time. But time is what we never seem to have, and deciding when the coals are ready is one of summer life's thorniest subjects. Remember the days when a bag of Rockford Quiklite or something like it answered all one's needs? Now we're hailing California for grapevine cuttings, denuding the Southwest of mesquite trees, and mail-ordering apple and cherry woodchips. When I got my first smoker, I brined and fumed just about everything but eggs. But I must confess that the flavor of woodsmoke can be definitely boring if it's too pervasive.

Mesquite, interesting though it can be, overwhelms a lot of foods, most fish for example. Apple chips and grapevine cuttings are better for more-fragile foods. But hickory and oak chips, found just about everywhere, are perfectly fine used in moderation. Some instructions on woodchip packets would have your grill looking like a fire in the Australian outback. Only one handful of chips, soaked for 15 or 20 minutes in water, makes great billows of smoke for flavoring (not for cooking—that's another subject). After the charcoal has burnt to a white ash over red glowing coals, throw on the damp chips, arrange the food on the grill, and cover for 5 minutes. (If your grill has no cover, it's easy to improvise one with a large, deep wok cover or heavy-duty foil.) Then uncover and continue grilling in the normal way for steaks, chops, or chicken. For large cuts and birds, covered barbecuing is recommended, with a pan under the food to catch good drippings and prevent a raging grease fire.

Steaks and chops for two or three people don't need a medieval fire wall for proper grilling. I use an ancient and very small hibachi for this and only fire up a big kettledrum-type or Texas doubledecker grill and smoker for parties. Hibachis of recent vintage seem to be both lighter and cheaper than the old ones—so easy to haul to the beach or on boats. They're practical to have around for small jobs and adjunct cooking when the main barbecue grill is occupied or a cooler temperature is needed. There are some sleek, compact, portable propane gas grills that are convenient for spontaneous picnics or for driving trips. They're great backups for major barbecue bashes too.

It is definitely untrue—no matter how much you may wish it so—that a barbecue grill doesn't need cleaning. It does. And it needs it every single time you use it. It's permissible to leave it crusty and black to prevent rust if you want to leave it outside. But few sights are more depressing to the eager cook. It's preferable to clean it, oil it, and put the grill back ready for the next use.

Covered grills don't really grill. They roast and they bake and they produce some great turkeys, capons, pork chops and loins, and whole fish. Never cover steaks, burgers, chops, etc., because this steams them to some extent. A wobbly, three-legged, flat-basin model can produce superb food if you get the heat and distance right. Experiment—outdoor grilling is a learning process, not an exact science.

Inevitably, the pyro tyro uses too much charcoal (although this is one of those rare instances in cookery where too much is preferable to too little). A 10-pound bag of it will burn and burn . . . and burn, until you get up in the middle of the night and kill it with a pail of water. Nearly everyone's first trials have enough firepower left over to cook for a three-day fiesta.

Gas-fueled grills big enough to roast a goat—complete with electric spits and ceramic "rocks" to hold or intensify heat—are popular with people who do a great deal of outdoor cooking. Hot ceramic rocks and damp chips add their woodsy appeal to the instant heat of gas.

But equipment really isn't the secret of successful barbecuing, although good stuff can make it easier and neater. Patience and vigilance—the salient characteristics of birdwatchers—are absolute necessities to the unruffled charcoal griller.

凃 SAIGON CHICKEN WINGS 佘

I called these "Saigon" because the flavors are hot and lemony, and somewhat reminiscent of Vietnamese cookery. The "recipe" is almost entirely technique. Marinate the chicken wings about 8 hours, or overnight if that's more convenient.

Serves 4

*2 pounds fresh small chicken
   wings
Juice of a large lemon
1/2 cup low sodium (Kikkoman
   Light) teriyaki sauce (or any
   Japanese soy sauce)*

*3 fat cloves garlic, pulverized
2 tablespoons Szechuan (hot)
   chili bean paste*

Chop the pinions off the wings and cut the skin away from the inside of them with kitchen shears and discard; the marinade will never penetrate the rather tough skin on a chicken's wing otherwise. Dry the pieces.

Mix the lemon juice, teriyaki sauce, garlic, and bean paste together, and roll each piece of chicken in this mixture, massaging it in well. Put the pieces into a large plastic bag and pour in the remaining marinade. Twist the bag shut and refrigerate. Turn the bag 2 or 3 times during the day.

Build a good charcoal fire and soak a handful of wood chips (cherry, apple, or hickory are best) in water for half an hour while the fire reaches the optimum cooking condition. It should not be so hot that the chicken skin burns black in the 20 minutes it requires on the grill. Some barbecues have adjustable gridirons, in which case, simply move them up if the coals are too hot. Unfortunately, a great many have fixed grids, so the fire must be judged more accurately. The skin should slowly turn brown and crisp; if it starts to blacken, remove the grid entirely and wait until the coals subside. After 5 minutes, turn the wings. After another 5 minutes, turn them again, then lift the grid and throw in the soaked wood chips; replace the grid and clap on the cover. (If you don't care for a smoky flavor, omit this step.) Cook with top vents closed for 5 minutes more, then remove the cover and turn the chicken pieces again. Continue grilling for a total of about 20 minutes, turning the chicken often with tongs. (A fork will puncture the skin and release all the juices.) When finished, the chicken should be smokelike dark, with a crisp skin and moist interior. Serve hot (the crispiness of the skin is lost when they cool) with the following dipping sauce:

SAIGON DIPPING SAUCE

Mix 2 tablespoons of dry wasabi powder with enough cold water to make a stiff paste. Let it mature, covered, for half an hour to develop its fiery flavor. Whisk as much as you like of it into some soy sauce, a teaspoon of dark Chinese sesame oil, and the juice of half a lemon. Mix in some toasted sesame seeds. Divide this among 4 small, flat dishes so that the wings can be rolled in it by each diner, Japanese style.

☆ FAJITAS AND SALSA PICANTE ☆

Fajitas were, so far as I can discover, invented in Texas and recently came north with the wild burst of Tex-Mex restaurants all over New York City. In Texas they're made with skirt steak (a richly beefy-tasting "inside" steak, well known to butchers but few others—there are only two of these long, tender, straplike steaks to a side of beef). Charcoal grilled strips of this are plonked, rare and juicy, into a large, soft flour tortilla and rounded up with the usual suspects: guacamole, fried onions, and a raw tomato sauce made with hot chili peppers, garlic, and lime juice. I like a dollop of refried beans on top of everything as a contrast to the guacamole; you can add just about any other element of Tex-Mex origin you like. This is amusing, delicious "hep yessef" food.

Serves 4 to 6

SALSA PICANTE:

*3 large, ripe tomatoes, skinned
  and seeded*
*2 medium-hot fresh chili peppers,
  seeded*
1 clove garlic, pulverized
4 to 5 scallions, minced
*1 tablespoon minced fresh
  parsley*
*1 tablespoon minced fresh
  coriander leaves*
2 teaspoons ground coriander
Salt to taste
Juice of 1 lime

*1 skirt steak (about 1 1/2 pounds
  trimmed)*
1 clove garlic, pulverized
1/2 cup olive oil
*Salt and coarsely ground fresh
  black pepper*
*8 to 12 fresh, warm, soft wheat
  tortillas*
Your favorite guacamole
*2 cups soft, browned, fried
  onions*
Refried beans

Finely chop the tomatoes, and mince the chili peppers, then combine with the remaining salsa ingredients. Make several hours ahead of time and let the flavors meld at room temperature or in the fridge if the weather's very hot.

Cut the skirt steak into large strips that will be manageable with tongs, and rub the meat with the garlic and oil. Broil it over a searing hot fire, only a few minutes on each side. Quickly slice it into narrow strips on a heated board.

Set out the meat, tortillas, guacamole, onions, and beans. Let everyone help themselves and build their own fajitas. This is the answer to a lazy host's prayer: meat, bread, and salad all in one course the guest has to put together. Definitely not black tie—paper plates and plenty of napkins.

☌ SAUSAGES AND OYSTERS ☌

Odd though this may sound, it is an old and venerable combination in French cuisine. The larger varieties of oysters are better than the smaller ones for this treatment, as they're easier to handle on a hot grill if you want them roasted. They need only to be scrubbed and set on the grill, deep shell down, until they open—that's cooked enough. Of course if you have succulent fresh, small oysters and a resident shucker, serve them raw on the half shell with lemon wedges only.

Grill hot or sweet Italian sausages about 10 minutes over a medium-hot bed of coals, turning them incessantly until you have an evenly crisped skin and they are just cooked through. Do *not* parboil them (a revisionist theory for me), as this dries them out, and don't overcook them for the same reason. Skillet-fried onions and sweet peppers are the best accompaniment along with new loaves of whole wheat Italian bread. This is hands-on eating: an oyster (either grilled in its shell or served cold and raw) alternated with a bite of juicy hot sausage. With this, serve a heady, rich dark beer like New Amsterdam Amber, Mexican Dos Equis, or Guiness mixed half and half with any decent lager, in big frosted mugs.

⚘ FRESH TUNA OR MAKO SHARK STEAKS ⚘

Fresh tuna has become increasingly available with its new popularity among American chefs. Previously it was left to the canners and the wise sushi lovers. Tuna steaks are the most meat-like of any creature of the sea. Mako is more like swordfish and needs the same care to avoid dryness. Skip mesquite and use plain oak charcoal. If you want a smoky flavor, throw some soaked herbs on the coals and cover the fish quickly for a minute or so. (When I cut back garden herbs in autumn I dry the scraggly stalks and vines to use on future fires.)

Buy steaks about 1½ inches thick—for 4 people, a piece that weighs about 1¼ pounds is generous, as there is no waste. Rub the fish well with oil and pepper (but no salt, as this draws out the juices), and let it marinate at room temperature for half an hour before grilling. Salt just before grilling over a medium-hot bed of coals, and keep the fish at least 6 inches from the coals. After searing on one side, turn and sear the other, switching the steaks at right angles to make a grid pattern. After 5 minutes, throw a large bunch of thyme twigs onto the coals and cover the fish briefly to let the herb flavor penetrate. (If you don't grow herbs, rub the fish before grilling with good, strongly scented dried thyme leaves.) Grapevine cuttings, soaked and tossed onto the coals, provide a gentle smoky flavor. Paint the fish with melted butter just before serving.

𝄞 SKEWERED JUMBO SHRIMP 𝄞

Shrimp of any size retains more of its natural flavor and juiciness if cooked in the shell—whether boiled or broiled. It's a bit messier to eat, but after all, barbecues are not for the wildly fastidious. Bamboo skewers need soaking before use so that they won't burn up; they're cheap and disposable, and food threaded on bamboo escapes any metallic flavor. Food also clings better to bamboo than metal, which facilitates turning. Jumbo shrimp are about 15 to the pound. As these are really giants, 4 per person is enough.

Serves 4

16 jumbo shrimp	*2 zucchini, about 5 inches long*
2 large bunches scallions	

MARINADE:

1 cup light, fruity olive oil	*1 clove garlic, crushed to a paste*
1 tablespoon minced fresh	*Pinch of salt*
marjoram	*Lemon wedges (optional)*
2 teaspoons freshly ground black	
pepper	

Rinse and dry the shrimp. Remove the legs and slit the shells down the back with sharp scissors. Do not remove the shell, but scrape out the large vein that runs down the back. Slice the shrimp open along the back about half an inch. Mix together the marinade ingredients. Marinate the shrimp with the scallions, cut in 1-inch lengths, and the zucchini, also cut in 1-inch lengths, for about an hour. Thread these ingredients on the previously soaked bamboo skewers, alternating shrimp, scallions, and zucchini. Brush the finished skewers with the reserved marinade and grill over a medium-low bed of coals for about 3 minutes per side. People seem to expect lemon or lime slices, but I try to discourage them, as they obliterate the haunting, low-country flavor of shrimp cooked in the shell. The shells are inedible, but true aficionados chew on them like rib bones to extract the last atom of flavor.

🎋 LAMB KIDNEYS AND ONIONS 🎋

Here's another kebab to excite the more adventurous. These are good with potatoes that have been parboiled, rolled in oil or butter, and crisped over a cooling grill. Vegetables grilled separately from meat are much simpler to time than complicated kebab combinations (though not so show biz, I'll admit). You will most likely have to order the lamb kidneys from your butcher, as they must be very fresh.

Allow 2 or 3 lamb kidneys per person. They should be well rinsed, the center button of fat removed, then each kidney butterflied. Dry well, then turn them in olive oil mixed with salt and pepper. Parboil some small yellow onions, then skin them, thread on skewers, and roll in oil or melted butter. They should be about 90 percent cooked. Place them at the outer edge of the grill; they will require about 5 minutes, the kidneys a bit less than that to reach the pink stage—overcooked kidneys are unpalatable.

🦊 GRILLED WHOLE TENDERLOIN 🦌

Nothing suitable for outdoor cookery could be simpler or more luxurious than this meltingly tender cut of beef grilled whole, then cut into succulent servings. Filet mignon, as this lean steak is also known, needs constant basting or barding to avert dryness. Larding the tenderloin with strips of porkfat threaded through its outer layer is ideal, but larding needles are about as hard to find in most kitchens as they are in haystacks, so we'll stick with the more probable: basting or barding.

Serves 4

*1/2 pound fresh pork fat, in thin
   sheets*
1 whole trimmed beef tenderloin
*2 tablespoons mixed peppercorns,
   green, white, and black*

1/4 pound butter, melted (1 stick)
*1/4 cup cognac or "fine"
   (optional)*
Coarse salt

Fresh unsalted pork fat in thin sheets of the type used to line pâté pans is what you need here. It is far more available than it used to be, but if your butcher can't oblige you, buy a slab of fatback (which is, unfortunately, very salty), have it sliced into large thin squares (not strips), then rinse it vigorously in cold water and dry it. Cut off the tail and scraggly butt end of the tenderloin and reserve them for a stir-fry. Crush the peppercorns coarsely, rub them into the meat, and let it rest at room temperature for an hour (while the coals are burning down to a steady glow). Tie the porkfat around the tenderloin at close intervals; otherwise it tends to curl up and away from the meat. Grill the fillet about 30 minutes, turning it and brushing it frequently with melted butter, then let it rest for 15 minutes to retract its juices. The interior temperature should read 125°F. for rare steak—it will cook a bit more while it is resting. (Do not be persuaded by anyone to omit the rest period; if you cut it immediately you will have 4 expensive but juiceless steaks.) Brush each portion (all strings discarded, of course) with some melted butter. Heat the cognac in a ladle, set it alight, and pour a little on each steak. Sprinkle with a little coarse salt just before serving.

You can cut the tenderloin into 8 pieces, or you can let it get cold and slice it thinly, in which case it will serve many more people. A charcoal-grilled tenderloin may be made in advance, cooled, wrapped in foil, and refrigerated until an hour or so before slicing for a buffet.

衤 THIRTY-MINUTE FILLET OF PORK 衤

The fillet of pork, which corresponds to the filet mignon in a side of beef, is a most versatile cut of meat, heretofore seldom seen in American markets. I "discovered" it in Ireland, where excellent pork is bred and much appreciated. This tender, small cut from the loin of the pig usually weighs no more than ¾ of a pound, enough to feed 2 people generously. Fortunately, I have an enterprising and talented young butcher who investigates new offerings from his supplier. Pork tenderloins can be ordered in relatively small quantities, so if you don't see them, pester your butcher to get them in. They make perfect quick-cooking, meltingly tender slices for stir-frys and the only 30-minute pork roast I know of—which makes it ideal for charcoal grilling as well as for conventional oven roasting.

Serves 2

1 whole pork tenderloin, about
¾ pound
1 clove garlic, in thin slivers
Softened butter

Salt and freshly ground pepper
2 to 3 tablespoons Madeira or
cognac

Preheat the oven to 450°F.

Spike the tenderloin all over with the garlic, inserting the slivers in tiny incisions all around the cylinder. Rub it well with butter, salt and pepper it, and lay it in a small, narrow pan, uncovered and with no added liquid. Put it in the center of the oven, roast for 8 minutes, then turn and roast 8 minutes more. When it has reached an interior temperature of 150°F., it will be tender, juicy, and very faintly pink. (The dreaded trichinae dies at 137°F., so have no fear.) Let the roast rest for 10 minutes on a warm board in a warm place. Cut into medallions about ½ inch thick and pour over them a short sauce made by deglazing the roasting pan with the Madeira or cognac and adding pepper to taste. This is utterly delicious and lightning fast.

Charcoal-Grilled Pork Fillet: Spike the meat with slivers of garlic rolled in minced fresh marjoram, thyme, rosemary, or sage, as you wish. Roll the meat in olive oil, cover it, and let marinate for half an hour. When your coals have burned to a white ash, adjust the grid to 6 or 8 inches from the firebed and put the tenderloin on it. Rotate it on the grill every 5 minutes until it is golden brown all over and cooked to an interior temperature of 150°F. Remove it to a warm board, cover it, and let it rest for 10 minutes. Carve in half-inch slices and moisten with whatever juices collect after carving. Thinly sliced cold pork tenderloin with a mustard mayonnaise is an interesting entry for a buffet platter.

Grilled Pork Kebabs: Tenderloin, alternated with summer vegetables, makes a lovely and easy-to-serve summer meal. Cut the pork fillet into cubes no larger than an inch so that they will be cooked to an interior temperature of 150°F. in about 15 minutes on the grill, turned often and basted with oil or butter. An almost instant sauce of soy sauce, lemon juice, and sesame oil or hot chili oil is delicious with pork. Put it into a shaker-spout bottle, Chinatown restaurant-style; it may lack elegance, but is handy for picnics and informal outdoor meals.

⚘ SMOKY HERBED CHICKEN ⚘

Things done in the name of "barbecued chicken" are so appalling—those dried-out little creatures turning on electric spits in supermarket delis throughout the land—that the delicacy has lost its dignity. Restaurants used to list it with the caveat "allow 25 minutes" rather proudly. Now it is precooked and reheated in a microwave. The charm of grilled chicken is in its freshness and juiciness—both of which fade within minutes off the grill. Though many claim to love cold leftover chicken, I am not one of them—refrigerating grilled chicken numbs it, though it is still passable cooled at room temperature. Serve this hot and crisp, and you'll be astonished at how good this simple American standard can be. ("American" doesn't have to mean slathered in dark red gooey sauce.)

Serves 4

2 broiler chickens, quartered
Juice of a lemon
1/2 cup olive oil
1/2 cup minced fresh tarragon
  and parsley, mixed

Salt and freshly ground pepper
Handful of grapevine or other
  wood chips, soaked

Chop off the backbones, flatten the breasts with the flat of a cleaver, and cut the pinions off the wings. Rinse and dry all the chicken and cut some slits in the legs. Mix the lemon juice, oil, and herbs, and rub it well into the chicken, under the skin as well as over it, working the mixture down inside the thigh pieces. Cover and let marinate for half an hour while you build a fire.

Grill the chicken pieces about 6 inches from the coals, turning every 5 minutes or so. Do not add the breasts until the dark meat is half-cooked. The dark meat requires about 25 minutes grilling and the white meat only about 12 minutes though it is impossible to be precise when there are so many variables: the size and heat of the fire, the outside temperature, the size of the chickens, and so on. When the breast pieces are added to the grill, throw the soaked vine cuttings or chips onto the coals, cover the grill, and let the smoke permeate the food for at least 5 minutes, then grill, uncovered, until the chicken is done. *Do not baste.* (Basting softens the skin and causes fat flare-ups from the coals.)

Use tongs to turn the chicken, as piercing with a fork causes a constant leaching of its juices. Chicken skin is very fat and provides self-basting, which keeps the flesh moist. Even if you are cooking for dieters, do not discard the skin (which contains most of the flavor and all the lubrication) until after the chicken is cooked. Grilled, it is crisp, almost fat-free, and it's a pity that it is so often ruined or thrown away.

GRILLED FRESH PINEAPPLE

Fresh pineapples from Hawaii and the Caribbean, once procurable only in fancy fruiterers, are often found in supermarkets. But they still retain their drama and exotic appeal. Choose a ripe one with a strong scent and an amber cast to the base. Or you can soften one at home in a warm, airy spot away from sunlight. When the fronds loosen and the bottom yields a bit to thumb pressure, it is ripe. Fresh pineapples usually come with a little hang-tag that explains how to cut them.

Be sure the pineapple is very ripe because this "grilling" merely heats it through and doesn't soften the fibers. Cut the pineapple through the fronds down to the the base into long quarters. Slice out the core with a sharp paring knife. Brush the cut surfaces with salad oil and sear them on the grill, first one surface, then the other. This takes up quite a lot of grill surface, so you may have to sacrifice some of the green fronds (they should overhang the edges to avoid burning them). To serve, slice down into the pineapple quarters at 1-inch intervals, then slice along the rind to release the flesh, but leave it in place for serving—on a large, impressive platter.

If the grill scene gets too hectic, remember that fresh pineapple really *needs* no cooking and is refreshingly tart with most grilled meats and poultry, although the heat does intensify the flavor immensely. Core, slice, and serve as above without grilling. In the absence of fresh pineapple, canned, unsweetened slices can be grilled, or blotted dry and skillet-fried in butter—not so thrilling visually, but still an unusual item at barbecues.

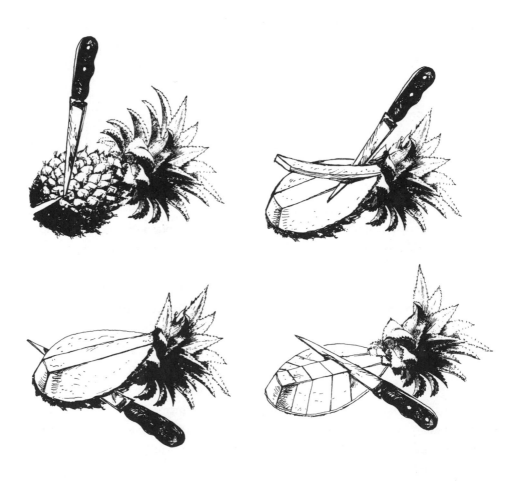

🌿 GRILLED LEG OF LAMB 🌿

The idea of grilling a whole leg of lamb was big news when I introduced it in an earlier book. It was a good idea whose time had come, and "butterflied lamb" remains a stalwart in the repertoire of many devoted fans. (An old friend who counts this among his favorite dishes even makes this in winter—broiled on a hibachi in his fireplace.) In the intervening decades, quite a few butchers have learned to bone the leg so that it is more or less the same thickness throughout. At best, a boned leg is a rather gnarled affair, and hard to grill evenly. Medium rare is optimum, but the shank end always gets a bit overcooked, and there are very few Americans left who prefer it that way. Lamb is much more popular now, and the demand for it is being met with a bigger and better-quality supply of fine U.S.-grown lamb. Those baby lamb legs from New Zealand don't have much flavor after their frozen journey from the antipodes.

Serves 6 to 8

*1 whole, fresh leg of lamb,
   butterflied*
2 cups dry red wine
2 cloves garlic, crushed
*4 or 5 sprigs fresh thyme or fresh
   marjoram (optional)*

*Salt and freshly ground black
   pepper to taste*
Olive oil

Open the leg flat and put it in a heavy plastic bag with the wine, garlic, and herb sprigs. (I never recommend rosemary with anything—though it is the traditional Anglo-Saxon seasoning for lamb, I prefer any other flavoring.) Close the bag tightly and lay the lamb in a flat dish. Turn the package whenever you think of it—at least 3 times in 24 hours. It can marinate longer, but tends to lose its lamblike taste after a couple of days and becomes more like venison. Let the lamb come to room temperature while you build a good fire, and let the fire smoulder to glowing red coals. Dry the lamb and rub it with oil and salt and pepper to taste; then stretch it over the gridiron, which should be raised to a height sufficient to prevent flaming. Broil the meat about 15 minutes on each side, or to an interior temperature of 150°F. at the thickest point. Let it rest in a warm place 10 minutes or so, then carve the meat rapidly, as thinly as you can manage. Arrange it on a hot platter and pour the juices over it.

Cold, charcoal-grilled leg of lamb is possibly even better than it is hot; the texture is finer and, like any cold roast meat, it is easier to carve. To serve cold, wrap the lamb tightly in foil after it reaches room temperature and carve just before serving. If the lamb must be refrigerated (no uncured meats should be left sitting on counters for more than an hour), bring it back to room temperature before serving.

My favorite side-kick for grilled lamb is still an eggplant soufflé, or thick slices of eggplant sautéed in garlic-scented olive oil. Baby zucchini, split, brushed with oil, and grilled face down for a few minutes, then on their backs, are a fail-proof quick vegetable that is also good with lamb. Even though the appeal of zucchini has been bludgeoned by restaurants that throw it on the plate with everything, give it another chance. Grilled, it has a smoky, nutty flavor, and a grating of Parmesan enlivens it too. Intersperse the green with the gold variety, sprinkle it with fresh herbs, and dear old zucchini can look quite new and fresh again.

STEAKS, PLAIN AND FANCY

Despite incessant disclaimers from an increasingly health-conscious population, we Americans still eat more red meat than any other nation. Well, maybe the Aussies beat us. Fish has risen astronomically in price, and cattlemen have had to lower theirs in the face of consumer resistance. No other country on earth enjoys such good meat at such low prices. Quality beef at decent prices makes the summer cookout season a time of simple pleasures attainable with only the most basic skills and equipment.

But not everyone is a devotee of the Weber and the hibachi—and there are many small steaks that always overcook on charcoal grills anyway. The old iron spider is still best for cooking individual club steaks, filet mignons, or "strip sirloins," as they are termed in New York. Deglazing the skillet with a little wine or spirits creates a little diversion from the run-of-the-grill steaks. To vary grilled meats, try some herb butters or some of the quick sauces included at the end of this chapter. I have never met a steak that wasn't significantly improved by a touch of Sauce Béarnaise (page 156) or a little pat of tarragon butter. Bare, ruined steaks are still perceived as virtuous, though I must warn that properly bred, aged, and marbled "choice" or "prime" beefsteaks really aren't for severe dieters. My philosophy is, go for broke or skip it.

Fine steaks are for healthy people, who should be able to eat, in moderation, whatever they like—though certainly less meat than has been the national custom. Frontier appetites may find my meat allocations somewhat on the mingy side, though magnanimous compared with the doll's teaparty portions of "nouvelle cuisine."

🌿 STEAK AU POIVRE 🌿

One of the great classics of French cooking, this simple preparation has suffered some mighty indignities—chief among them, glutinous cream sauces for added effects of "fanciness." This heavily peppercorn-encrusted steak is only for true aficionados; it loses its point if modified for tamer palates.

Serves 4

*4 small, boneless club
(Delmonico) steaks, about 1
inch thick, well trimmed
3 tablespoons whole black
peppercorns*

*Salad oil
Salt to taste
Softened butter
3 tablespoons cognac or bourbon*

Blot the steaks dry. Pound or grind the peppercorns very coarsely, then press them evenly onto all sides of the steaks. If there is time, leave them in the refrigerator for a few hours so that the pepper can penetrate. Heat two cast-iron skillets rubbed with salad oil to smoking hot. (Open all windows and turn on the exhaust fan; also put on your *gros bonnet* or a scarf; this is an unavoidably smoky technique.) Slap in the steaks, 2 to a pan, sprinkle with salt, and sear; after about 2 minutes, turn and sear for an equal time on the opposite side. (This is rare steak; cook it a bit longer if you wish, moderating the flame.) Lift the steaks onto hot plates and smear with a little softened butter. Heat the cognac in a ladle over a gas burner or in a small pan, light it, and pour it over the steaks.

🌿 GREEN PEPPERCORN STEAKS 🌿

Green, red, and Szechuan peppercorns have had their fads, but, though recklessly overdone, green peppercorns are too interesting to be abandoned. The soft, immature berries of the pepper tree, which provides the usual black and white dried pepper-corns, are imported packed in brine. Their unique bite bolsters the flavor of tenderloin steaks—expensive, but a flashy dish in minimum time.

Serve 4

4 center cut tenderloin slices,
1 1/2-inch thick (a.k.a. filet
mignon or chateaubriand)
Sweet butter
2 shallots, minced
Salt

Splash of cognac
1 cup Crème Fraîche (page 123)
or reduced heavy cream
1 small tin green peppercorns,
drained
Watercress (optional)

Whole tenderloins are frequently offered in supermarkets. If you can get one, strip it completely and render some of the suet—it is unbeatable for sautéeing beef, as well as onions and potatoes. Take 4 thick slices from the center and reserve the butt and tail pieces for kebabs or stir-frys.

Dry the fillets well. Melt some of the suet, or a spoonful of good sweet butter, in a cast-iron skillet, put in the steaks, and sauté them over a medium-high heat for about 5 minutes. Turn them, add the shallots, and cook sautéeing until done to your liking. Push the shallots around so that they don't burn—neither the steaks nor the shallots should be blackened. Lightly salt the steaks when finished and put them on hot plates. With the cognac, deglaze the skillet off the heat (otherwise the cognac could leap into raging flames) and stir in the *crème fraîche,* scraping up the shallots and meat juices from the bottom of the pan. Add the green peppercorns and mash some of them into the sauce. Bubble the sauce for a few seconds, then divide and pour over the steaks. (It is more fashionable to put the sauce under the steaks, but this method imparts little flavoring to the meat—suit yourself about this.) Branches of watercress, large stalks removed, are enough adornment and one especially delicious with these steaks.

𣴎 BACKYARD BARBECUED STEAK 𣴎

Although not even saloons list "London Broil" on their menus anymore, it is still one of the most popular steaks for home barbecuing. Originally "London Broil" meant flank steak, but because there is only one of these to a side of beef and the butcher can cut a great many "London Broils" from the round, that is the "LB" most commonly found now in supermarkets. Try to get the first cut of the top round, which, because it is closest to the sirloin, is the most tender. This cut is much easier to carve at a slight angle in thinnish slices than the flank, which has to be carved almost parallel to the board to render it chewable. (Flank steak has a wonderful, intense beef flavor, but should only be broiled briefly and fiercely to blood rare. It used to be "po' folk's" steak but is now mysteriously scarce and expensive.) A "first cut" top round steak of choice or prime grade, cut about 2 inches thick, will feed about 6 people magnificently—a good family steak, succulent and tender.

Soak the meat in olive oil or plain salad oil flavored with crushed garlic or herbs of your choice for an hour before grilling. As this thick solid muscle requires about 10 minutes per side, adjust the rack so that the steak doesn't char in that time. Keep a close watch and douse any flames with a bulb baster filled with water. Remove it to a warm carving board, salt and pepper it well, and let it rest in a warm place for 10 minutes before slicing. The plain version gains new meaning with a post-grill flaming of cognac or bourbon. Also, this Eliza Dolittle steak can be turned out as a duchess by adding unexpected flavor via herb butters spread on during its "rest" period.

Top round isn't cursed with the stringiness of flank steak, so it needn't be sliced less than a quarter-inch thick. However, this steak can be sliced almost transparently thin when it is cold and makes a superb buffet dish. For this purpose, the meat profits immensely from a day in a marinade of garlic, green gingerroot, soy sauce, pepper, and mirin or a dash of sherry.

The pitfall of grilling top round, because it is so lean, is dryness. Give it plenty of lubrication and don't cook it too long—the rarer the better. If you fail to allow the rest period, the juices pour out, leaving you with a listless, tasteless, though diety, steak.

COUNTRY HAMBURGERS

Sometimes there's a rainy day or firing up any kind of grill seems just too much trouble for a couple of hungry people. That's when these old-fashioned skillet burgers seasoned with onion and parsley are ideal. Serve them with mashed or baked potatoes or fresh French bread, split and warmed, which sops up the juices nicely and makes an attractive platform. A big dish of new cucumbers and ripe tomatoes in a vinaigrette perfectly completes this quick summer meal.

Serves 4

1 1/2 pounds ground chuck or
   sirloin
1 large onion, finely minced
1 tablespoon butter
1/2 cup minced fresh parsley

1 large egg, beaten
1 slice firm bread, trimmed
Coarsely cracked pepper to taste
Coarse salt to taste
Plain salad oil

Put the meat in a large bowl. Sauté the onion in the butter and scrape it into the ground meat along with the parsley and egg. Spin the bread to crumbs in the food processor and add it. If there's no bread or no processor, sprinkle in a little flour to bind the ingredients. Mix the ingredients as lightly and quickly as possible—overhandling toughens burgers. Form into large thick patties and sprinkle well with salt and pepper. Heat the oil in a black cast-iron skillet to very hot, plop in the burgers and sear on both sides. Turn again half-way through cooking, which should be for about 4 minutes on each side; this amount of meat should make 4 burgers about 1 1/2 inches thick. The thick vs. thinnies can fight this out.

Purist Burger: If you prefer beef and nothing but the beef, mix it first with a little crushed ice for very rare, juicy hamburgers. Sear them in a smoking skillet (keeping your face away) over high flame. Open all windows and turn on exhausts.

Mushroom Burger: Finely chop some fresh mushrooms and sauté them in butter. Mix into the Country Hamburger. In a separate skillet, sauté more mushrooms, roughly chopped, for just a couple of minutes. Add a splash of red wine and stir in some softened butter. Season to taste with salt and pepper. Put the mushroom burger on a thick toasted slab of French bread and pour the mushrooms over it. This is no break-through combination but it's amazingly good and seldom served.

🎋 SHORT-CUT SAUCE BÉARNAISE 🎋

With fresh tarragon so easily found in summer it's a pity to pass up this glorious sauce that elevates just-another-grilled steak, chicken, or hamburger into elegant eating. Never try to hold egg-liaison sauces (such as this and Hollandaise) for any length of time over hot water. It will separate and worse still, create a friendly environment for hostile bacteria. This only takes a couple of minutes to make anyway.

For about 1 cup

2 tablespoons wine vinegar
1/4 cup dry white wine
1 1/2 tablespoons chopped fresh
   tarragon leaves
1 tablespoon minced shallots or
   scallions

1/2 pound sweet butter (2 sticks)
3 egg yolks
Salt and white pepper to taste

Combine the vinegar, wine, tarragon, and shallots in a small saucepan and simmer 5 minutes. Reduce liquid to about 2 tablespoons. Barely melt the butter. Put the yolks in a blender and turn it on high speed with the cover on. Remove center and, with the motor running, slowly trickle the liquid butter into the vortex. When the sauce begins to thicken, you can add the remaining butter more quickly. Strain the tarragon mixture into the sauce, season it with salt and pepper, and spin smooth. You can leave it in the covered blender sitting in a pan of warm (not simmering) water for half an hour. Reblend briefly and put the Béarnaise into a small warmed bowl.

Blender Hollandaise: Prepare as above, omitting the tarragon/wine mixture. Season at the end with a little fresh lemon juice. (Don't overdo this; packaged dried Hollandaise mixes taste hideously of artificial lemon, which does not disguise its fundamentally vile taste.) Fresh, homemade Hollandaise is terribly simple to make, so why not do it? You can lighten it with a half cup of whipped cream folded in at the end (Sauce Mousseline) and you can change it to a Sauce Maltaise by substituting orange juice and a teaspoon of red wine vinegar for the lemon juice with some of the orange rind grated in for piquance and color. These are useful sauces to know for enhancing poached and grilled fish, poached eggs and asparagus, as well as steaks and grilled leg of lamb.

I realize that many people look upon these triumphs of the culinary art as deadly potions, but they are not meant to be eaten every day or in anything but small, accenting amounts. It should be pointed out that two ordinary chocolate chip cookies have the same caloric value as one tablespoon of Hollandaise Sauce.

VEAL, "BOB" VEAL, AND BABY BEEF

Veal has priced itself right out of existence in average households. At best, its appearance in the marketplace is by happenstance and its quality unknown. There's a giant chain supermarket in the village next to mine that occasionally comes up with a shipment of shanks, stew meat, breasts for stuffing, or shoulder chops—the choice loin and rib chops, and fine escalopes that can only be cut from the leg have been shipped off to some more worthy neighborhood, I guess. Occasionally I splurge on priceless loin chops *schlepped* from an Italian butcher in my old Greenwich Village neighborhood.

Other likely sources of veal are butcher shops in German neighborhoods. Their veal is usually fresh and the best available, but American veal is simply not the same as the pale, white, milk-fed veal of Europe. Different grass, different breeds of cows— and we don't have many dairy-wives to coddle the little animals along to market, either. Veal is a dairyman's product, not the cattlemen's, and its production has tended to fall between the economic cracks except for a few specialists like the "Plume de Veau" people.

"Bob" veal is much pinker, from an animal that has grazed a bit; it is almost as tender as "milk-fed" and has more flavor. The cuts marketed under the name "baby beef" are from grass-fed animals in their sixth or seventh month, frequently casualties of hard times in the cattle business when the cattleman has to unload some of his stock early.

Dairy farmers in the Great Smoky Mountains, where I spent many childhood summers, supplied us with bob veal steaks that I wish I could lay my hands on again. We ate pork, ham, chicken, and bob veal and lots of fish, shrimp, and oysters, but hardly any beef. It was a priceless luxury—which is probably what gave rise to the infamous "Chicken Fried Steak" throughout the South (a thin sliver of round steak beaten to a shadow, dredged in flour, and fried in lard—tough as saddlebags).

In France and Germany I learned how splendid veal could be in *blanquette de veau* and *wienerschnitzel*. Returning home I still found soggy breaded veal cutlets and wispy, wizened little scraps called *scallopinis*. If fortune brings you some first-class veal chops or escalopes, they need only the simplest, quickest sautéeing in butter or olive oil. Consult French and Italian cookbooks for ways to flavor this tender but timidly flavored meat. *Osso bucco* is my favorite veal dish, but slow simmered to sticky succulence, it's a winter feast.

HAM

A ham is one of the two hind legs of the pig; after that you run into "picnic shoulders" and all manner of euphemistic "hams." There are a bewildering number of them, both foreign and domestic, to choose among. They come raw, semi-cooked, and fully cooked; hickory or corn-cob smoked, pepper-cured, quick-smoked, liquid smoke injected, brine-cured, and canned, some of which require refrigeration and others not. One of the most delicious ready-to-eat "hams" is smoked pork loins chops (called *Kassler Rippchen* in Germany, where they originated).

Bayonne, Westphalian, and Parma are imported hams of reliable high quality. The legendary York hams from England are one of Britain's finest foods but seldom seen here. These hams are eaten "raw"—that is, they have been so thoroughly cured and aged they require no further cooking. All are shaved in paper-thin slices and served, like prosciutto, as is. American packers (Hormel, I think) are offering a consistently lean, dry but tender prosciutto that may not totally duplicate the Italian original, but it is very good indeed and available everywhere. Our own chaps in Chicago also put out a creditable smoked beef that imitates the Alpine wind-dried Rindnerfleisch of Switzerland.

American country hams from Virginia, Kentucky, and Tennessee (the most familiar to me) are extremely fine and one finds exceptional smokehouses from Texas to New Hampshire. Our country hams are highly regarded in Europe though most Americans these days opt for those dreary, ready-to-eat "hams" in supermarkets. Most of them are about as exciting as corn flakes.

Country hams are not in the least difficult to cook and I don't really understand why soaking something in cold water is so taxing; hams can do this unassisted and unobserved. They will keep in their cotton bag in the refrigerator for many months so it's pointless to freeze them. Hams can be hung in a cold, unheated but airy garage or toolshed for a couple of months. City dwellers rarely have space enough to concern themselves with this, although ham does keep perfectly under refrigeration for many weeks. However, the flavor begins to go a bit off and the saltiness seems to concentrate unpleasantly in interminably refrigerated leftovers. Cooked ham (and bones) should be frozen for long-term keeping.

How to Cook a Country Ham in an Average Kitchen

Scrub the ham with a stiff brush under tepid running water. Get off all the pepper or mold or ashes and put the ham in a large roaster or a big plastic container. Cover it completely with cold water and let it soak 12 hours. Change the water and soak a further 12 hours. I have a deep sink in my greenhouse that I use for this purpose—you might commandeer a bathtub overnight.

The beautiful copper ham boilers of the nineteenth-century kitchen have become plant cachepots in country houses, and nothing has come along to replace them. However, we can make do with one of the old-fashioned, blue speckled, graniteware roasters still sold in hardware and dime stores, should you be lucky enough to have one in these terrible times of giant shopping malls. Huge foil roasting pans can be found in similar stores. As they aren't very strong, buy two and place them one inside the other on a heavy baking sheet. Put the ham in whatever vessel you've got, cover it with cold water, cover with foil if there is no top, and put it in a cold oven. Turn the thermostat to 325°F. and bake 4 hours for a whole ham, turning it once midway in the cooking. Pierce it with sharp tines to be sure it is tender. Remove the ham to the top of the stove and let it cool in its liquid (now called "likker") to tepid. Remove the rind carefully and let the fat solidify. Pare the fat evenly—this is easier than soap carving—leaving about a half-inch layer. This helps to preserve the ham's freshness and moisture—a completely scalped ham will dry out. Wrap the ham in heavy foil and refrigerate it overnight.

Carving—not cooking—is the tricky aspect of a country ham. Use a supersharp, thin, long knife and keep resharpening it as you go. Cut a wedge from the hock on the top side of the ham and set it aside. Begin making transparently thin slices at a 45-degree angle from the bone and make as many as you can; then turn the ham and carve the other side.

Dryness is the bête noir of country hams. It is caused by either undercooking, undersoaking, removing the ham before it has cooled in its cooking liquid—or maddeningly, overcooking until all the flavor and texture have been boiled away. So stick to the age-old traditional routine and let no one persuade you to "try something new" with a valuable aged country ham. Even after you have successfully cooked, cooled, and carved a ham, dryness is still to be guarded against. Cover the sliced ham with airtight plastic wrap until serving (or arranging) time.

Supermarket Hams

Many of these are excellent and I don't mean "supermarket" as a term of opprobrium (I think supermarkets are pretty good things as long as they don't cover more than one entire county). Supermarket hams are those offered by large commercial meatpackers, generally as "ready-to-serve." They seldom really are, but always ask the butcher if you're uncertain about exactly how much heating or cooking the ham you're buying requires. Most of them look absolutely flawless, and many are as tasteless as they are tantalizing. I do wish there could be a little order brought to the chaotic ham scene.

Meat packers are permitted legally to inject up to 10% of the ham's total weight with water. Some of these should be labeled "Ham Drink." There is no way of distinguishing these precooked, often unlabeled hams except to beware of extreme wetness and mushiness. Some of the nameless hams offered by big chains are of better quality than some of the relentlessly ballyhooed "name" brands. Chains have a nasty little trick of removing the center cut steaks when the butcher parts the leg to sell as a "butt" or "shank" half. If you want to be absolutely clear about getting your center slices, either ask to have one cut before your very eyes (the butcher may or may not agree to this) or enlist a friend to share one and the market cannot refuse to halve it for you.

I have never seen the point of canned hams except for extended canoe trips or in localities where fire has not yet been discovered. Smoking preserves and flavors a ham; the canned ones are only cured—barely. If it isn't smoked, it isn't ham to me. And country ham is really the only ham what am.

🦋 FRESH HAMS 🦋

A ham is the hind leg of a pig, and before it is brined, cured, or smoked, this cut of fresh pork is designated "fresh ham" in most parts of the country. It is an immense piece of meat and even a half leg will serve 16 to 20 people as a cold buffet entree. While it takes a long time to cook, nothing could be simpler. Slowly roasted in its own juices, the meat is as pale and fine-grained as veal and much tastier and juicier than the loin of pork at less than half the price—a thing to consider when you're faced with a large buffet-cocktail summer bash.

½ leg of "fresh ham," about 7 pounds	2 medium onions, thinly sliced
2 cloves garlic	Several sprigs of fresh thyme or marjoram
Salt and freshly ground pepper	1 cup Madeira

Wipe the ham with damp paper towels and score the rind through to the fat in a diamond pattern. (When roasted, the rind becomes the delicious "crackling," the dark brown, crisp skin chopped into choice fragments that will be immediately appropriated by the cognoscenti.) Cut the garlic into slivers and insert it all over the leg with the point of a small knife. Rub the meat well with salt and lots of fresh pepper. Lay the leg on a bed of sliced onions, the heavier side up, and tuck the herb sprigs into the gashes in the rind. Pour on about half the Madeira and roast, uncovered, in a very slow oven of 300°F. for 25 minutes to the pound. Add a bit of water to the pan if the juices seem to be burning, though they should not at this gentle temperature. Halfway through the roasting time, baste with a quarter cup of Madeira and use the remainder for a basting about half an hour before the ham is done. It should be tender and register 165°F. on an instant-read meat thermometer when done. Let the meat cool on its onion bed for at least an hour. Remove the rind and cut it into pieces with scissors—it can be recrisped under a moderate broiler flame for serving later. Pare the fat to about a quarter-inch thick when the pork is cold, and either serve it carved like a cured country ham (though it needn't be so thin) or chill it, well-wrapped in foil. It is much easier to carve after 24 hours of chilling. Decorate the platter of fresh ham with summer herbs tied in little bouquets and a dilled mustard mayonnaise sauce.

🌿 PERFECT FRIED CHICKEN 🌿

"We'll just fry up a chicken" is the Carolinian equivalent of the French "Oh, we'll just have an omelette." It's a little more time-consuming, but even less difficult. The best fried chicken is not deep-fried, but pan-fried, which requires watching and frequent turning with tongs (so that the gradually hardening crust is not pierced; that would make it soggy).

A frying chicken should weigh about 2½ pounds minus giblets. It should be disjointed, not hack-sawed into quarters. Tell the butcher you want everything except the "Pope's Nose," and to cut the backbone in half crosswise. You should have 2 thighs, 2 drumsticks, 2 breast halves, 2 wings, and 2 pieces of bony back that will become hotly contested once they're fried to crisp deliciousness.

Trim off any excess skin or fat. Trim out the tough connecting skin that joins the 2 parts of a chicken wing and slit each part so that it fries fairly flat. Bash the breast pieces with the flat of a cleaver to flatten them for quicker and more even cooking. I cut each half-breast once again horizontally to make 4 pieces of white meat; they cook faster and are juicier, and prevent white-meat squabbles at table. Rinse the pieces in cold water and shake dry.

Soak the chicken pieces for about 15 to 20 minutes in milk splashed with 10 or 12 drops of Tabasco sauce. (If you haven't time for "perfect," skip the milk bath.) Put peanut or vegetable oil to a depth of about half an inch in a heavy cast-iron skillet or *sauteuse.* Heat it slowly. Put about 1 cup of flour into a brown paper bag, add lots of freshly ground black pepper and a tablespoon of coarse salt, and shake the bag well to mix.

When the oil is hot but not smoking, shake the thighs and drumsticks in the seasoned flour, remove the pieces one by one shaking each lightly to remove excess flour and patting it quickly so that the flour adheres, slide each piece into the hot oil. After about 3 minutes, once all the pieces are in the pan, reduce the flame to medium-low. (A spatter screen is immensely helpful for keeping your stove and floor fairly grease-free while frying chicken.) Turn the pieces with tongs after 8 to 10 minutes, turn up the flame for a few minutes, then turn it down again to medium-low. Continue frying for another 10 minutes, turning the chicken again during the last 5 minutes. Drain on thick layers of crumpled paper toweling.

Shake the remaining pieces of chicken in the flour and fry them following the above procedure (small breast halves or quarters should not be fried for more than 15 minutes, total). The bony wings and back pieces, however, need 20 minutes frying to arrive at that state of crispiness that makes even the small bones edible. Fried chicken should be roughly the color of a brown paper bag, but don't mind if there are some small darker spots here and there. Uneven color is a characteristic of carefully hand-turned, pan-fried chicken—crisp outside and juicy inside.

One fryer-sized chicken (don't buy larger ones or the outside will be burnt before the inside is done) feeds only 2 or 3 people of good appetite. You can keep the dark meat, which is fried first because it takes the longest, warm in a low oven very briefly. If the chicken can't be served right away, serve it at room temperature, as trying to "hold" fried chicken for any length of time makes it soggy. It will also become soggy if you refrigerate it, though I seldom have any left over. Although it will never be quite as good, there *is* a way to reheat fried chicken that has been refrigerated. Let it come to room temperature. Put the pieces under a low-flame broiler, at least 4 inches from the flame, and turn after about 3 minutes to crisp up the other side.

CHICKEN BREASTS

Few subjects have occupied the commercial food press more intensely than America's favorite diet food: the chicken breast. Something called a "paillard," which is just as dry and tasteless as its paradigm, the veal "paillard," is a skinned, boned, half-breast, cross-hatched with brown grill marks that is served up as "spa food." This penance is an idea that could never work, because the delicate white meat deprived of its flavor-giving bone and lubricating skin cannot survive the charcoal grill. With skin and bone, chicken breasts can be delicious and juicy if flattened to cook evenly, brushed with butter or oil and seasoning, and cooked only about 4 minutes on each side. Dieters can feed the crisp, tasty skin (which is now off guard duty) to any lucky animals patrolling the outdoor grill area.

✺ BONED CHICKEN BREASTS WITH ✺ MUSHROOMS AND CREAM SAUCE

As chicken "cutlets" (which is the name most butchers seem to have settled on) are handy for speedy summer meals, here's an old and often repeated dish that's always welcome because it's so easy to vary with different herbs and spices.

Serves 4

4 tablespoons butter (1/2 stick)
2 fryer breasts, split, skinned, and
   boned
1/2 pound fresh mushrooms,
   sliced
Salt and freshly ground pepper
Juice of 1/2 lemon
4 slices dry white toast

1/4 cup chicken stock
1/4 cup dry white wine
1 cup heavy cream
1 tablespoon minced fresh
   tarragon leaves (optional)
2 tablespoons minced fresh
   parsley

Heat the butter in a heavy skillet and add the chicken pieces, which have been blotted very dry. Sauté on both sides until lightly browned, then add the mushrooms, salt, pepper and lemon juice, and shake the pan to distribute them well. Cover securely and turn the heat down very low. After 6 minutes, press the meat with your finger. If it is firm and springy to the touch, it is done. The smallest overcooking will dry and toughen chicken cutlets, but of course, be sure they are not pink inside. (Years ago it was hard to get anyone to believe that 8 minutes was long enough to cook a chicken cutlet; these days rare chicken has its fans, but I persist in the belief that there is only one way to cook chicken: perfectly—moist but done.)

Lay one chicken fillet on each piece of toast, put the plates in a warm oven (hot sauce on cold plates becomes a congealed disaster), and prepare the sauce, which takes about 2 minutes. Add the stock and wine to the sautéeing pan and reduce to a syrup over high heat. Stir in the cream and tarragon, if used, and reduce rapidly, stirring constantly, until thick. Pour over the chicken, sprinkle with parsley, and serve.

RICE AND PASTA

R ice and pasta are among the most versatile foods in the world and, since they keep indefinitely under almost any conditions, are an ideal base for the impromptu meal. What is nicer than linguini with fresh clam or mussel sauce, spaghetti carbonara, or a saffron rice pilaf with shrimp—all of them effortless?

The Italians make their splendid risottos, the Spanish their national dish, paella, and much of Oriental cookery is designed as a complement to the rice bowl. American converted long-grain rice is almost foolproof and is essential to nearly every rice recipe that follows. The best utensil for cooking rice is a heavy cast-iron skillet with a cover. The reason rice is all too often a gummy mess is that it has been cooked in a deep, narrow pot or has been cooked with more liquid than the rice can absorb. Long-grain rice cooks dry and tender in 20 minutes or less, thus obviating the use of "instant" rice.

Our admiration for pasta seems second only to that of the Italians, and we've even learned not to overcook it. It should be *al dente* ("to the tooth"), barely tender and firm, but not hard in the center. (Some reactionaries have begun cooking spaghetti only to the "soft crack" stage.) The water—lots of it—must be boiling "like a volcano," in the words of an Italian friend, before the pasta is added.

There are quite a number of lighter, more interesting, things to do with pasta other than smother it under a heavy meat and tomato sauce. The famous Genoese pesto is an aromatic basil and olive oil sauce delicious on spaghetti as well as on fish. The varieties of noodles and pasta manufactured in the United States are truly staggering, but the packages, excepting spaghetti, rarely give cooking times. The only way to determine when pasta is cooked *al dente* is by eating a piece from time to time during the cooking process. Dried fettucine, for instance, cooks in about 5 minutes, while cavatelli (small shells) may not be done for 15 or even 20 minutes. Fresh egg-dough pastas cook almost as soon as the water returns to the boil.

Although pasta is undeniably calorific, it is a quick, delicious summer meal when served with a light sauce, and the rest of the meal can be compensatingly low calorie. At any rate, the trend has moved away from those gargantuan Neopolitan restaurant portions to small ones, often delicately sauced.

UNCOOKED TOMATO SAUCE
(SALSA CRUDA)

The surprise of this tartly fresh sauce, which can only be made in summer with ripe field tomatoes, is a large part of its charm. It's also incredibly simple to make, so it runs the danger of being over-exposed. But it hasn't been yet—perhaps because its essential ingredient is unavailable most of the year.

Serves about 4 as a main course, 8 as a first course

4 pounds ripe, meaty tomatoes	*Freshly ground black pepper*
2 tablespoons minced shallots	*12 or so imported black olives,*
1 tablespoon minced fresh basil	*stoned*
or marjoram	*Salt to taste*
1 tablespoon minced fresh thyme	*4 to 6 tablespoons cold-pressed*
leaves (optional)	*olive oil*
1 tablespoon minced fresh	*1 small tin drained anchovy*
parsley	*fillets (optional)*
1 or 2 hot fresh chili peppers,	*1 pound pasta*
seeded and minced (optional)	

Scald the tomatoes in boiling water for 15 seconds, then plunge them into cold water at once to halt the cooking. Skin and core them and scoop out most of the seeds with your thumb. Dice the tomato flesh rather small. Combine them with all other ingredients except the salt, oil, or anchovies. *Do not add salt* as it draws all the juice out of the tomatoes and makes a watery sauce. Cover with a dishtowel and leave at room temperature for about an hour. (Sealing tight with plastic wrap causes the tomatoes to ferment in hot weather.)

If you want to make this sauce earlier in the day, refrigerate it at this point and let it come back to room temperature before serving. Salt to taste just before serving and divide the sauce over a pound of very hot pasta tossed with olive oil and divided into 4 portions. (For a first course, use only 2 ounces of pasta per person.) Add the anchovies, cut in half, last. Serve in well-heated pasta bowls, although this dish won't ever be truly hot. Grated cheese therefore isn't recommended, because it won't melt at all, but in any case this summer specialty is supposed to highlight the taste of scrumptious ripe tomatoes and fresh herbs.

⚘ QUICK NO-COOK SAUCE ⚘

If you keep some compound butters in the freezer or even a little dish of simple parsley butter in the fridge, this might qualify as an "instant" sauce.

Parsley Butter: To ¼ pound (1 stick) softened, fresh sweet butter, beat in 1 tablespoon finely minced fresh Italian flat leaf (or regular) parsley. Add freshly ground white pepper and a bit of salt to taste. Mound into a small dish to serve with steaming ears of corn, or pack it into a small jar or crock for use as needed.

For Pasta Sauce: Put a rounded tablespoon of parsley butter in each pasta bowl and set them in a 150°F. oven to warm and melt the butter lightly—it should not get greasy and separated. Cook some fresh (or dried) fettucine in boiling salted water. Plunge a large red, ripe tomato (per 2 servings) on a fork into the boiling pasta and count to ten by thousands . . . one thousand, two thousand, etc. Run cold water on the tomato and peel it quickly. Cut it in sixths and scoop out the seeds and pulp. Dice the remaining tomato flesh into small squares, and salt and pepper it.

Scoop out the pasta into the hot bowls and mix it quickly with the parsley butter. Divide the diced tomato over the pasta and serve at once. The pasta will warm the tomatoes. This very light herb butter and fresh tomato dressing is startlingly good, especially on egg noodles. This pasta goes with just about any fish or flesh one might ordinarily serve in summer—I can't vouch for its suitability with jugged hare or grilled ortolans.

🐦 PINK PAPPARDELLE WITH DRIED TOMATOES 🐦

Pappardelle are wide, flat ribbons of egg noodle, in this case tinted with a bit of tomato paste (they could also be left their natural pale yellow or shaded green with spinach puree). Pappardelle are easily made at home because the shape is so simple, and once in a while you'll find them at specialty food shops.

Serves 4

THE PASTA:

Olive oil

1 cup unbleached flour

2 large eggs, room temperature

1 teaspoon tomato paste

Put the flour in the food processor and pulse it a couple of times. Add the eggs and the tomato paste and process until the dough cleans the bowl. Remove the dough to a lightly floured board and knead it about 5 minutes by hand—this produces a better texture. Cover with a bowl or wrap in plastic and let rest for an hour. (This step is necessary to relax the gluten; otherwise the dough will be too elastic and difficult to roll out.)

If you have a pasta machine, follow the manufacturer's directions, running the dough through the rollers at progressively lower settings until you have several long, thin rectangles. You may also divide the dough into thirds and roll it out with a rolling pin (though in this case, don't say I promised you a rose garden).

Roll up the dough and, using a very sharp knife, cut the rectangles into long ribbons about an inch wide. Let these dry, hanging up or loosely coiled, for at least an hour. You can make the pasta in the morning and leave it, uncovered, in a cool airy place until evening. Pasta cooked immediately after it's made is extremely soft and difficult to cook *al dente*.

THE SAUCE:

2 large fresh shallots, minced,
   about ¼ cup
2 tablespoons olive oil
8 Italian sun-dried tomatoes
   in oil

1 cup heavy cream
Salt and freshly ground white
   pepper to taste
¼ cup tightly packed fresh basil
   leaves

Sauté the shallots in the olive oil in a small, heavy pot until just transparent. Cut the tomatoes into little pieces with scissors, catching their oil in a bowl. Add the tomatoes with their oil and heavy cream to the shallots, and heat through, stirring constantly. Season with salt and pepper.

Shred the basil leaves with a stainless steel knife, and not very far in advance, as the cut edges tend to darken. Before cooking the pappardelle, cut it into 4-inch lengths, then throw it into a large pot of boiling salted water with a little oil in it. (The sauce must be ready before the pasta is cooked, which takes only 2 or 3 minutes.) Stir the pasta constantly, as these large noodles have a tendency to stick together or sink to the bottom. (Note: you can test-boil a single noodle to determine just how long to cook this pasta.) When the noodles are done, drain them and return to the hot pot with enough olive oil to keep it slippery. Toss the pasta immediately with the sauce and divide it among 4 hot pasta bowls with the shredded basil strewn on the top.

This is a remarkably delicate color study, with the dark red of the glistening dried tomatoes dotting the pale apricot-colored pasta, and the sauce of pale pink, flecked with the fresh green of the basil. Do not add cheese—it will make the dish heavy and gummy. Serve a salad of fresh summer lettuces—American style—*with* the pasta course for maximum pleasure in the contrast of flavors and textures.

Nectarines are normally in good supply by late June and they're superb with a fresh, mild goat cheese for dessert. The fresh fruit ending to this meal is in the Italian style, though the rest of it is my own American invention.

⚶ FRIED SPAGHETTI ⚶

A very few Italian-American friends have admitted bashfully that they heated up leftover spaghetti (already sauced) in a skillet for a quick lunch. It's really delicious. The sauce penetrates and concentrates and the strands get slightly crusty. Here's another idea you won't find in any Italian cookbooks either (our more recent Italian cookbooks seem devoted to proving that Italian food can be just as complicated as French cuisine). It is from *Nika Hazelton's Pasta Cookbook.* Mrs. Hazelton is a no-nonsense German-Italian who, in an aristocratic fashion, finds all food snobism unbearable.

Use fresh or leftover, plain or sauced, long or short pasta that is already cooked. You might serve this with slices of cold lamb, chicken, or ham and some cucumber or green salad.

Serves 4

3 cups cooked spaghetti or other
  pasta
2 or 3 eggs
1/3 cup milk
1/3 cup freshly grated Parmesan
  or Romano cheese

Lots of freshly ground pepper
2 tablespoons minced fresh
  parsley or chives, or both
  mixed
4 tablespoons butter (1/2 stick)

Have the pasta at room temperature in a large bowl. Beat together all the remaining ingredients except the butter, which should be slowing melting in a heavy nonstick skillet. Pour the egg mixture over the pasta and toss it well. Turn this into the skillet when the butter foams and clears. Spread and flatten the pasta into a pancake and cook over low heat until the bottom forms a golden crust. Flip it over and cook the other side to form another crust. Slide out onto a hot plate and sprinkle with additional grated cheese if you like. Cut it in wedges and serve hot or warm.

🌿 SALSA AL PESTO 🌿

The main ingredient of this sauce is a fine, fresh bunch of sweet basil. This is to serve on fish or 4 servings of pasta as a main course. Do keep pasta servings rather small, because no matter how fine or delicate the sauce, mountains of pasta leave a leaden feeling. This sauce comes from Genoa, a city famous for its cuisine.

Serves 4

*1 bunch fresh basil, about 1
  packed cup of leaves
2 cloves garlic
10 to 15 pine nuts*

*Dash of salt
3 tablespoons freshly grated
  Parmesan or Romano cheese
1/2 cup olive oil*

Pound the basil leaves with the garlic, nuts, and a dash of salt in a mortar. (If this much classicism doesn't appeal to you, use a blender or a food processor, but don't puree too finely.) Pound in the cheese, and when it forms a thick puree, run in the oil slowly, as if you were making mayonnaise. The sauce should be very thick and creamy. It can also be made with parsley if basil is unavailable, but it will have a completely different flavor. My preference is for a 50–50 proportion of parsley and basil.

✺ SALSA VERDE ✺

"Green sauce" is made in much the same way as Salsa al Pesto but tastes more like an especially good vinaigrette dressing. It too, can be used on boiled meat or fish as well as pasta.

Serves 4

1 cup lightly packed parsley leaves
2 or 3 anchovy fillets
2 cloves garlic
1/2 teaspoon salt

Freshly ground black pepper
Juice of 1/2 lemon
1/2 cup olive oil
1 tablespoon soft green peppercorns (tinned)

Pound the parsley leaves, anchovies, garlic, salt, pepper, and lemon juice in a mortar. When it is a paste (this takes only a few minutes, so don't panic), pound in the olive oil by droplets. (This sauce may also be made in an electric blender or processor.) Stir in the whole green peppercorns last.

✻ SPAGHETTINI CARBONARA ✻

Even bacon and eggs are combined with pasta by Italian cooks. Have whatever pasta you have chosen cooked, and very hot, before you start the sauce. Fettucine or small macaroni are some other pastas to use this way.

Serves 4

¼ pound double-smoked bacon   *Pasta, 4 servings*
Butter   *3 tablespoons freshly grated*
3 eggs, beaten   *Parmesan cheese*

Cut the bacon into matchsticks and fry it in a little butter until almost crisp. Drain off all but 2 tablespoons of fat, cool the pan slightly, and add the bacon and fat to the beaten eggs. Pour *at once* onto the hot pasta and toss vigorously, being careful not to mash the pasta. (The heat of the pasta should cook the eggs.) Sprinkle with cheese and serve immediately. Pass more cheese at the table.

☀ SPAGHETTI WITH CLAM SAUCE ☀

American clam sauce for spaghetti is usually made from large chowder clams, or quahogs. To prevent the texture from becoming like shredded tires, they are always finely chopped. This sauce is made with tiny, tender whole clams or mussels very briefly cooked and is, to my mind, immensely better. It is also labor-saving, since you neither have to pry open the clams nor chop them. Small mussels need only a brisk washing—no debearding.

Serves 4

3 quarts littleneck clams or 3 quarts small mussels	*1 teaspoon flour*
1/4 pound butter (1 stick)	*Spaghetti for 4 servings, cooked and hot*
1/2 onion, chopped	*Minced parsley (optional)*
2 cloves garlic, minced	*Dried red pepper flakes (optional)*

Scrub the shellfish, put them in a pan with 1/2 cup water, cover, and set over high heat. Cook, stirring occasionally, about 5 minutes, until all are opened. Set aside shellfish and strain the broth through cheesecloth to remove any sand. Reserve 1/2 cup for the sauce and keep the rest to make Court Bouillon (page 103) or soup.

Melt the butter in a small, heavy saucepan. Simmer the onions and garlic in the butter until soft. Do not allow either the butter or the vegetables to brown. Stir in the flour (this thickens the sauce a trifle) and cook, stirring, for 3 to 4 minutes. Whisk in the clam or mussel broth and whisk over medium heat a couple of minutes. Add the shelled clams or mussels and heat through. Toss with hot spaghetti or linguini and more butter if necessary. Strew a little minced parsley over the dish if you like, but never serve cheese with this. A light sprinkle of crushed hot red pepper is an attractive addition.

❧ PIZZAIOLA SAUCE ❧

Fresh tomatoes are the dominant flavor of this sauce, which is traditionally used to cover small steaks (in one of the least appealing dishes in the Italian repertoire—and one that used to be on every Italian menu in New York City). A much better use for this sauce is with pasta. You will be disappointed if you expect a rich, thick puree, for the point of this sauce is the freshness of the ripe, barely cooked tomatoes. It is a simple dish that will be appreciated by people who like plain spaghetti with butter or oil and garlic. This is also the ideal sauce for homemade pizzas.

Serves 4 to 6

*1 1/2 pounds ripe tomatoes
(Romas are best for this)
3 cloves garlic, minced
1/4 cup olive oil*

*Salt and freshly ground pepper
2 tablespoons chopped fresh basil
or parsley*

Plunge the tomatoes into boiling water for 20 seconds, then immediately in cold, and peel them. Coarsely chop in a wooden bowl, being careful not to lose their juices. Soften, but do not brown, the garlic in the olive oil over medium heat. Add the tomatoes, salt and pepper to taste, and the fresh basil and/or parsley. Simmer, uncovered, for about 30 minutes. Stir the sauce occasionally to prevent scorching or sticking.

This sauce has been rechristened "tomato fresca" in newer restaurants, but it's the same old pizzaiola.

🌿 FETTUCINE ALLA ROMANA 🌿

A Roman chef created the original of this dish, simplicity itself, which numerous restaurants have been trying to complicate ever since. The myth that something occult is involved is perpetuated by the waiter ministering to the pasta over a spirit lamp before your very eyes. *All* pasta has to be quickly tossed with its sauce and served immediately, very hot! Unless you live in a castle, it doesn't matter whether the dish is mixed in the kitchen or at the table. Fettucine are egg noodles and the sauce is simply butter, cream, and cheese. Serve as a first course—this dish is too heavy and becomes boring as a main course.

Serves 4

*1/4 pound sweet butter, melted
    (1 stick)*
1/2 cup heavy cream, hot
*1/2 pound fettucine, cooked
    and hot*

*1/2 cup freshly grated Parmesan
    or Romano cheese*
Freshly ground black pepper

Pour the butter and heavy cream over the fettucine and mix gently. Mix in the grated cheese with a generous amount of pepper. Mix lightly but well in a hot dish. The pasta must be hot enough to melt the cheese slightly. Serve on hot plates and pass more cheese at the table.

☈ CANNELLONI I ☈

My cannelloni is in no way to be construed as authentic. I have never been able to discover exactly what *is* authentic, because it has never been served to me in the same way twice. The most marvelous cannelloni I have ever tasted was in Rome, probably because the noodles were homemade. But let no one deceive you; rolling out pasta needs the combined muscle power of a sculling crew. A small pasta machine can fill in here, though. This recipe calls for store-bought lasagne noodles, or large flat noodles about 3 by 4 inches, if you can get them. Allow about 2 per person as a first course, or 3 for a luncheon.

Serves 3 to 6

*Lasagne or egg noodles 3 by 4
   inches*
1 pound ricotta cheese
1/2 cup melted butter (2 sticks)
*1 cup freshly grated Parmesan
   cheese*

*3 tablespoons minced fresh
   marjoram or oregano*
1 cup heavy cream

Cook the pasta according to the package directions, or until barely tender. Slip it into cold water as soon as it is cooked. Drain and spread each noodle with about 1 tablespoon of ricotta. Roll up, jelly-roll fashion, and lay each noodle seam side down in a buttered oven-to-table dish. Drizzle melted butter over all. Sprinkle with the grated Parmesan and marjoram. Pour the cream over and around the cheese-filled rolls. Bake in a 400°F. oven 15 minutes, basting frequently with the sauce in the pan to prevent the cannelloni from becoming dry and crusty. When golden, bubbly, and heated through, serve immediately with more grated cheese passed at the table.

❧ CANNELLONI II ❧

This is an utter bastard in that it is not made with pasta at all, but with crêpes (thin pancakes). Actually, you may stuff the crêpes with any filling you fancy and give it any name you like—creamed spinach, mushrooms, or minced chicken or veal are all very good alternatives to ricotta. Make this dish exactly the same way as Cannelloni I, except substitute these crêpes for the pasta.

Makes about 20 crêpes

CRÊPES

1¾ cups cold milk	*3 tablespoons melted butter or*
4 eggs	*salad oil*
½ teaspoon salt	*Salad oil for greasing pan*
1 cup sifted, all-purpose flour	

In a blender, combine the milk, eggs, and salt. Put in the flour and butter, and blend at high speed for 1 minute. Cover the batter and let it rest in the refrigerator for 2 hours. (This step improves the texture, but can be skipped if time is short.)

Rub a little oil all around a small, heavy skillet or omelette pan, about 6 inches in diameter. Heat it to nearly smoking and pour in a bit less than ¼ cup of batter. Pick up the pan and roll the batter around to completely coat the bottom of the pan with a thick film. (These pancakes are more like tortillas than our thick breakfast pancakes; they should be almost paper thin.) Return to the heat and shake the pan back and forth over high heat about 60 seconds. Take the pan off the heat and turn the crêpe by grasping the edge nearest you with the thumb and forefinger of each hand, or flip it over with a toss of the pan, *voila!* and all that. Most times you have to sacrifice a couple of trial crêpes to the God of Whimsy. (The second side needs only a few seconds cooking and is not too attractive. Put the filling on this side.) Slide the crêpe onto a plate and stack them up as you make them. Cover the stack with a cloth napkin. Oil the skillet before making each crêpe. It does not matter if the crêpes get cold, since they will be reheated. (If you want to use the crêpes in some other way, stack them on a damp dish towel, fold it up gently, and reheat in a 350°F. oven about 5 minutes.)

Crêpes are an extremely useful thing to master. They can be used for *hors d'oeuvre,* the main course, or dessert, depending on what you care to fill them with. (A tablespoon of sugar is essential to dessert crêpes.)

Shrimp, lobster, crab, or fish in a good cream sauce are excellent fillings. Leftover bits of ham, veal, or chicken can be also put to good use as crêpe fillings. Crêpes filled with cooked, chopped vegetables covered with a Sauce Mornay make a delectable luncheon dish. Dessert crêpes are a perfect foil for summer's fresh fruits and berries (see Dessert). Crêpes may be made ahead and either refrigerated or frozen. But thawing frozen crêpes can take longer than it does to make them fresh.

⚡ PAELLA ⚡

The Spanish national dish is made with or without chicken, sausages, ham, garbanzos (chick peas), lobster, shrimp, scallops, clams, and mussels. In Madrid, I have even had it served with tiny, purple fiddler crabs. It *always* is cooked in a good chicken stock, flavored with saffron, and decorated with roasted red pepper strips and a few green peas, and has, as its chief ingredient, rice. My preference is for the seafood version, given here. However, if lobster or another shellfish is unavailable or too pricey, add 8 small, sautéed chicken thighs along with the shellfish. Paella is a marvelous entree for a dinner party—it pleases everyone.

Serves 8

1 lobster, 1 1/2 pounds or more	1/2 pound shrimp, shelled and
2 ounces smoked bacon, diced	deveined
1 large onion, chopped	1 quart hard-shell clams
2 cups chicken stock	(little-necks)
2 cups clam juice	1 quart mussels (in shells)
1/2 teaspoon saffron	Small can pimentos
2 cups converted rice	1 cup freshly shelled (or thawed)
1/2 pound scallops	baby green peas

You will need a large, heavy skillet plus a large, shallow (3-inch-deep) oven-to-table casserole in which to bake and serve the paella. (In Spain the dish is cooked on the stove, not baked, but Spanish cooks have a special paella pan that hardly seems worth the shelf space unless you serve it incessantly. Half the recipe—for four—may be cooked entirely on top of the stove in a large pot, but otherwise, dividing all the ingredients between 2 pans becomes rather complicated.

Preheat the oven to 400°F.

Either kill the lobster yourself or have the fish dealer do it for you. (You must cook the lobster within a few hours once it is killed, so it's a good idea to learn to do the job yourself.) Remove the sac near the head and cut the lobster into pieces: the body in 4, the tail in 4, the claws cracked and separated from the second joints. Pack the lobster on a bag of crushed ice.

Put the bacon in a cold skillet and fry it slowly until crisp. Reserve. Sauté the onion and lobster in the bacon fat until the onion is transparent and the lobster turns red. Add the chicken stock, clam juice, and saffron. Bring to a boil, add the rice, pour into the ovenproof casserole, and cover with a double thickness of aluminum foil, tightly sealing the dish. Bake for 15 minutes. Remove foil and add the shrimp and scallops, but do not stir the rice. Recover with foil and return to oven for another 5 minutes. Meanwhile, put the clams and mussels in a pot with a little water, cover, and steam open over a brisk flame. Remove casserole from oven, stir in the peas, and add the clams and mussels in their shells. Decorate with strips of red pepper. Heat, uncovered, another 5 minutes.

The rice should be tender and dry, each grain separate and all the seafood thoroughly hot. The total cooking time in the oven is 25 minutes, but if you allow the dish to cool off when adding ingredients, you may have to increase the baking time. It is advisable to taste a few grains of rice before adding the cooked clams and mussels, which must not be overcooked or they will be dry and tough. Just before serving, stir up the rice to distribute the seafood evenly.

Do not attempt to make paella in a deep, narrow dish or pan or the rice will be sticky.

Do not cook the mussels and clams with the paella. There is no way of gauging how much liquid they will release.

Do not use any rice other than American converted long-grain rice because it must cook tender in 20 minutes and absorb all the liquid. Short, stubby rice will be starchy and sticky, and unless you're a veteran rice cook many things can go awry in using plain long-grain rice in paella.

Variations: Chicken must be sautéed until golden as the first step in the paella. When cut in serving pieces, the chicken will be done in 20 minutes in a 400° F. oven.

Ham should be precooked, diced, and sautéed with the onion.

Sausages should be the hard, dry Spanish chorizos or Italian smoked sausages of the same type. Cut in slices ¼-inch thick and add to the paella with the rice.

Garbanzos must be fully cooked (canned ones already are), drained, and added with the rice.

🦐 CHICKEN AND RICE WITH MUSHROOMS 🦐

Quick and uncomplicated, this is a dish even the dedicated noncook can easily master. It can be made more exotic by using distinctively flavored mushrooms such as cêpes or *chanterelles*. These usually come from France or Switzerland and are available in cans, dried, and occasionally fresh. Reconstituted dried Chinese black mushrooms are good, too.

Serves 4

1 2½-pound fryer, disjointed*
4 tablespoons butter (½ stick)
1 small onion, chopped
1 cup rice
2 cups boiling chicken stock
1 teaspoon salt

⅛ teaspoon freshly ground black pepper
½ pound mushrooms, sliced
Lemon juice
Chopped parsley

Rinse and dry the chicken pieces thoroughly on paper toweling. Melt the butter and sauté the chicken until golden on all sides. Add the onions and sauté until transparent, for about 2 or 3 minutes. Drain off excess fat, if any. Add the rice, boiling chicken stock, salt, and pepper. Lightly brown the mushrooms in butter with a squeeze of lemon juice in a separate pan and add them to the chicken. Cover tightly and cook over low heat for 18 minutes. Remove cover and test rice. It is done when you can bite through a grain easily but the rice is not mushy. All the liquid must be absorbed. If it is not, continue cooking uncovered over low heat until the excess liquid evaporates. Sprinkle with parsley and serve very hot.

*A disjointed chicken means that the breast is split, wings removed, wing tips cut off, legs detached from thighs, and back cut into 2 or 3 small pieces, if used (usually the back, neck, and giblets, except the liver, are stewed in advance to make the stock, then discarded). It does not mean hacked into 4 quarters on a buzz-saw.

Note: This may be made in advance, then reheated, loosely covered, in a moderate oven. In this case, the initial cooking period should be reduced by about 5 minutes so that the chicken will not be dried out, nor the rice overcooked.

Chicken Broth: Either make your own with the neck, back, and giblets (excluding the liver), an onion, some celery and a little salt stewed together about an hour or use a good, clear canned chicken stock, undiluted. In either case it should be an aromatic, strongly flavored broth because the rice will be tasteless otherwise. Canned stock is improved by boiling it for 5 to 10 minutes with a few sprigs of parsley, an onion, and some celery tops to flavor and concentrate it. Make certain the stock is accurately salted.

⚘ PERFECT COOKED RICE ⚘

The pot in which rice is cooked has more to do with its success than most other foods. One of the reasons for "Oryzaphobia" (my made-up word for fear of rice) is that cooks have been advised to use too much water by too many books for too many years. Choose a pot wider than it is deep. It should have a close-fitting cover and a fairly heavy bottom. A thick *sautoir* or a well-seasoned Dutch oven or chicken fryer are good choices.

Yields 5 cups

2 1/2 cups long-grain "Carolina" rice
2 tablespoons plain salad oil

2 teaspoons salt
4 1/2 cups water

Rinse the rice with cold water in a basin, pouring off the powdery water several times. Drain. Turn the rice into a tea towel and rub it fairly dry. Heat the oil in the pot and add the rice. Stir it over low heat to coat all the grains. Add the salt and water, turn heat to high, and stir. When the water boils, lower the heat to minimum, cover tightly, and cook for 15 minutes. *Do not stir.*

When you remove the cover, steam will rise and there should be little holes across the surface of the rice. Tilt the pan to see if there is any water left; if there is, raise the heat and evaporate it. Put a paper towel between the rice and the pot lid and let stand, off heat, for 5 minutes. The rice is now ready to serve hot.

For a salad, turn the rice out onto a tray or a wide, flat colander to cool it quickly. Flip the tray or colander up and down so the rice moves and is aerated. When cool enough to handle, pour on some olive oil and lift and turn it into the rice with both hands, fingers spread.

Alternatively, you can use Uncle Ben's converted rice (which is more expensive but less work than regular long-grain rice) and cook it according to package directions *except:* Reduce the water by one third and the cooking time by 5 minutes.

❋ PERSIAN RICE ❋

Here is another way to cook long-grain white rice, either basmati or Carolina. Nowhere on earth is more care lavished on the cooking of rice than in Iran (once the Persian Empire) where it is central to the most refined cuisine in the Middle East. This technique is a little more trouble but it produces amazing rice (*chelo*) with a crisp bottom crust to be served sparingly to honored guests. Traditionally, a raw egg yolk in a half shell and a pat of sweet butter accompany rice, which is eaten in prodigious quantities several times a day by Iranians. The following amount has been reduced to circumspect American servings.

Serves 4

1 cup long-grain white rice

2 tablespoons coarse salt

4 quarts boiling water

2 tablespoons water

6 tablespoons melted butter

Rinse the rice in 3 changes of cold water, until it runs fairly clear. (If using basmati rice, soak it 6 hours in cold, salted water; Carolina rice does not need soaking.) Add the 2 tablespoons salt to the boiling water and slowly dribble in the rice grains, stirring them around so that they move constantly. Boil for 8 to 10 minutes; test by biting a grain to insure the center isn't hard. The rice should be slightly underdone and by no means should the grains split open, at least until after steaming. Drain the rice and rinse it in warm water in a strainer. Pour half the melted butter into a heavy-bottomed pot with a lid. Add the rice, pressing it lightly across the bottom of the pot, then add the 2 tablespoons water and pour on the remaining butter. Put a double thickness of paper towels between the rice and the pot lid. Steam over medium-low heat about 15 minutes. The rice should be white, dry, and fluffy with a golden crust on the bottom. Sometimes thinly sliced or shredded potatoes are put on the bottom to enhance this crust. If you don't want any crust at all, bake it in the oven at 400°F. for 15 minutes.

Green Chelo: Fresh herbs have always had a large role in Persian cookery and the *chelo* is sometimes turned green with them. Throw into the boiling rice just before draining about 4 tablespoons of mixed minced fresh herbs—parsley, chives, plus one other. Iranians would choose mint; I would choose tarragon or marjoram. The herbs will cling to the rice and you'll have green *chelo*.

☀ PILAF ☀

Pilaf differs from plain white rice only in that the rice is cooked in a stock—chicken, beef, veal, or fish—instead of plain water. Use whatever stock best suits the course the rice will accompany.

Serves 4

1 small onion, chopped
1 tablespoon butter
1 cup rice

2 cups boiling stock
1 teaspoon salt

Sauté the onion in butter until softened. Stir in the rice and cook until it looks slightly opaque. (Converted rice becomes transparent.) Pour on the boiling stock and stir once around with a fork. Cover and cook over low heat about 20 minutes.

𓇬 PICADILLO WITH RICE & BEANS 𓇬

You need no special pots, foods, or devices to make this Mexican dinner. Since the Mexican food craze of a couple of years ago, you no longer have to hunt around for cominos, or ground cumin. A dish of red hot pepper sauce is nice to serve with this.

Serves 8

Olive oil
2 cloves garlic, minced
2 cups cooked pinto or red beans
Double recipe Pilaf cooked with
  chicken stock (page 189)
2 pounds lean, ground chuck
1 large onion, chopped

2 medium tomatoes, peeled and
  chopped
1 tablespoon ground cumin
Salt and chili powder to taste*
2 tablespoons capers, drained
4 tablespoons minced scallions
1 hard-cooked egg, minced

In a heavy pot, heat 1 tablespoon olive oil and garlic. (If you like a stronger garlic flavor, use more, but the beans are supposed to be quite bland.) Add the drained beans and cook over low heat, stirring with a wooden spoon from time to time to prevent sticking. They will gradually dissolve into a lumpy puree, ugly but good.

Make the rice while the beans are cooking and begin the Picadillo: Sauté the ground beef in a little olive oil until crumbled and lightly browned (not hard or dried out). Add the onion and cook, stirring, for 3 to 4 minutes. Add the tomatoes and seasoning and cook, stirring occasionally, until the liquid has almost evaporated. Place in the center of a large, preheated platter and sprinkle with the capers, scallions, and hard-cooked egg. Surround with the rice and serve the bean puree in a heated bowl. Corn bread and cold beer are delicious with this meal, which definitely throws weight-consciousness to the winds. And most people do—I can't recall ever having any leftovers, no matter how much I've made.

*Here you can get as plain or fancy, as you like. You can use any seeded dry chilies, soaked and minced. The introductory version I tasted in Oaxaca was not at all spicy, but that has never deterred me from experimenting with different chilies.

🌿 JAMBALAYA 🌿

This ancient Creole dish is sort of a Southern paella—and it varies from region to region just like the Spanish dish. Mine changes too. Sometimes I add shrimp or lobster as garnish, but this is the basic. You will need a large, shallow oven-to-table casserole.

Serves 6

½ cup clarified butter (page 126)

6 to 8 chicken thighs, skinned and boned

½ inch center-cut slice country ham*

½ cup finely diced celery

2 large cloves garlic, minced

1 very large onion, finely chopped

1 jalapeño or other hot fresh chili, seeded and minced

1 bay leaf

1 pound tomatoes, peeled and chopped

3 cups chicken broth

2 cups converted white rice

Salt to taste

1 teaspoon chopped fresh thyme leaves

12 hot Italian sausages

1 large red bell pepper

¼ cup minced fresh parsley

Dried red pepper flakes (optional)

Heat the butter in a large, heavy sauté pan. Add the chicken and ham, and sauté until lightly browned. Remove. Add celery, garlic, onions, and jalapeño pepper. Stir and "sweat," covered, over low heat, about 5 minutes. Add bay leaf, tomatoes, chicken broth, and rice. Stir and taste for salt. (The ham and broth are great variables in

*Center-cut slices of uncooked country ham are not easy to come by in all localities. It needs to be poached in barely moving hot water for an hour before it is dried, trimmed, and cut into small chunks. Precooked ham needs only to be chunked and turned in butter with the onions and garlic.

determining how much salt will be needed.) Return the ham and chicken thighs to the pan, add the thyme, bring to a simmer, cover, and cook over low heat 15 minutes. Insert a double thickness of paper towel between the pan and the lid, turn off heat and let the Jambalaya steam for another 10 minutes. (All this can be done ahead and reheated, covered loosely with foil, in a 325°F. oven, making this a convenient dish for parties.)

Prick each sausage a couple of times and broil over very low heat (or a charcoal fire, if available) for about 15 minutes, turning frequently. (Sausages, unfortunately, do not reheat well.)

Put the sweet pepper on a long fork, char its skin over an open flame, and place in a paper bag for 10 minutes, after which the skin can easily be rubbed off with a paper towel or blunt knife edge. Slice the pepper in long strips and use it to garnish the Jambalaya after you have arranged the sausages over the rice. Sprinkle the whole thing liberally with minced parsley. Pass a shaker of dried red pepper flakes at the table for the heavy-duty fire eaters.

Note: Chicken breasts may be used instead of thighs, but they dry out so easily they should be sautéed in butter separately and only added (buried in the rice) to the Jambalaya for the last 5 minutes or so of cooking.

✿ HOPPIN' JOHN ✿

It isn't likely that everyone will fall into ecstasies over this, but it is a novelty and may easily be adapted to other kinds of beans if you do not happen to be a black-eyed pea aficionado. In South Carolina it is served on New Year's Day and is supposed to bring good luck. Dried peas are commonly used, but fresh ones are better. Frozen black-eyed peas are available in any supermarket.

Serves 4

3 strips thick bacon, sliced into matchsticks
1 onion, chopped
1 cup diced precooked ham
2½ cups water

1 package frozen black-eyed peas
Salt and freshly ground pepper to taste
1 cup converted rice

Fry the bacon until crisp and remove. Drain off all but 2 tablespoons of fat and sauté the onion and ham in this for about 5 minutes. Add the water and, when it comes to a boil, the frozen peas. Cover and cook 15 minutes, or until tender, over medium-low heat. Taste for salt and sprinkle with pepper. Add the rice, cover tightly, and cook over low heat for 20 minutes. The rice should be dry and fluffy, the peas tender. (Be sure the peas are almost done before adding the rice. If using dried peas or beans, make sure they are fully cooked.) Crumble the reserved bacon and sprinkle over the Hoppin'john.

I've probably included this favorite of mine in all my books hoping for converts. Obviously, I'm no St. Paul (the great proselytizer), because I have yet to see this dish on anybody else's table.

🌿 RED RICE AND BEANS 🌿

Throughout the Caribbean Islands, Mexico, and South America some form of rice and beans comprises a major part of the diet. Sharing the climate and economic conditions of these regions, many parts of the Southern United States have their rice and beans dishes, too. This recipe is a combination of several low-country recipes. It is quite different from the "red beans and rice" of New Orleans. Here the *rice* is red.

Serves 4

½ cup diced smoked bacon
1 large onion, chopped
2 cloves garlic, minced
3 very ripe tomatoes, peeled
1 cup (or more) chicken broth
Sprig of sweet basil
1 teaspoon salt
1 tablespoon tomato paste

1 cup converted rice
2 cups cooked beans: garbanzo,
    white marrow, or kidney
    beans; red kidney beans; pinto
    beans; or California pink beans
2 tablespoons chopped fresh
    parsley

Fry the bacon slowly in a heavy skillet until nearly done. Add the onions and garlic, and sauté until soft. Chop the tomatoes and squeeze as much juice as possible out of them into a bowl. Add enough chicken broth to make 2 cups of liquid. Put the tomatoes, basil, salt, and tomato-and-chicken broth into the skillet with the vegetables and bacon. Stir in the tomato paste and bring to a boil. Add the rice and cooked beans. Cover and cook over low heat until the liquid has evaporated and the rice is tender. (The heat should be adjusted so that this takes 20 minutes or less.) Turn into an earthenware casserole and sprinkle with parsley. This is a main dish, but you may also serve some ham, chicken, fish, or shellfish with it if you like. Pass some hot pickled peppers.

VEGETABLES

Truly field-fresh vegetables, which seemed headed for extinction except in remote, backward countries, are in new demand. Undoubtedly we will now enjoy a greater supply, at least in summer. There are, of course, "fresh" vegetables in supermarkets most of the year around. But most of them were harvested weeks, or even months, before and "life extended" Lord knows how. Some even look good in a garish sort of way, but after you get them home and into the cookpot, they reveal their cottony textures and wispy flavorlessness. Greenmarkets and an avalanche of well-managed Korean produce shops have improved the quality of vegetables in New York City, at least, remarkably.

Only in the upper echelons of expensive restaurants does one find fresh-picked young produce. Baby vegetables are the status symbols of our newfound red-white-and-blue native cookery. A national preoccupation with bigness—county fair giant pumpkins, tomatoes, whatever—distorted agricultural aims. Year after year after year, zillions of bushels of tough overgrown greenbeans are harvested, sold, cooked, and thrown away. (One perceives dimly that the reason old-fashioned cooks stewed those enormous veggies for hours was to make them at least chewable.)

Only recently have Americans come to grips with "small is better" and more beautiful. (Though "small" should not mean ripped from the ground untimely before any flavor at all can form.) In France and the Orient this has always been the case, with premium prices paid to farmers for the youngest, finest, and freshest vegetables. But unless you live in an area with rather sophisticated farmers and local farmstands, you still have trouble finding anything but overgrown produce. A whole new, highly food-conscious and knowing segment of the population is creating a demand, though, and someday, I hope in the next several years, size standards will change among big, commercial growers. Overgrown vegetables are, of course, cheaper to harvest whether by hand or machine, so don't hold your breath.

Frozen peas, both green and black-eyed, and lima beans seem to be fairly successful, but the more watery items, such as asparagus and string beans, for instance, don't make it. Canned vegetables, except for beets and tomatoes, are more or less appalling. Therefore, I long ago came to grips with cooking whatever is in season and enjoying it more. The first tomatoes, acid-sweet and slippery fleshed, and the first milky kerneled green corn, are well worth waiting for through the winter.

Most fresh summer vegetables need very little cooking, and they're a wonderful change from the soft lettuce salads whose wonder begins to fade as the umpteenth one appears in mid-June. Though it is not within the living memory of most Americans, there was a time—only a generation ago—when green salad was not a mandatory part of every dinner. Here are just a few alternatives—or additions, if you feel that life without salad is unthinkable. The small vegetable selection here has been chosen because they're at their best in summer and they are grown locally in nearly every region of the country. Even the commonest vegetables, small and freshly harvested, have a special taste of summer that can't be duplicated.

CORN

Mark Twain, a man who knew his victuals, said that the only way to fix corn was to boil a pot of water in the field and shuck the ears into it. He was right; aim at that ideal even if you haven't got your own corn field. Our local farmers do such a sensational job of growing many varieties of superior corn that few amateur gardeners try to plant it.

Get to your favorite farmstand early in the day or for the late afternoon picking. Take a big Styrofoam hamper with some ice or a plastic "blue ice" square to keep the corn cool. Heat is the enemy of corn; it should be kept out of the sun (never buy from a pile of corn that is lying in the sun) and refrigerated until the moment it is to be cooked. Start boiling the water before you start shucking the corn. Add nothing, *no! nothing,* not milk, sugar, or salt, to the water. Great big ears of yellow corn, while some people prefer them, tend to be rather starchy and tough. I prefer the first young, slender ears and pale, small kernels. They can be white, gold, or a mix of the two. Whatever your choice, corn-on-the-cob should be the main event of a summer meal, rushed from boiling pot to table set with plenty of fresh sweet whipped butter, coarse salt, and fresh pepper.

⅋ FRIED CORN ⅋

"Fried corn" is not really "fried" now that we've all learned the word "sauté." In old-fangled redneck cooking, it was often made with canned "Niblets" out of corn season. The corn season goes on here on the East End of Long Island all September long, so people do get the urge to do something with it besides corn-on-the-cob. Slicing the kernels off is not a hard job if you have a sharp knife. There is a gadget made for this but not worth buying unless you're getting into an operatic freezing fit.

Serves 4

4 cups fresh corn kernels
1 large red onion
2 to 3 tablespoons butter
Salt and freshly ground white
   pepper to taste
Dried red pepper flakes or seeded
and minced hot fresh chili
pepper to taste
1 teaspoon minced fresh
   coriander or parsley, or ½
   teaspoon ground coriander
   (optional)

Shuck the corn and cut it from the cobs shortly before you wish to serve this dish or refrigerate the cut corn, tightly covered, until mealtime. This is quick to make but impossible to keep warm—it's better to give up and eat it at room temperature.

Thinly slice the onion and break it into rings. Melt the butter in a wok or large skillet and add the onions. When they are limp, add the corn and all remaining ingredients, and stir-fry just until the corn is hot and gives up a bit of juice—about 3 minutes.

Fresh coriander, which looks much like parsley, is a brassy tasting herb sometimes known as Chinese parsley and in Spanish as cilantro. People either love it or hate it, so it's best to be cautious and use parsley unless you know your corn eaters' tastes very well. Ground coriander has a markedly different, but interesting flavor much more universally liked than fresh coriander. Don't overdo either, as freshly picked corn has such charm all on its own. You might want to try it just plain "fried" with butter, salt, and pepper.

ZUCCHINI THE INESCAPABLE

This relative newcomer to the American table must be as easy to grow as crabgrass; even the neighborhood Black Thumbs have such success they can't find takers for the excess. Local restaurants seem to have forgotten that there is any other vegetable. But there is hope.

An Italophile friend of mine sat patiently stuffing the blossoms, freshly picked from his own garden one July evening, and thus did I discover one of the best things I've ever eaten anywhere. Not only that, but I could see in a flash that my campaign to suppress the zucchini population had a solution. Here was a delicious and humane way to control the little buggers. Dipped in batter and deep-fried to a crisp exterior, the brilliant yellow flowers of the zucchini plant are utterly delicious. The blossoms are so incredibly perishable they should be used within several hours. (Although I did keep some successfully in the fridge overnight, laid in a single layer on damp newspaper spread on a jelly roll pan, the surface lightly covered with plastic wrap.) As planting too many zuke vines is a peril common to most gardeners, taking some of the incipient vegetables off their hands should endear you to your friends.

Some years ago, I spent half a summer trying to work out recipes for the zucchini running wild in the vegetable patch of my landlady, the late but vividly remembered writer Jean Stafford. Had I only known the joys of flower fritters, we might have been spared some of my zucchini pickles, zucchini soup, and zucchini stuffed a hundred ways.

🌿 FRIED STUFFED ZUCCHINI BLOSSOMS 🌿

Inspect each blossom's interior for insects. Don't wash them; keep them in a dry, very roomy, plastic bag in the fridge if you can't cook them shortly after they are picked. Make your batter* and slowly heat your oil. Line a tray with crumpled paper towels to drain the fried blossoms.

1 package "Zebbie's Mushroom Batter Mix" or about 1 1/2 cups homemade fritter batter (page 201)

1 quart fresh safflower oil (or other light, plain cooking oil)

16 zucchini blossoms

16 cubes (1/2-inch or less) mozzarella

8 anchovy fillets, halved lengthwise

The package directions on the batter mix say to add one cup of water, but it seems too thick for these fragile bundles so I thin it with an additional 1/4 cup of water. Whatever batter you use must be just thick enough to keep the blossoms completely enclosed while they are frying.

Start the oil heating to 385°F. (Or the fritters may be shallow-fried in 1/2 inch of oil in a black cast-iron skillet, taking care not to crowd them or they will stick to-gether.)

Gently unfurl the petals and poke the mozzarella cubes and bits of anchovy down into the cups of the flowers. (They twist themselves back into position, more or less.) Dip each blossom in batter, holding it by the stem or the occasional infant zucchini attached to it, and fry them a few at a time for a few minutes on each side. Remove them to paper towels with a slotted spoon and serve them smoking hot with salt. Fried

---

*I have found a highly successful group of batter mixes from a small factory in Memphis, Texas. "Zebbie's" makes onion ring and mushroom mix, among several other dried products. Some-times you find these hanging over the fresh produce they're designed for and not in the dried mix department as one might expect.

stuffed zucchini blossoms are a delicacy to concentrate on and should be enjoyed all by themselves. They're a great backyard treat before the barbecuing begins.

When the oil cools, strain it, rebottle it, and keep it refrigerated until the next mess of zucchini blossoms comes your way.

✳ FRITTER BATTER ✳

Here's a light, delicate batter to use with most vegetables and seafood. It must be made at least 1 hour in advance to relax the gluten in the flour before folding in the egg whites.

Makes about 1 1/2 cups

1/2 cup cold beer
1 large egg
1 cup flour, after sifting
3 tablespoons melted butter or
  Crisco shortening

1/2 teaspoon salt
2 egg whites

Beat the beer and whole egg together in a processor, then add the flour. When blended, add the melted butter or shortening and salt, and run the processor briefly until the batter is smooth. Cover and refrigerate for at least 1 hour. When ready to fry fritters, beat the 2 egg whites until stiff but not dry. Fold into the batter and use it at once.

❧ SAUTÉED ZUCCHINI AND/OR ❧ CROOKNECK SQUASH

Difficult though it may be to believe, the ubiquitous green squash was unknown outside Italian neighborhoods until about a decade ago. There is now even *gold* zucchini. Yellow squash, with a slender crooked neck on its fat oval body, has been neglected but is returning to favor. It tastes much the same as zucchini, and both cook in the same time if they're about the same size.

Serves 4

2 pounds baby zucchini or yellow crookneck squash, or a combination of the two
2 tablespoons butter
1 tablespoon vegetable oil
Juice of ½ lemon

Salt and freshly ground pepper to taste
1 tablespoon fresh thyme leaves
2 tablespoons minced fresh chives or parsley, or both

Rinse and dry the vegetables, but do not peel. Slice in ⅛-inch rounds. Heat the butter and oil in a deep, heavy skillet or wok until it foams and clears. Scatter in the squash and sauté over medium-high heat, turning almost constantly, for about 5 minutes. Neither of these squash has any flavor at all raw, so they must be cooked enough to bring out their shy, delicate taste. Sprinkle with salt and pepper to taste and mix in the herbs. Serve at once. If you want to serve the squash at room temperature, it should be cooled quickly on a cold tray. Otherwise it will wilt in its own heat and become watery.

☆ ZUCCHINI FINGERS ☆

A simple accompaniment to summer meals, especially grilled fish, this is quickly and easily assembled. For a crowd, much of the prepping can be done in advance. Lightweight and light work, but don't shirk the blanching step or the zucchini will be tasteless.

Serves 4

*4 small zucchini, about 5 inches
long
1 tablespoon softened butter
Salt and freshly ground pepper*

*3 tablespoons freshly grated
Parmesan cheese
(approximately)*

Scrub the squash with a soft brush but do not peel. Blanch them in boiling water for a couple of minutes. Refresh in cold water, dry, and split them lengthwise. Dry the cut surfaces. Spread with softened butter, salt, and pepper them (use cayenne for a spicier effect), and cover with a light layer of Parmesan. Run under a broiler until the cheese melts and the edges are golden. The zucchini fingers may be prepared in advance, up to sprinkling them with salt. This cannot be done more than a few minutes before cooking because salt draws out moisture, making the vegetable limp.

STUFFED TOMATOES

Against every region's boast of "the best tomatoes in the world" I back the beauties of Eastern Long Island. The days are just hot and sunny enough, and the nights just cool enough, to sharpen the flavor. Tomatoes grown in really hot climates just aren't in the same class as the fruits from temperate zones (neither are the fish from warm seas, but that's another dispute). Nonetheless, no matter how divinely pure, plain sliced tomatoes can get boring after a month or two. (You can, though, vary them with different cheeses, olive oils, and occasionally, toasted pine nuts and summer herbs.)

Fortunately, tomatoes keep their appeal because, both cooked and raw, they go with so many other tastes and textures. Some of the fillings for tomatoes appropriate for summer luncheons include leftover baked or poached fish in vinaigrette or aioli, curried egg salad, shrimp or tuna salad, and fresh young vegetables lightly steamed or raw (or a mixture of several) in a mayonnaise or vinaigrette, Stuffed tomatoes may not surprise anyone but they'll please more people than tabbouleh with cilantro. (Exotic food shock has to be halted somewhere and it might as well be in the home.)

There should be some crisp ingredients in any of these fillings, as a contrast to the voluptuous tomato texture. Dried legumes such as chick peas, lentils, or great Northern or pinto beans make wonderful salads for strict vegetarians.

Basic Stuffed Tomato Preparation

Tomatoes to be stuffed should be firm, red-ripe and blemishless. It's best to select them a day or two in advance and keep them at room temperature in the dark. If raw tomatoes are not skinned and seeded, they are difficult to cut (especially at forks-only buffets) and impossible to stuff. Drop them into boiling water, count to 20, then plunge them immediately into ice water. Cut out the core and the skins will pull off easily. Cut off the top third of the tomato, scoop out the seeds and pulp with your thumb, sprinkle the insides with a little salt and set them upside-down to drain on a rack. Blot the interiors with a ball of paper toweling before filling them. Small tomatoes—cherry or Tiny Tims—that can be eaten in one or two bites needn't be peeled, but of course, must still be seeded if you hope to put any stuffing into them.

ROASTED BELL PEPPERS

Plain old green bell peppers, mild and burpy, are one of the Holy Trinity in traditional Southern cooking. (The other two are celery and onions; hundreds of recipes begin, "Take a bell pepper, some celery and onions . . . ") I was bored blue by them before I was 14, and I was at least 30 before I could bear celery in anything! But I've rediscovered the old bell pepper because its taste is so wonderful once the skin has been scorched and removed. No one ever did this in old recipes—peppers were seeded, but that's all.

Now we have red, yellow, and chocolate brown peppers in the markets. These have been allowed to ripen—though not all green peppers turn another color when ripe. Red and yellow taste best to me and the colors remain glorious. They will keep several days in a little oil, but have the finest flavor freshly roasted either over charcoal (best) or a gas flame (second best, but still very good indeed).

Although sweet peppers are the confetti of modern cuisine and have been egregiously overused, let's not abandon this wonderful accent for chicken, eggs, and pasta in particular (peppers overwhelm fish, as a rule). Charcoal-grilled chicken positively levitates when fresh roasted peppers are scattered over it.

The technique seems complicated—skinning those convoluted shapes!—but it isn't. Get 3 or 4 cheap green peppers and practice before investing in the red and the gold—rather wildly expensive, for some unaccountable reason. Once yours, the mastery of roast peppers lets you dress up all manner of dull little recipes—people don't really need many recipes if they have good techniques in the kitchen.

Charcoal Grilling: Rinse and dry the peppers but do nothing else. Put them on the grill and roast until the skins puff and turn dark brown or even a bit black, turning them very, very often for even cooking. Wrap each in thicknesses of paper toweling (or put several in a heavy brown bag, twisted shut) and leave alone for about 10 minutes. (They will steam slightly, which loosens their skins.) Wipe off the skin with paper toweling, cut the pepper in half, and discard the stem and top. Scrape out the seeds and inside veins. The peppers can be served in halves, quarters, strips, or squares. Halves give a beautiful bright tulip effect on the plate with other food.

Flame Roasting: Pierce the stem end of the pepper with a long cooking fork. Hold it over the highest flame of a gas burner, turning it to blacken all sides. Let steam in paper and skin as described in Charcoal Grilling. Peppers are terribly easy to grow, so undoubtedly they'll one day be cheap even in winter markets if their extreme popularity with the New American chefs hasn't worn out their welcome with the public.

Keeping Roast Peppers: Of course the best-tasting peppers are the ones you buy straight off a farmstand. These have not been stunned with refrigeration. But wherever you buy them, try to use them as soon as possible because the flavor starts dying the minute they're picked. They must be kept quite cool from field to stove. After roasting and skinning, put them in a jar with some good olive oil—no salt, no vinegar, because both leach out the color and juices.

✣ REVISIONIST RATATOUILLE ✣

A Mediterranean mélange of summer vegetables, this is exquisite served hot or cold. It may be a separate course and it makes a marvelous dish for the buffet table. My new version is quickly stir-fried and therefore radically different in texture from the soft, long-cooked traditional dish. If there is any left over, ratatouille makes an interesting filling for omelettes.

Serves 6

1/2 pound zucchini
1/2 cup olive oil, approximately
1 medium eggplant
2 cups sliced yellow onions
2 green peppers, cut in strips
2 cloves garlic, minced

1 pound ripe red tomatoes,
  peeled
Salt and freshly ground pepper
3 tablespoons minced fresh
  parsley and basil, mixed

Rinse the zucchini, dry it, and slice in ⅛-inch rounds. Put a little oil in a heavy skillet or wok over high heat. Sauté the zucchini a layer at a time, then remove to a side dish. Peel the eggplant and slice it into matchsticks. Add more oil to the skillet and sauté the eggplant, then place it in the dish with the zucchini. Add more oil and sauté the onions, green peppers, and garlic until softened. Cut the tomatoes in half and squeeze out the juice and seeds. Chop them and add to the vegetables in the skillet. Season with salt and pepper to taste, and cook rapidly, stirring constantly, until the juice from the tomatoes has almost evaporated. Return the eggplant and zucchini to the skillet with the other vegetables. Adjust salt and pepper, sprinkle with herbs, and cook over medium heat about 5 minutes, lifting the vegetables and turning carefully with a spatula until all the juices, except for a few tablespoons of the richly flavored oil, have evaporated. Set aside, uncovered, until serving time, then reheat; or serve at room temperature. It is important that each vegetable retain its own texture and flavor, so be careful not to overcook.

🌿 BRAISED PEAS À LA FRANÇAISE 🌿

The ultimate preparation for fresh garden peas, these are worthy of being presented at court—and they were. In the court of Louis XIV, this delicacy became as chic with the ladies as eating nothing is today in America. Only very young, tender peas, shelled just before cooking, should be used. There are only a few weeks a year that fresh young peas are available, and there's a heap of shelling involved, so they deserve star billing as a hot first course.

Serves 4

3 pounds fresh, tender green
  peas, in the pod
10 sprigs parsley
2 bunches scallions
6 tablespoons butter (3/4 stick)

1/2 cup water
1 tablespoon sugar
1/2 teaspoon salt
Freshly ground black pepper

Shell the peas and tie the parsley in a bunch. Trim the scallions and cut off the tops so that only the bulbs—about 3/4 inch—remain. In a heavy, enameled skillet or saucepan, place 4 tablespoons of the butter, with the water, sugar, salt, and pepper. Bring to a boil and add the peas. Shake the pan to coat the peas. Lay the parsley then the scallion bulbs on the peas. Cover with a heavy, domed lid or an inverted shallow bowl so that the condensed steam will fall back on the vegetables. Braise over very low heat about 5 minutes. Remove the cover and continue to cook, shaking the saucepan occasionally so that the vegetables cook evenly. When the peas are tender, the cooking liquid should have nearly evaporated. Discard the parsley. Toss the peas and scallions with the remaining 2 tablespoons of butter.

⚘ BLANCHED SPINACH ⚘

Presumably everyone has some method of cooking spinach. But since frozen spinach (because of its availability and cheapness) has all but obliterated fresh spinach, I offer this recipe to remind you of how amazingly good the fresh article can be.

Serves 4

3 pounds young, fresh spinach
1 teaspoon salt
1/8 teaspoon freshly ground
* pepper*

1/4 cup melted butter (1/2 stick)
2 hard-cooked eggs
Lemon wedges

Wash the spinach by lifting and swishing it through 3 changes of cold water, leaving the sand at the bottom of the sink each time. Do this even if the spinach is said to have been "prewashed." Discard large, tough, or blemished leaves. Break off the stems with a slight pull upward to remove some of the spine of the leaf. Blanch the spinach in a large amount of boiling salted water for about 2 minutes after the water returns to the boil. Remove at once, drain well, mix with the butter, add pepper, and serve garnished with egg and lemon wedges.

❧ CREAMED SPINACH ☙

Cook fresh spinach as in preceding recipe. Drain well and chop with a stainless steel knife; carbon steel discolors spinach. Do not use a processor unless your control of this machine is quite precise; you do not want a puree. When it is cold, add it to the sauce.

Serves 4

3 tablespoons butter
2 tablespoons minced onion
2 tablespoons flour
1 cup boiling milk or light cream
1/2 teaspoon salt

1/8 teaspoon pepper
Nutmeg
2 cups spinach, cooked, cooled,
  and chopped

Melt 1 tablespoon of the butter in a heavy saucepan and gently cook the minced onion in it. Do not brown. Add the remaining butter and melt. Stir in the flour and cook, without browning, for 2 minutes. Pour in the boiling milk or cream and cook, beating rapidly with a wire whisk, until the sauce is smooth and thickened, about 3 minutes. Remove from the heat, add salt and pepper, and grate in a little nutmeg. Add the spinach and reheat in this sauce. (If the spinach is still hot when added to the sauce, it will overcook.) This is a good filling for Crêpes (page 181) as well as an ideal accompaniment to fish or veal. Creamed spinach is also a fine base for poached eggs; sprinkle them with grated Parmesan and run quickly under a hot broiler to glaze.

❧ PARSLIED GLEANERS (NEW POTATOES) ❧

Another lovely vegetable and simple pleasure is a dish of tiny, really new potatoes. Buy small, shiny, pale beige potatoes. On Long Island sometimes the farmers will allow you to glean these after their big machines have harvested the larger potatoes. Red Bliss potatoes are an alternative that is available most of the time.

Serves 4

2 pounds small, whole new
   potatoes, not more than 2
   inches in diameter
2 cups water
1 tablespoon salt

2 tablespoons butter
Freshly ground pepper
3 tablespoons chopped fresh
   parsley

Scrub the potatoes under running water with a soft brush. Bring the water and salt to a boil in a large saucepan. Add the potatoes and boil them in their jackets just until tender, about 15 to 20 minutes. Drain, then put them back in the pot and shake over low heat to evaporate excess moisture. Add the butter and shake the pot to coat all the potatoes evenly. Grind on pepper and sprinkle with the parsley. The more quickly they're served (eating a couple straight from the pot is the cook's special perk), the better they are. Potatoes can get soggy if held at low heat, but new potatoes are delicious served at room temperature with Sauce Aioli (page 82).

☆ GREEN BEANS WITH EGG AND LEMON SAUCE ☆

The kind of slender, immature beans needed for this dish are almost an oddity, but if you have a garden this is another way to enjoy the brief season of early summer vegetables. The beans should be picked when they are about ¼ inch in diameter and about 3 inches long. It is nearly impossible to get commercially grown beans of this size, but a few farm stands have them. Select the smallest, youngest beans even if it involves picking them out one by one.

Serves 4

2 pounds tiny, whole green beans
2 eggs
Juice of ½ lemon

3 tablespoons melted butter,
slightly cooled

Trim just the stems of the beans and drop them into boiling salted water. They should still be deep green and slightly crunchy but tender, in 3 to 5 minutes. Test by eating one. Drain the beans and keep them hot, reserving ½ cup of the cooking water. In a small saucepan, beat the eggs and lemon juice together with a wire whisk until frothy. Add the butter and a few spoonfuls of the bean water, whisking rapidly over low heat until the sauce thickens. Pour over hot beans and serve at once.

TIMBALE D'AUBERGINE

If I called this "eggplant custard," who would eat it? That's what it is, but the French name suits the elegance of this dish, which is inspired by both French and Italian cookery. It's very good with roast meats and broiled steaks and chops.

Timbales, incidentally, are gaining popularity in American cookery. You can use this recipe to make nearly any kind of vegetable timbale, so long as the vegetable is first cooked and excess moisture removed from it

Serves 4

2 medium eggplants, about 6 inches long
1 tablespoon coarse salt
2 tablespoons olive oil
1 clove garlic, minced
3 eggs
1 cup milk or light cream
1/2 teaspoon salt
1/8 teaspoon pepper
1/2 cup freshly grated Parmesan cheese

Peel the eggplants, slice them, and sprinkle with the salt. Let them drain for half an hour. Rinse and press the slices to remove excess moisture, then dry with paper towels. Cook them gently in the olive oil in a skillet until most of their moisture has evaporated. Puree the eggplant with the garlic and combine it with the eggs, milk, and seasonings. Pour into a well-buttered 1 1/2-quart soufflé dish or casserole. Sprinkle with the grated cheese. Set in a pan of hot water and bake in a preheated 350°F. oven until set, about 1 hour. Serve immediately.

🌿 BEAUTIFUL BROCCOLI QUICHE 🌿

The fickle winds of fashion may blow away all their chic, but feathery-crusted, rich quiches are entrenched in our cookery now. And when they're properly made, none but the most intractable snobs can resist their appeal. In summer, keep a supply of good pie shells in the freezer, and you'll have the foundation for many quick, consoling (if not startling), good old-fangled quiches. This one uses broccoli, which, once an autumn vegetable, seems to have become a year-round crop.

1 pie shell, prebaked blind
1 1/2 cups tiny fresh broccoli
    florets
2 tablespoons minced scallions
2 extra-large eggs and enough
    heavy cream to make up a
    volume of 1 1/2 cups liquid

Grating of fresh nutmeg
1/2 teaspoon white pepper
1 teaspoon salt
3 to 4 tablespoons coarsely grated
    Gruyère or Swiss cheese

Preheat the oven to 375°F.

Put the pie shell, in its tin, on a baking sheet. (Really high, fluffy quiches are temperamental and, at times, rise a bit too exuberantly over their pans.) Blanch the florets in a lot of salted boiling water for just 2 minutes. Drain and toss onto a kitchen towel to dry. Arrange the broccoli in the pie shell and sprinkle over the scallions. Whisk the eggs and cream with the nutmeg, pepper, and salt, and pour it over the broccoli. Sprinkle the top with the Gruyère.

Bake the quiche in the upper third of the oven for about 25 to 30 minutes; it should be puffed and light brown and still quivery in the center. Let the pie cool out of a draught for 10 minutes before attempting to cut it into wedges.

For finger food servings, cook the filling in an oblong pastry case and cut it into squares when it is at room temperature. Reheat them quickly to serve.

⚜ BLACK BEANS WITH ANCHOS ⚜

I include this dried vegetable dish because it is a perfect sidebar for summer barbecues of all kinds. One pound of black beans is usually enough for 8 (but maybe not, if some of them are Texans). These are extremely tasty beans, but not at all spicy. Anchos are mild but mellow chili peppers that burnish the color and flavor of many Tex-Mex dishes. Dried anchos, the only kind I've ever seen, are almost black, but after soaking become a dark brick red. Anchos should be leathery when bought, not brittle.

Serves 6 to 8

1 pound dried black (turtle) beans

2 dried ancho chili peppers

1 or 2 stalks celery

3 small strips smoked country bacon (speck)

1 cup minced onion

2 or 3 cloves garlic, minced

Salt to taste

Coarsely ground black pepper to taste

Pick over, rinse, and soak the beans in cold water to cover overnight. (Or bring to a boil, simmer one minute, turn off heat, and let soak for 1 hour before proceeding.) Drain. Wash the anchos, split them, and discard the stems and seeds. Pour on just enough boiling water to cover them, weight them under it, and leave to soak for an hour. Then puree them along with their soaking water.

Cover the beans and celery with fresh water, bring to a boil, and let simmer for 1 hour. *Do not add salt.* Add the bacon. Sauté the onion and garlic in a little oil and add them to the beans along with salt and coarsely ground pepper to taste.

Continue to simmer the beans until tender, which usually takes about 2 hours, sometimes less. It's a good idea to bake them for the latter hour—because they'll be less apt to stick. Black beans should be a little soupy; the juice cooks to a dark, thick pot liquor treasured by most bean fanciers.

❧ SEPTEMBER MIXED FRY ❦

Here's a chance to indulge one's irrepressible urge to buy some of everything on the farmstand. The bright colored peppers and squashes of this selection lend it a Southwestern tone, though it's stir-fried in a wok and the vegetables I use are native-born Long Islanders. All the cutting and just a tad of the cooking can be done in advance, but the final cooking is only a 3-minute job.

Serves 8 to 10

2 tablespoons olive oil

1 large yellow onion, peeled and
   coarsely chopped

3 cloves garlic, peeled and
   minced

1 long, thin eggplant, about ½
   pound, cut into ½-inch cubes

1 mild Italian green pepper,
   seeded and cut in large dice

2 large ripe bell peppers, 1 red
   and 1 yellow, roasted, skinned,

cut into strips (page 205), and
   mixed with a little oil

2 golden zuccini, about 6 inches
   long, sliced

2 green zucchini, about 6 inches
   long, sliced

6 ears bicolored young corn,
   shucked and cut from the cob

6 leaves fresh basil, shredded fine

Salt and freshly ground pepper to
   taste

Unless you're as fast with a knife as a sushi master, it's probably best to get all the peeling and chopping done with before you begin cooking. Place the vegetables in separate bags and refrigerate until you're ready to proceed.

Necklace the wok with some of the oil, place over medium-high heat, and add the onion and garlic, while stirring. Cover and cook over low heat for 2 minutes. Raise the heat and add the eggplant. Stir rapidly to coat, then add the green pepper, lower the heat, and cook, covered, for 5 minutes. Remove all to a strainer set over a pot.

Add more oil to the wok, throw in the zucchini and stir-fry over highest heat for about 2 minutes. Add the corn. Return the eggplant mixture to the wok with the roasted peppers, tossing and turning together. Sprinkle with the shredded basil and salt and pepper to taste. Serve at once.

DESSERT

It seems to me that there has been a real rejuvenation of public interest in this area of cookery in recent years. In a society that has markedly cut down on drinking and gone mad for "fitness," the reasons for this increased popularity of sweets are puzzling. Perhaps dessert has become the reward (like "time-off") for good behavior.

At any rate, my own interest in the subject has burgeoned dangerously in the past couple of years, though I have grown thinner. Maybe it all makes sense somehow; I am certainly enjoying my newfound passion in this part of gastronomy as the length of this chapter attests when compared with my previous books. I am particularly taken with the possibilities in homemade ice cream, where adult tastes have been so little taken into account by commercial manufacturers. Peanut butter candies or peppermint sticks crumbled into innocent ice cream do not fit into my idea of grown-up food. Pistachio ice cream with raspberry puree and a splash of framboise, a great summer dessert, definitely does. Ice creams and sherbets, which can be made out of anything that can be frozen, are fun to make at home using your imagination on the galaxy of possibilities unexplored by commercial ice cream producers. You may think they have explored plenty, but the flavors are aimed at a child market. Though there are many terrific ice creams to be bought, few of them come without a lot of additives and preservatives necessary to mass distribution and a good profit margin. At the very least one can take pleasure in knowing and tasting the purity of one's own homemade confection.

Fruit, berries, and the ice creams made with them, are particularly appealing in summer. The season obliges first with magnificent crops of strawberries glittering in the late June sun. Then come the blueberries, blackberries, and raspberries in July, and the glory of the stone fruits—delectable peaches, plums, and apricots—in August. Of course all these things are wonderful as is or simply bathed in a little heavy cream with a sprinkle of sugar. But what cook can resist making pies, tarts, and ice creams when all this glorious fruit presents itself? With progeny and all their friends home from school and the season's innumerable weekend guests milling about, summer is the perfect time for sweet indulgences.

THREE PASTRY RECIPES

Any pastry can, of course, be made entirely by hand. But the food processor is a big help with most, even if you finish the job by hand—a combination of techniques I also use with yeast doughs and fragile Italian cookie-type pastry. Unless you are able to feel the dough, it's almost impossible to know when enough water has been added. Too much water makes pastry shrink excessively and also makes it tough. Too little water makes pastry impossible to roll out, as does too much warmth. *Any* type of pastry should be chilled for an hour before you try to roll it. The rolled dough should be fitted into its pan or tart mold, pricked and frozen for 10 minutes before baking. Pastry is undeniably a tricky thing to master—but anyone can, with diligent practice. As with omelettes, just keep making pie shells and tossing them out until they come out perfect.

There are different types of pastry for different purposes, but once the basic technique is learned, they're all easy. Pastry should be refrigerated or frozen in summer, because all forms of shortening deteriorate rapidly in hot weather. Since this is a summertime cookbook, readers may have neither the time nor the inclination to stand in a warm kitchen trying to make puff pastry for hours on end; I therefore recommend buying the frozen raw dough, which is quick and simple to roll out the way you want it.

⚵ GOOD QUICK PIE CRUST ⚶

This type of pastry is appropriate for most pie recipes. Use the processor to cut in the shortening, then finish the job by hand to insure against adding too much water.

Makes 1 9- or 10-inch shell

1 cup unbleached flour plus ½ cup cake flour or 1½ cups unbleached flour
4 tablespoons salted butter, chilled (½ stick)
2 tablespoons solid vegetable shortening or lard, chilled

2 teaspoons lemon juice or white vinegar
Approximately 2 tablespoons ice water

Put the flour into the processor bowl. Cut the chilled butter and shortening into pieces and add. Pulse to cut in the fats until the size of split peas. Add the lemon juice or vinegar, pulse a couple of times, then add the ice water in dribbles, pulsing the machine just until the dough is a shaggy mass. Turn this out onto a floured surface and push it away from you with the heel of your hand to blend it lightly. Add more ice water if necessary to make the ingredients hold together. Quickly shape into a ball then flatten the mass. Wrap in plastic wrap and refrigerate at least an hour, or overnight.

Let the pastry warm up slightly at room temperature so that it can be worked. Place on a lightly floured board and roll out, turning the circle after each 2 strokes, until it is 2 inches larger than the circumference of the pie pan. Gently lift it into the pan and press it lightly into place. Trim the edges, leaving a half-inch overhang. Fold this over the rim of the pie tin and crimp the edges. Prick the pie shell, then put it in the freezer for 10 minutes.

Preheat the oven to 375°F. Line the pastry shell with oiled aluminum foil and some pie weights, dried beans, or rice. Bake on the lower rack of the oven for 15 minutes. Reduce heat to 350°F. and remove the weights and foil. Continue baking for another 10 minutes or until dry and firm. Cool thoroughly before filling.

To retain a crisp crust, paint the shell with a thin glaze of apricot jam or currant jelly before filling, or with a thin layer of slightly beaten egg white before baking. I prefer all pies, even fruit pies, to have a prebaked bottom crust. Though many traditional recipes for custard pies don't call for prebaking, they will have soggy bottoms if the shell isn't baked twice, once "blind" (empty) and again after filling.

❧ ITALIAN-STYLE PASTRY FOR TARTS ☙

This recipe is intended for special heavy, open metal forms that are placed on heavy baking tins lined with parchment paper, which do not bend and sway like thin aluminum jelly roll pans. The forms, tins, and parchment paper can be bought in any serious cookware shop. They are worth having if you wish to exhibit your handiwork properly, but, lacking them, you can improvise a tart mold with aluminum foil or create a freeform tart, as described below.

Makes 1 16- by 5-inch oblong tart shell

1 ¼ cups unbleached flour

2 teaspoons sugar

Pinch of salt

¼ pound chilled sweet butter
  (1 stick)

1 egg

1 teaspoon lemon juice

Put the flour, sugar, and salt in the processor bowl. Cut the butter into 8 pieces and add it. Pulse the machine until the butter is cut in coarsely. Add the egg and lemon juice and process briefly. Turn the mass out onto a floured cloth or board, shape it into a ball, flatten it, and wrap in plastic wrap. Refrigerate at least 1 hour, or overnight. (Or freeze the dough for up to three months.)

Remove the dough and let it soften at room temperature for 15 minutes. Now the tricky part: between sheets of plastic wrap, roll out the chilled dough into a rectangle a couple of inches larger than your tart mold. Fit it lightly into the mold and trim to fit. Lacking a mold, cut the pastry into an oblong and build up a border by laying thin strips of pastry brushed with ice water along the sides and ends of the oblong. Press them down lightly and build to a height of three or four strips, gluing them together with egg wash (an egg yolk beaten with a bit of water) as you go. You can also create an oblong tart mold with folded strips of heavy aluminum foil. Prick the pastry well with a table fork and chill in the freezer 10 minutes.

Preheat the oven to 375°F. Line the pastry with oiled aluminum foil and fill with pie weights, dried beans, or raw rice. Bake on the lowest rack of the oven (not the floor) for 15 minutes. Remove the foil and weights and lower the oven temperature to 350°F. Bake for 10 minutes longer. The blind shell should be pale gold, not brown. This very short, crisp crust, can nevertheless support rich cream fillings.

⚹ SHORT PASTRY FOR SWEET ⚹
AND SAVORY FILLINGS

Lard is used in this flaky pastry recipe and it has an excellent flavor, especially for empañadas and other meat pies. Use a larger proportion of lard and less butter for an even flakier crust. Some people object to its slightly meaty taste, but I do not, even in sweet dessert pies. Diet watchers can substitute a hydrogenated vegetable fat such as Crisco for the lard, though the result is not as good. I have no idea what happens if margarine is substituted for the butter—you're on your own. This recipe makes enough pastry for a large 9- to 10-inch double crust pie or a whole lot of meat-filled turnovers or half-moon pies.

2 cups unbleached flour*
1/2 teaspoon salt
1/4 pound chilled sweet butter,
  cut in 8 pieces (1 stick)
3 tablespoons chilled lard, cut in
  4 pieces

2 eggs, beaten with 1 tablespoon
  lemon juice
Ice water (if necessary)

Use the processor technique to cut in the fats, as described (page 221) or put the flour and salt in a large bowl and cut in the butter and lard using 2 table knives in a crisscross action. When the fat is the size of small peas, dribble in the eggs beaten with lemon juice, and lightly and quickly gather the dough together with your finger tips. (The warmth of your hand must not soften the shortenings.) Press the dough into 2 flat balls, then wrap and refrigerate them for at least an hour.

Roll out each ball of dough on a floured pastry cloth with plenty of flour rubbed on the pin, as this dough can be sticky. (It does not matter if the dough absorbs a little

---

*Whole wheat flour adds an interesting flavor, but makes the dough hard to work, so always use it in the proportions of 1 part whole wheat to 3 parts unbleached white flour.

of the extra flour.) Always roll away from your body; after every 2 or 3 strokes with the pin, lift the dough, dust more flour under it, and rotate it a quarter turn. Each round should be a couple of inches larger than the pie plate. Lift the bottom crust and drape it in the pie dish. (If you are making a very large pie, it's best to fold the dough in the center before moving it.) Fill the pie as directed, then cover with the top crust, trim off the excess dough, seal, and crimp the edges.

You can roll out any leftover scraps of dough to make leaves or other decorations. Fasten these to the top crust by dabbing a little egg wash on the back of them. Chill the pie briefly, then brush it with egg wash and bake according to your recipe. The bottom crust will bake crisper if the pie is set on the lowest oven shelf, at least for the first 15 minutes. Turnovers, such as the Mexican meat-filled empañadas, are easiest to bake on parchment paper. Egg-wash glaze gives all pastries a beautiful high gloss, but care must be taken not to brown them too much. If this threatens, cover the pastry loosely with a sheet of foil.

❧ COBBLER DOUGH ❧

This is a rich biscuit to be used as a topping for cobblers or baked in traditional rounds for all sorts of shortcakes. Lindsey R. Shere, head pâtissière at the restaurant Chez Panisse since its opening in Berkeley, California, in 1971, is the source of this recipe, which I have modified very slightly, using sour cream instead of heavy cream (because that's what I had on hand). I liked the result.

1 1/2 cups unbleached flour
1/4 teaspoon salt
2 1/2 teaspoons baking powder
1 1/2 tablespoons sugar

6 tablespoons chilled sweet
   butter, cut into 6 pieces
1/2 cup sour cream

Sift the flour, salt, and baking powder together or blend them in a food processor. Pulse in the sugar, then the butter until it is the size of those peas again. Blend in the sour cream lightly and, handling the dough as little as possible, pat it out on a floured surface to half-inch thickness. Cut out rounds with a small floured glass and lay them on top of your berries or fruit mixture in a gratin dish. The biscuits should not be touching, or they may become soggy. Bake immediately in the center of a 375°F. oven for 30 to 35 minutes. If baking as biscuits, lay the rounds on a parchment-lined baking sheet about 2 inches apart and bake only about 15 minutes, or until pale gold on the outside and dry in the center.

When making several batches of this recipe, you can save time and ingredients by patting the dough out into a rectangle, arranging it on the baking sheet and then cutting it into small squares with a large sharp knife. After baking the biscuits will break apart easily. Biscuits are at their best eaten directly out of the oven, but these can be made, left at room temperature, and reheated in a microwave.

❧ PASTRY CREAM ❧

Pastry cream, or *crème pâtissière,* is one of the most basic building blocks of the pastry maker's art. It is used as the base of fruit tarts, to fill cream puffs, and in many, many classic desserts. Pastry cream is quite simple to make and keeps well in the refrigerator.

Makes about 2 1/2 cups

6 egg yolks
1/3 cup sugar
1/4 cup flour
2 cups milk or light cream, or

use 1 cup heavy cream and 1
cup of milk
1 1/2 teaspoons vanilla extract, or
half a vanilla bean, split

Beat the egg yolks until light; then beat in the sugar gradually. Beat in the flour. Scald the milk (if using the vanilla bean, add its contents and the pod to the milk and remove after steeping it for 10 minutes in the hot milk) and pour it in a stream into the egg mixture, whisking rapidly. When smooth, put it in the top of a double boiler and cook it over barely bubbling water, stirring constantly. This may be cooked faster over direct heat using a moderate flame, stirring constantly with a wooden spoon. Lift the pot from time to time to avoid scrambled eggs in the bottom of the pot. It is done when you can mark a track with your finger drawn across the back of the stirring spoon—it should not be allowed to boil or the yolks will curdle. Beat in the vanilla extract and taste. You may prefer a sweeter pastry cream. Or you might want to flavor it with a liqueur or some melted semi-sweet chocolate.

🌿 CRÈME ANGLAISE (CUSTARD SAUCE) 🌿

The custard sauce, called *crème anglaise* in French (I've always thought this was faintly contemptuous as the French have always maintained that the English have many religions but only one sauce) is a thinner version of *crème pâtissière* and is splendidly complementary to things like apple crisp, gingerbread, various fruit cobblers, or just stewed fruits. Missing for some time in American cookery, I think custard sauce is due for a revival.

About 2 1/2 cups

2 cups milk or half-and-half	*1 teaspoon vanilla extract*
1/4 cup sugar	*1 tablespoon rum, bourbon, or*
4 egg yolks	*cognac*

Scald the milk or half-and-half (a richer sauce). Beat the sugar and egg yolks together well, then beat in the scalded milk with a wooden spoon. (A whisk can raise so much foam that it is impossible to see when the custard has cooked enough.)

Place this in a small saucepan over moderate heat and stir constantly until the mixture thickens. (I use the top of a stainless steel double boiler which has a rounded bottom, thus no crevices for the custard to overcook in—be sure to stir in the corners if using a regular saucepan.) When a trail may be marked on the spoon back with your finger, the custard is done. Set the bottom of the pan in another pan of cold water and stir until the custard ceases cooking—a few minutes. Beat in the vanilla extract and spirits. Pour into a glass or stainless steel container, cover, and refrigerate until needed—it will thicken further when cold.

A lighter, more translucent sauce can be made using the same basic method but a different formula.

🌿 LIGHT CRÈME ANGLAISE 🌿

¹/₂ cup sugar

2 teaspoons arrowroot

2 egg yolks

2 cups milk, scalded

1 teaspoon vanilla

1 tablespoon rum, bourbon, or

    cognac

Mix the sugar and arrowroot together, then whisk in the egg yolks. With the wooden spoon, stir in the scalded milk and cook over a moderate flame a few minutes until the sauce thickens. Do not overcook or the thickening properties of the arrowroot will weaken and the sauce will thin out. Off-heat, flavor the custard sauce with vanilla and whatever spirits you have chosen. Store as in the foregoing recipe. This *crème anglaise* isn't classic (and I will not pretend that it is just as good) but it's a lot easier on the arteries than the emulsion of egg yolks and milk that comes down to us from the time of Careme . . . some of those recipes started with "Beat 32 egg yolks . . ."

⚘ HOT STRAWBERRY DUFF ⚘

Strawberry season is short but vivid. It takes only a couple of beastly thunderstorms to waterlog the fields, so get out there with all hands picking fast. This is the time to enjoy the brief season of strawberry spillover.

My grandmother made hot lattice-top pies from little wild berries gathered in the North Carolina mountains. She made a lot of other things too—the usual hundred or so pints of preserves, and jars of berries mixed with rhubarb for winter pies, ice creams in summer, and fried half-moon pies on her busier days.

Serves 6 to 8

2 pints strawberries

1 cup sugar

1 tablespoon cornstarch

4 tablespoons sweet butter, barely melted (1/2 stick)

BISCUIT DOUGH:

2 cups flour

3 tablespoons sugar

1 tablespoon baking powder

1/2 teaspoon salt

1/4 pound very cold butter (1 stick)

1/3 cup milk

Rinse, drain, and hull the berries, twisting out the cores with the leaves and stems. If large, quarter them. Mix the berries with the sugar and cornstarch and pour into a shallow, ovenproof glass or china casserole. Drizzle the melted butter over the berries.

Preheat the oven to 425°F.

Place the flour, sugar, baking powder, and salt in a food processor workbowl and pulse a few times to mix. Chop the butter into about 8 pieces and add it to the dry ingredients. Pulse off and on until the butter is the size of small peas. Turn into a bowl, add the milk and blend with a spoon. (If you haven't a food processor, cut the butter into the flour the old-fashioned way with criss-crossing table knives.) Drop the batter by spoonfuls onto the berry surface, leaving the shapes rough—they will bake into golden brown, spiky biscuits. Bake with the top of the cobbler in the center of the oven for 20 minutes; cover with loose foil if the biscuits brown too fast. Serve hot or warm, with plain or whipped cream.

Note: The berries should be at warm room temperature, otherwise they will not cook at all in this length of time. To be on the safe side, you can heat them up in a small, heavy saucepan until the juices begin to flow before putting them in the baking dish, which should be rather wide and shallow so that there's plenty of biscuit to soak up the juices.

☀ FRIED HALF-MOON PIES ☀

These have to be filled with fruit cooked to a jammy consistency, as they're too dangerous otherwise (wet mixtures sometimes explode during frying). They're dangerous to have around the house too—irresistible to pick at, since they're "finger food."

Makes 6 to 8

1 recipe Short Pastry (page 163)
1 pound peaches, apricots, or
 plums
Sugar to taste
Pinch of salt

Scant ¼ teaspoon freshly grated
 nutmeg
Juice and grated rind of half a
 lemon
Clarified butter (page 126)

Make the pastry and let it rest, tightly wrapped, in the fridge. Put the fruit (cut in half but with peels and stones intact, as these add greatly to the final flavor) into a small, heavy pot. Stir in sugar to taste—usually about half the weight of the fruit. Cook over low heat until juices run, stirring often. When the fruit is soft and pulpy, add the spices and lemon juice and zest. Turn into a cold shallow dish and pick out the stones, then mash the fruit roughly with a fork. Let cool.

Preheat the oven to 400°F.

Roll out the pastry to ⅛-inch thickness and cut into 5-inch circles. Put a dab of the cool, thick fruit compote in the center, then fold one half of the dough over to meet the other, which has been moistened with cold water. Crimp the edges. Place on a greased jelly roll tin and, when all the pies are made, drizzle melted clarified butter over them. Bake for about 15 minutes, or until crust is pale brown and crisp. In the original recipe, these half-moon pies were fried in something like Crisco in a cast-iron skillet. This technique is very tricky, as the pies sometimes leak their filling and this causes the frying fat to explode—but if you're brave, go ahead and try it. In winter, fried pies are delicious made with a compote of dried apricots, apples, or pears.

❧ CHOCOLATE CHINCHILLA MOUSSE ❧

A "chinchilla" used to mean any dessert made with whipped egg whites. This is a light, simple, relatively low-cal chocolate mousse, owing to the absence of egg yolks and flour. It is, in fact, mostly air, and must be served rapidly or turned out after it is cold—but then it is collapsed, of course. Served hot with barely whipped brandied cream it is divine.

6 to 7 egg whites, at room
   temperature
Pinch of cream of tartar
1/3 cup unsweetened cocoa
   powder

1/2 cup sugar
1/2 teaspoon ground cinnamon
1 tablespoon instant espresso
   powder

Preheat oven to 350°F.

Butter a 1 1/2-quart soufflé dish or tube pan and coat with superfine sugar. Chill. Beat egg whites with the cream of tartar until stiff. Sift the cocoa, sugar, cinnamon, and espresso powder together, then return it to the sifter. Sift over the egg whites and fold in by halves. With a broad rubber spatula, scrape this mixture into the buttered and sugared mold and set into another pan half filled with hot water. Bake in the lower third of the oven for 45 minutes. Rush the soufflé to the table and pass some lightly whipped heavy cream, with a little rum or brandy added.

To serve the chinchilla cold, let it cool to room temperature, then turn it out onto a round platter. Decorate with stiffly beaten whipped cream forced through a star tube or other fancy tip of a pastry bag.

⚘ BUTTERMILK PIE ⚘

An old Southern "hard times" pie seldom seen anymore, this country dessert is simply wonderful in good times or bad. You can use a little less sugar or reduce the amount of butter somewhat to suit your taste or the times. Haters of buttermilk can rest assured that a light tartness is the only vestige of it that remains in the finished pie.

Makes a 9-inch pie

1 prebaked 9-inch pie shell (pages 220)
2 tablespoons flour
1¼ cups sugar
Pinch of salt
¼ pound melted sweet butter (1 stick)

3 large eggs
1 cup buttermilk
1 teaspoon vanilla
Freshly grated nutmeg

Bake the pie crust "blind" until it is crisp and pale (use lard or solid vegetable shortening such as Crisco for optimum flakiness). Cool and freeze if you want to get this step out of the way in advance. The filling must not be baked in the shell until the day it is to be served, but the frozen prebaked shell need not be thawed before filling.

Preheat oven to 350°F.

Blend flour and sugar with salt, then whisk in the melted butter (it should be just liquified, not sizzling). Beat the eggs and whisk them in, then add the buttermilk, the vanilla, and a few gratings of nutmeg. Pour into the baked pie shell, grate some nutmeg over the surface, and place the pie on a heavy baking sheet (to prevent the already-baked shell from burning). Slide it into the lower third of the oven and bake about 1 hour, or until a knife inserted in the center comes out clean. Cool on a wire rack and serve at room temperature. Any leftover pie may be refrigerated, but the texture becomes denser.

🌿 SIESTA KEY MOUSSE 🌿

Some friends lent me a house one winter on the Gulf Coast of Florida. To celebrate their homecoming (and repossession of their house), I left this dessert in their fridge. I'd gone a little berserk in the orange groves and had, just *had,* to use up some of my fridge-full of tree-ripened oranges. They are incredibly different from those we usually can buy, which are picked somewhat green and sent on a long journey by refrigerated boxcar. Like avocados, they ripen after picking, but also like avocados, their flavor is best if left longer on the tree. The recipe almost fills a 6-cup mold.

Serves 6 to 8

1 1/2 envelopes (1 1/2 tablespoons) unflavored gelatin

3/4 cup fresh orange juice with pulp, or substitute 2 tablespoons frozen concentrate mixed with 1/2 cup cold water

Thin rind of 1 orange, cut in fine julienne

1/2 cup sugar mixed with 1/2 cup water

2 cups ricotta cheese

1 cup sour cream

1/2 cup heavy cream, whipped

1 navel orange

Cointreau

Almond slices or slivers

Soak the gelatin in the orange juice for 5 minutes, then warm it just enough to dissolve the gelatin. Stir well and cool to tepid. Sauté the orange rind in a little butter and sugar until it caramelizes slightly—this burns easily, so be careful. Add the sugar-water and simmer until the orange rind is tender.

Beat the ricotta smooth and blend in the sour cream, orange juice and gelatin, and the orange rind and syrup. Finally, fold in the whipped cream and scrape it all into a 6-cup oiled mold—fluted or melon-shaped, but not a ring. Lightly press plastic wrap onto the surface of the orange creme and seal it over the edges so that other fridge flavors can't penetrate. Chill overnight or up to 4 days.

Peel and section the orange, ridding it of all skin and pith. Put the sections into a small dish with enough Cointreau to bathe them in, cover, and refrigerate until serving time. (You can substitute canned mandarin orange segments, well drained.) Toast the almonds not too long before serving the dessert.

Dip the mold in hot water, put a plate over it, and invert; if you're lucky, the molded creme will drop onto it. If not, try again. Decorate with the macerated orange slices and toasted almonds. Some kind of thin, crisp sugar cookie is nice with this. Although this mousse doesn't depend on seasonal fruit (oranges seem to make it through plague and drought somehow) it seems, in its lightness, to go especially well with summer meals. The dessert is only faintly sweet and fills the place of both the cheese and dessert courses. In August, try making it with fresh peaches.

⚡ CHEESE PUDDING ⚡

This is a Passover dessert from *Jewish Cookery* by Leah W. Leonard, originally published in 1949, reprinted by Crown in 1977. This basic Jewish cookbook contains all the best known traditional dishes from Europe, as well as American-Jewish Kentucky Fried Chicken and homemade peach butter. I have added the dried cherries in Kirsch; otherwise the recipe is unchanged. Use a 9-inch square Pyrex cake pan.

Serves 8

4 matzohs

1 pound dry cottage cheese

4 eggs

2 cups milk

Grated rind and juice of 1 lemon

¾ cup sugar

1 teaspoon salt

1 cup dried Montmorency
    cherries, soaked overnight (or
    longer) in Kirsch to cover

Soak the matzohs in lukewarm water to cover for 15 minutes. Drain them and care-fully press out the excess moisture, so as not to break the matzohs. Generously butter a 9-inch square, deep cake pan. Place 1 matzoh in the bottom of the pan and spread it with a third of the cheese. Add another matzoh and spread with cheese, the third matzoh and more cheese, and finally, the fourth matzoh. Beat the eggs with the milk, lemon rind and juice, sugar, and salt. Pour over the cheese and matzohs. Bake at 375°F. for 45 minutes or until firm. Serve warm or cold, cut in squares, with a spoonful of macerated cherries on each serving.

🌿 ALMOND CRÈME CHANTILLY 🌿

Crème chantilly means slightly whipped cream in classic French cookery, but this one is firmed up with unflavored gelatin. It's a lovely, airy, almond confection that actually improves overnight, so make it a day before it's to be served.

1 cup whole or chopped blanched almonds

1 cup milk, scalded

2 egg yolks

1/2 cup sugar

Pinch of salt

1 envelope unflavored gelatin

1/4 cup cold milk

1 or 2 leaves rose geranium (optional)

1 tablespoon rose flower water

1 cup whipping cream

1/4 teaspoon almond extract, or more

Rose geranium leaves, almond slices, raspberries, or halved strawberries (choose one only)

Toast the almonds in a dry heavy skillet over low heat for 5 minutes, stirring them once or twice. Cool them and grind in a food processor. Steep the ground almonds in the scalding hot milk for at least an hour, covered. Reheat to scalding.

Beat the egg yolks with the sugar and salt, beat in the scalding almond milk, and cook over low heat in a very heavy saucepan until the custard coats a spoon. (Do not boil or the yolks will curdle.) Remove from heat.

Soften the gelatin in the cold milk for 5 minutes, then stir into the hot custard along with a rose geranium leaf or two, if desired, and the rose flower water. Set aside to cool or stir over ice until cold, which is much quicker and keeps the custard smooth. Whip the cream until fairly stiff and flavor with almond extract to taste. Remove the geranium leaves and discard. Fold the whipped cream into the cooled custard, turn it into 6 individual coupe glasses or a single glass bowl, cover with plastic wrap, and chill overnight. Just before serving, decorate the dessert with whichever garnish you have chosen.

❧ CREMETS D'ANGERS ❧

This is a very old French farm dessert that is easy to produce with no notice (if you live on a farm—otherwise it means a little shopping). It is simply fresh cream cheese lightened with egg whites and served with fruit or jam, or just more heavy cream.

Serves 4

1 cup heavy cream
2 egg whites

Coarse brown sugar, jam, or
plain cream

Whip the cream until stiff, then whip the egg whites with a clean beater in a separate bowl, until stiff. Fold the two together, then turn the mixture into a small basket lined with wet cheesecloth. Set this over a bowl, cover the "cremet," and let drain overnight. This is much prettier if you have little individual round or heart-shaped baskets to work with. If you don't, though, just cut the cremet in 4 wedges and serve with brown sugar and cream or with some good fresh jam or berries.

❧ FARMER CHEESE WITH SEEDLESS GRAPES ❧

Unexciting though this may sound, fresh white farmer cheese (which is not the same as "cream cheese") served with a glittering bunch of red or green seedless grapes makes a surprisingly satisfactory ending to a dieter's meal.

❧ LEMON TEA CAKE ❧
(GÂTEAU AU CITRON)

A version of this quick little cake was included in the very first Cuisinart pamphlet cookbook that came with the machine. It can be made, start to finish, in about 1 hour and makes a great little gift. It's very lemony—drenched in lemon juice along with some Cointreau, *after* baking. If I were only permitted one cake for the rest of my life, this might be it. It is beguiling with almost any kind of ice cream or sherbet and wonderful with just a cup of tea.

Makes an 8-inch square cake

Grated rind of 1 lemon and 1
   orange (optional)
½ cup sugar
¼ pound unsalted butter (1
   stick)
2 large eggs
1 teaspoon baking powder

Juice of 1 lemon
1 cup less 2 tablespoons
   all-purpose or cake flour
1 tablespoon Cointreau, Triple
   Sec, or Grand Marnier
½ cup confectioners' sugar

Preheat oven to 350°F. Butter and flour an 8-inch cake pan or, better, a small loaf or fancy flute pan of equal volume. Place the grated lemon and, optional, orange zest in the work bowl of a food processor with the sugar. Process 20 seconds. Add the butter, cut in quarters, then the eggs, one at a time. Process in pulses for about 15 seconds, until smooth. Scrape down the sides.

Mix the baking powder into the flour. Add this to the processor, distributing it around evenly. Cover and pulse *only* until flour disappears—2 or 3 times. Further action will produce a tough cake. (This cake is like a quick bread—quick cake!)

Bake the cake on the center rack of the oven for about 25 minutes. (The exact time will depend on the depth of the pan; test by inserting a skewer, it should come out clean. Remove and cool in the pan for 5 minutes, then turn out onto a rack to finish cooling. Mix together the lemon juice, confectioners' sugar and liqueur. Prick the cold cake all over with the sharp tines of a long cooking fork. Dribble the lemon juice mixture over the surface, then turn the cake over and do a second side as well, so that the cake is completely penetrated. Wrap in plastic and refrigerate, unless the cake is to be eaten the same day. This cake keeps well for several days, but it should always be served at room temperature. It is excellent plain, but really entrancing with a blumpf of whipped cream. It's an oddity, both rich and sharp tasting.

🌾 OLD-FASHIONED LEMON TARTS 🐿

This is a very old favorite that seems to be making a comeback. It has many variants, but the recipe I like best comes from an entry by Jack Lenor Larsen in the Guild Hall cookbook, *Palettes on Palates*. The tarts are riveting. Sophisticates slaver over them. These tarts are twice baked: First the crust, then the filling. They can be made one day ahead if the weather isn't too humid. They do not freeze well . . . although they are still delicious, the crust does not stay crisp. But they do stay wonderful for two or three days in the fridge, if they ever last that long.

1/2 pound cold sweet butter　　　　*all-purpose flour plus 1/2 cup*
　(2 sticks)　　　　　　　　　　　*cake flour*
1/2 cup confectioners' sugar　　　　*Pinch of salt*
2 cups flour, or 1 1/2 cups

Cut the butter into eighths and put it into a food processor with the sugar, flour, and salt. Pulse to a rough dough, remove, and quickly knead together lightly on a cold floured surface. Wrap in plastic and chill.

Preheat the oven to 350°F.

Roll out between two sheets of floured plastic wrap or carefully pat out onto a greased, oblong baking pan, 7½ by 11 inches, or a bit larger, and bake for 15 minutes. Cool thoroughly. The pastry should be pale gold—shield it with a loose covering of foil if it starts to brown. (If using a convection oven, bake at 325°F.)

FILLING

4 extra-large eggs, beaten
2 cups sugar
¼ cup flour

6 tablespoons lemon juice and
the grated rind of 3 lemons

Preheat oven to 350°F.

Beat all the filling ingredients together. Pour over the baked crust. Return to the lower third of the oven for about 20 minutes or just until set. Remove and let cool completely. When cold, cut into 2-inch squares, dipping the knife in hot water if necessary. A very thin white crust will form over the tart.

If desired, sift a light snow of confectioners' sugar over the squares after they have been cut and put on wire racks. If they must be refrigerated—with this egg content, they should be refrigerated if not to be served the same day—store them on tissue paper arranging them in a single layer.

🌿 PEACH SHORTCAKE 🌿

I'm amazed that this great American classic is so seldom seen anymore—especially in August when fragrant peaches beckon from farmstands and are cheap and lovely even in supermarkets. Perhaps it's because the knack of skinning peaches is one of those kitchen skills that got lost in the rush to canned and frozen products. It's as simple as skinning a tomato (or onion): Drop ripe peaches, a few at a time, into boiling water. Remove after 15 seconds to a basin of ice water to prevent cooking. Make an incision along the natural dividing line of the peach, slip off the skins, halve and stone them, and turn the halves around in water acidulated with lemon juice to prevent them from discoloring.

1 large peach per person
1 teaspoon sugar per peach
1 teaspoon bourbon per peach
Hot biscuits (homemade, from
*   ready-to-bake canned dough, or*
*   bought)*

Whipped cream
Spearmint sprigs or peach leaves
*   for garnish (optional)*

Skin and slice the peaches, then mix them with the sugar and bourbon. Split and butter the hot biscuits and divide the peaches between the bottom layer and the top layer. Stack the layers and garnish with lots of whipped cream and top with spearmint sprigs (peach leaves are pretty, if you should have some).

⚘ BAKED PEACHES AND CREAM ⚘

A simple, good country dessert to make when the peach crop is in. Allow 1 large or 2 medium peaches per serving. Skin, stone, and slice the peaches. Drop them into acidulated water as you work, to keep them from darkening. Arrange them in a buttered gratin dish, sprinkle with sugar mixed with half as much soft, fresh white breadcrumbs, and dot liberally with butter. Bake in the center of a preheated 350°F. oven until peaches are tender. Sprinkle with brown sugar and glaze under the broiler. Serve with a spoonful of brandied whipped cream.

⚘ PEACH AND GREENGAGE TART ⚘

Good peaches are obligingly available where I live, but greengages (large, pale green, yellow-fleshed plums) are rare. The jade green of the greengages combines well with rosy yellow peaches in this elegant tart. If you can't find any greengages, use another large, ripe plum in their stead.

1 1-pound package frozen puff
  pastry, defrosted
2 cups Pastry Cream (page 227)
3 medium peaches
3 or 4 greengages

Approximately 2 tablespoons
  granulated sugar
2 cups whipped cream
Sugar and Mirabelle eau de vie

Preheat the oven to 375°F. Roll out the puff pastry and cut it to fit either a long oblong or round tart ring. Put the ring on a heavy baking sheet and fit the pastry in, cutting the edges off evenly. Bake until pale and crisp in the center of the oven. Cool.

Make the Pastry Cream and line the tart shell with it. Slice the peaches and greengages and lay them in alternate clumps the length of the shell. Sprinkle with sugar and glaze very briefly under the broiler. Remove at once and chill. Serve with whipped cream flavored to taste with sugar and a tablespoon or so of Mirabelle (a superlative Alsatian *eau de vie* made from small yellow plums).

☆ CLASSIC STRAWBERRY SHORTCAKE ☆

Strawberry shortcake, pure and simply made with berries, biscuits, and sweetened whipped cream, must be reiterated from time to time lest a great dish strays too far from its roots. The Presbyterian Church in East Hampton has a "strawberry tea" every June and that's really the way to eat this dessert: at mid-afternoon, with tea or coffee. When making biscuits from scratch seems too much like work, use one of the ready-to-bake biscuit doughs that come in 10-to-a-tube in the refrigerated case in supermarkets.

Serves 5 to 10

10 hot biscuits
10 pats sweet butter
2 cups chopped fresh
strawberries
2 tablespoons superfine white
sugar

4 cups lightly sweetened whipped
cream
10 whole strawberries

Have all ingredients ready before baking the biscuits. While they're hot, split and butter them and cover until the butter is melted. Sweeten the chopped strawberries with the sugar a little in advance—not too long, however, because the sugar draws the juice from the berries. Ladle on the berries, put the tops of biscuits back on, and slather, really lavishly, with whipped cream. Top each biscuit construction with 1 perfect whole berry.

☙ CHOCOLATE BAVARIAN MOUSSE OR PIE ❧

Bavarois is a classic of traditional French cooking, a relic of a more generous age (both in figures and in desserts), and it remains a big hit with me. Friends love being forced to eat this. You can serve it in little soufflé dishes, a large fancy mold turned out, or piled high into a crisp baked pie shell. As there is bit too much for 1 pie, you'll have a lagniappe for somebody.

For a 2-quart mold or 10-inch shell

2 envelopes unflavored gelatin
1/2 cup cold espresso or milk
1 2/3 cups milk
8 ounces semi-sweet chocolate, or
   6 ounces semi-sweet and 2
   ounces bitter chocolate
2/3 cup sugar
8 egg yolks

1 teaspoon vanilla or a split
   vanilla bean soaked in brandy
Cognac or other liqueur to taste
1 cup chilled heavy cream
Sifted cocoa
5 egg whites
Pinch of salt
1/4 teaspoon cream of tartar

Make the custard base: Sprinkle the gelatin over the cold espresso or milk. Heat the 1 2/3 cups milk slowly with the chocolate, broken in small pieces, in a small, heavy pot until the chocolate melts. Beat the sugar with the egg yolks until thick. Slowly add the chocolate and milk mixture to the sugar and yolks, whisking constantly, or use an electric mixer with the balloon whip.

    Cook, stirring constantly with a wooden spoon, over medium heat in a heavy-bottomed pan until the custard thickens enough to coat a metal spoon. (Do not allow the custard to boil or the eggs will curdle, and this cannot be undone.) Stir to cool for a minute or so, off the heat, then stir in the softened gelatin and blend well. Stir in the vanilla and any liqueur you like—cognac, Kahlua, and rum are all compatible with chocolate.

Whip the heavy cream until doubled in volume but not rigid. In a separate bowl with clean beaters, whip the egg whites stiff with the salt and cream of tartar. Fold the egg whites into the warm custard, then cool this mixture completely by folding it up and over while the bowl is set in a basin of ice mixed with a little salt and water. Fold half the whipped cream into the custard base. Flavor the other half with additional liqueur and a little sugar, if desired, and set aside to use as a garnish.

Either fill a prebaked pie shell with this Bavarian cream or turn it into a 2-quart soufflé dish. Chill for at least 4 hours (and up to 24 hours) before unmolding. To serve as a "soufflé," choose a small deep soufflé dish (3 inches deep by 7 inches in diameter), heightened with a foil or wax paper collar tied around the rim to make the "soufflé" rise 2 or 3 inches above the rim of the dish. Just before serving, sprinkle the "soufflé" with a little sifted cocoa. This presentation is easier than having to unmold the dessert at the last minute and decorate it with whipped cream, but the soufflé is not so attractive when scooped out onto a plate as are the neatly unmolded slices topped with whipped cream.

FROZEN DESSERTS

THE COLD FACTS

When this basic recipe of mine was developed (in 1980 for an article in *The New York Times*), ingredients came to under two dollars for half a gallon of vanilla ice cream. Food prices have gone up and down (mostly up) since then, but this excellent ice cream, pure and homemade, varied with any fresh, seasonal fruit, is a bargain in quality anyway. Commercial ice creams—often more than 50 percent air—range from *el cheapos,* constructed of God knows what, to the creamiest grand luxe compositions at princely prices. Homemade "from scratch" ice cream is far richer with an overrun (air percentage) of only about 20 to 30 percent.

Unfortunately, high price is not a guarantee of quality—even if ice creams are made of premium ingredients, they are often stored too long. In chichi little ice cream boutiques, I've often noticed a distinct "off" taste to pistachio, a favorite of mine, but not a best seller. Especially when buying from bulk ice cream bins it's probably wise to stick with buying the top-of-the-charts flavors at high turnover stores.

You'll never be disappointed if you make your own ice cream and you don't need an expensive machine either. For many years I've used an inexpensive electric machine that requires only table salt and ice cubes to turn out 2 quarts of splendid ice cream in about 30 minutes. When using machines that require salt, keep in mind that too much salt causes the ice cream to freeze too fast and makes it grainy, too little salt slows the process—you will have creamy ice cream but it may have an excessive overrun (percentage of air) and will not firm up. Undeniably, these machines are messier (although larger and the results more predictable) and more trouble than the nifty little freon-lined machine (called "Wizard," similar to the better known "Donvier") I have recently acquired. It demands 12 hours chilling in the freezer, but plug it in and *voila!* you get 1½ quarts of ice cream in about 45 minutes. With an extra freezing chamber you can have the capacity to make ice cream for a party without the inconvenience of starting the project 3 days in advance. Although, come to think of it, making the dessert course way in advance has its merits. Homemade ice cream is best eaten within 24 hours but is okay for a week before the flavor deteriorates.

Some expensive state-of-the-art ice cream machines are limited to making only 1 quart at a time, but can be used continuously. I grew up in a region where no one ever considered making less than a gallon. Of course, I'll have to admit that ice-cream making then was a very big, messy undertaking, so little bits weren't feasible. (I've still got one of those massive old ice-cream churns that I simply can't discard—inexplicable but for nostalgia.)

Do not reduce the sugar—I've already done that—in these recipes, or your ice cream will taste flat and bland. The mixture before freezing always tastes a little too sweet. The gelatin stabilizes the melting point of the ice cream and smooths the texture by preventing the formation of large ice crystals. (This can be caused by overchurning too.) Automatic turn-offs fail often (in my experience), so keep a timer on the churning duration recommended by the manufacturer. The recipes in this chapter demonstrate most of the techniques and various formulas for ice-cream making. The yield is difficult to reckon as so many things can affect it: the coldness of the ingredients, the temperature of the kitchen, the performance of each type of ice-cream machine, so yields are approximate to the nearest cup in the following recipes.

🌿 GREAT VANILLA ICE CREAM 🌿

Vanilla is always in season, and is basis of all fruit flavors. It's necessarily the starting point of any ice-cream making career—which, once begun, soon becomes a passion. Pomegranates, passion fruit, and exotic melons all are fodder for the imaginative (some say obsessed) ice-cream and sorbet designer. The gelatin enhances the smoothness of the ice cream, but it can be omitted if you prefer. You can make an almost equally creamy but lower-calorie "ice milk" with this recipe substituting milk for the half-and-half or light cream.

Makes 2 quarts (approximately)

¼ cup cold milk
1 envelope unflavored gelatin
  (optional)
4 extra-large or jumbo egg yolks
1 cup sugar

½ vanilla bean or 2 teaspoons
  vanilla extract
2 cups half-and-half
Pinch of salt
2 cups heavy cream

Pour the milk in a small bowl, add gelatin, and set aside to dissolve. Beat the egg yolks with the sugar until light. Split the vanilla bean and scrape its contents into the half-and-half, then add the pod halves. Bring it to the boiling point and cover to steep off-heat for 10 minutes. (You may wish to use more or less of the bean as vanilla beans vary wildly; they are native to Mexico—the cured seed pods of an orchid species—but some of the biggest and best pods, 8 to 10 inches long, come from Tahiti.) Remove, rinse, and dry the vanilla bean for another use (e.g., bury it in sugar to use for baking or pour vodka or brandy on the split bean and store it in a small bottle to make your own vanilla "extract"). Add a pinch of salt to the yolks and sugar and beat the hot vanilla cream into them with a whisk. Cook over moderate heat in a heavy saucepan, stirring constantly, until the custard coats a wooden spoon. This stage is reached when a finger drawn across the spoon leaves a definite trail. Overcooking or too high heat will cause this to curdle irredeemably, so slow and easy does it.

If used, beat in the softened gelatin until thoroughly dissolved in the hot custard, then stir in the heavy cream (and vanilla extract if a bean wasn't available). Cover with plastic wrap laid directly on the surface of the custard to prevent a skin forming. Seal thoroughly to ward off any refrigerator odors that could invade the delicate custard/ cream. Chill thoroughly, then whisk smooth again and pour into the ice-cream churn. Freeze according to the manufacturer's directions.

Homemade ice cream is very soft and needs to be stored (airtight of course) in the freezer for a couple of hours to firm and mellow it before serving.

Besides tasting flat, insufficiently sweetened ice creams are apt to develop large ice crystals from the mixture freezing too fast. Remember that freezing vitiates all flavors.

☙ LIGHT VANILLA ICE CREAM ☙

Make Great Vanilla Ice Cream (page 251) substituting plain whole milk or low-fat milk for the cream and half-and-half in the recipe. You can replace ¼ cup of the sugar with honey or white corn syrup, but these two items are still sugar though in another form.

The villains in rich, luxurious ice cream are the egg yolks and cream but this "lean" version of vanilla ice cream is still fairly irresistible.

To make "anyberry" ice cream—actually ice milk or sherbet—replace 1 cup of milk with 1 cup of pureed or well-mashed ripe berries of your choice. Freeze according to the manufacturer's directions.

⚜ PHILADELPHIA VANILLA ICE CREAM ⚜

The "City of Brotherly Love" claims to be the birthplace of ice cream in the Colonies though there were already ice-cream parlours in New York City in 1770. But "Philadelphia" ice cream has become a generic term for ice creams made solely of frozen pure cream. It is a lovely dessert and while it lacks a certain *je ne sais quoi,* "Philadelphia" ice cream is certainly the simplest of all ice-cream formulas. Ice cream of some sort is recorded in Chinese gastronomy over three thousand years ago so they really beat the world on inventing what has come to be regarded as a quintessentially "American" food.

Makes 1 1/2 quarts

1 cup superfine sugar   *Dash of salt*
1 quart heavy cream   *2 teaspoons vanilla extract*

Stir the sugar into the cream along with a dash of salt and the vanilla extract. Pour it into an ice-cream maker and freeze according to the manufacturer's directions.

☙ BARBADOS NUTMEG ICE CREAM WITH RUM ❧

Make Great Vanilla Ice Cream (page 251) and add ½ teaspoon of freshly grated nutmeg to the custard while it is cooking. This is a large amount of nutmeg—the greatest quantity of that ebullient spice you're ever likely to use in any one recipe; it was more popular in many dishes a few centuries ago. Beautiful people of the Elizabethan era carried their own silver graters.

After the ice cream is scooped, either individually or mounded up in a crystal bowl, heat a large ladle containing about 2 jiggers of Barbados's Mount Gay Eclipse rum (or look out for some Cockspur, another great Bajun rum), set it alight and "flambé" your nutmeg ice cream. I've tried adding spirits to ice creams and it has very little effect on the flavor and inhibits the freezing process as well. Add any spirits you fancy to vanilla ice cream, but pour it on at the last minute. Chartreuse and crème de menthe go back to the dawn of American ice cream. Try out the Italian nut liqueurs Nocelle (walnut) and Frangelico (hazelnut) for an out-of-the-way ice cream trip. My favorite spirits toppings are the Alsatian and Swiss *eaux de vie* such as Poire, Kirsch, Framboise, and Mirabelle.

❧ BLUEBERRY ICE CREAM ❧
WITH MIRABELLE CREAM

There is no gainsaying the drab blue of blueberry ice cream but its flavor is simply astonishing. Here we will hide its color, until people get used to it, under a cloak of whipped cream studded with blueberries and flavored with Mirabelle, a miraculous *eau de vie* distilled in Alsace from small yellow plums. Small wild blueberries are best (the canned wild berries from Maine are fine out of season); very large cultivated blueberries may need a short ride in the food processor to avoid large frozen lumps in the finished ice cream.

Makes 1 1/2 quarts

4 extra large egg yolks
1 cup sugar
3 cups half-and-half
1 teaspoon vanilla extract
1 envelope unflavored gelatin
  (optional)

1 1/2 cups fresh small blueberries
Whipped cream, lighty sweetened
  with sugar and flavored with
  Mirabelle
Blueberries, for garnish

Whisk the egg yolks with ¾ cup sugar. Scald the half-and-half and beat it into the egg mixture. Cook until thickened, then add the vanilla. (At this point you may add a package of softened gelatin if you like the very smooth *gelato* texture it gives.) Sprinkle the blueberries with the remaining ¼ cup sugar and heat them in a skillet until they burst, shaking the skillet fairly often. Stir this into the custard mixture and chill it thoroughly. Freeze according to the manufacturer's directions.

To serve, scoop out the ice cream into wine glasses and cover with a blanket of lightly sweetened whipped cream, flavored with a generous lashing of Mirabelle, then topped with a spoonful of fresh blueberries.

CANTALOUPE ICE CREAM WITH RASPBERRIES

Raspberries are like the Scarlet Pimpernel in my region—appearing suddenly and disappearing equally suddenly. Blackberries—even rarer nowadays—are beautiful with this melon ice cream, but so are good fresh peaches, which are much more accessible for a much longer period in summer. When our local crop of sweet cantaloupes are in, I puree and freeze a few quarts to enjoy a summer flavor in winter.

Makes 1 1/2 quarts

1 large cantaloupe
1 cup superfine sugar
3 cups heavy cream
1/8 teaspoon grated nutmeg

Pinch of salt
Raspberries or blackberries, or
  fresh peach slices

Select a ripe melon, halve and seed it, then puree the flesh. Measure out 2 cups and combine it with the sugar, cream, nutmeg, and salt. Pour it into an ice-cream maker and freeze according to the manufacturer's directions. After it has firmed up and ripened for at least 6 hours, serve in large wine glasses with a spoonful of fresh raspberries or blackberries on top. Lacking berries, the taste and texture of ripe peaches are surprisingly amenable to cantaloupe ice cream and the pale colors complement each other. Frozen berries are a reasonable substitution if the brief berry season has passed.

✻ PISTACHIO ICE CREAM/RASPBERRY PUREE ✻ WITH FRAMBOISE

Fresh pistachio nuts—the best come from Lebanon—make the best ice cream, of course. Despite the wars in the Middle East, the pistachio connection seems unbroken and good ones are fairly easy to get. Freeze them when you find a supply and they will stay fresh for months.

Makes 2 quarts

1 cup shelled pistachio nuts	*1 cup sugar*
2 tablespoons butter	*1/2 teaspoon almond extract*
2 cups half-and-half	*1 teaspoon vanilla extract*
4 egg yolks	*2 cups heavy cream*

Chop the nuts coarsely, then toast them in the butter in a heavy skillet. Empty them into the half-and-half in a saucepan and bring this to a simmer. Turn off heat and steep for 10 minutes. Beat the yolks with the sugar, then beat in the half-and-half and stir constantly over moderate heat until the custard thickens enough to coat the spoon. Beat in the almond and vanilla extract, then the heavy cream. Chill well and freeze according to the manufacturer's directions. A few drops of green food coloring will turn this a pale celadon green that is traditional for pistachio because the nutmeats are greenish.

RASPBERRY SAUCE WITH FRAMBOISE

If fresh raspberries are unavailable—as is usually the case—buy two boxes of frozen raspberries and stir into them, when thawed, about 1/4 cup of Framboise. Add no sugar. If you have fresh raspberries you will need an extravagant-but-worth-it quart of berries. For 8 ice cream servings, reserve 24 whole berries and coarsely mash the remainder. Lightly sugar them and refrigerate. Just before serving, stir in ¼ cup of Framboise and ladle on the ice cream. Decorate each serving with 3 whole raspberries. Serve some plain sugar cookies that do not distract the palate's perception of this marvelous ice-cream dessert.

⚘ CHOCOLATE ICE CREAM ⚘

Chocolate ice cream can be made by melting 6 ounces of semi-sweet chocolate in 1 cup of cream, then adding it to the hot custard in the recipe for Great Vanilla Ice Cream (page 251). Serve to those who concentrate on chocolate with a fulfilling:

BITTERSWEET CHOCOLATE RUM SAUCE

Buy the best quality semi-sweet dark chocolate you can find, as the flaws of cheap chocolate will be all too apparent in this warm sauce.

Makes about 1¼ cups

4 ounces dark semi-sweet
  chocolate
2 tablespoons sweet butter

¼ cup heavy cream
2 teaspoons rum

Melt the chocolate, cut in small pieces, in a heavy saucepan with the butter (or melt it in a dish in a microwave), then thoroughly blend in the cream and finally the rum. Serve warm over ice cream. If not all used, it should be refrigerated. (I have given this to friends at Christmas, warning them on the gift tag that it needs refrigeration.)

❧ GEORGIA PEACH ICE CREAM ❧
WITH WHITE CHOCOLATE SAUCE

Make Great Vanilla Ice Cream (page 251). Skin, stone, and mash 3 medium-large ripe peaches, about 1 pound. Add the juice of half a lemon to prevent discoloration as you work with the peaches. Puree the peaches in a food processor for best results. Chill thoroughly. Fold the pureed fruit into the vanilla ice cream when it is almost frozen. Freeze according to manufacturer's directions. The addition of the peach puree will increase the volume of the ice cream so divide the recipe if necessary to meet the capacity of your ice-cream maker.

WHITE CHOCOLATE SAUCE

The flavor of this pale sauce is a delicious surprise on the pale peach ice cream. It goes equally well, however, with a dark chocolate ice cream.

Makes about 1 cup

6 ounces white chocolate   *1 teaspoon vanilla extract*
1/2 cup heavy cream

Melt the white chocolate in the heavy cream in a heavy saucepan, then blend in the vanilla extract. Serve warm. Add almond extract and a tablespoon of white rum or cognac to vary the sauce if you like.

⚜ PEACH SHERBET WITH PEACH PUREE ⚜ AND BOURBON

Particularly invigorating on a hot August day, peach sherbet is rare commercially and well worth making at home when orchards are full of ripe peaches.

Makes about 2 quarts

3 cups fresh peach puree
Juice of half a lemon
3/4 cup superfine sugar, or

granulated sugar
2 cups milk
1/2 teaspoon almond extract

Skin, peel, and puree enough ripe peaches to make 3 cups of puree (about 4 medium-large peaches). Have the lemon juice waiting in a bowl as you skin and stone each peach, then cut it into quarters before pureeing in a processor. Stir in the sugar, then the cold milk. If you are using granulated sugar, melt it first in 1 cup of the milk stirred over heat. Add the remaining cup of cold milk to cool the mixture, which should be cold before it is added to the peach puree. Stir in the almond extract and chill the mixture thoroughly. Freeze according to the manufacturer's directions.

PEACH PUREE WITH BOURBON

If you've ever wondered how intense the flavor of peaches could be, here's the answer in a sophisticated sauce to pour over peach sherbet.

Makes about 2 cups

3 large, ripe peaches
Juice of 1/2 lemon
1/2 to 3/4 cup superfine sugar

1/4 cup best-quality bourbon
(Wild Turkey)

Skin, stone, and slice peaches into the lemon juice. Puree in a food processor adding sugar to taste. You will need more or less depending on the condition of the fruit. Stir in the bourbon and serve the sauce at room temperature over peach sherbet. The sauce is also marvelous with peach or vanilla ice cream.

✑ BLACK WALNUT ICE CREAM ✎
WITH TIA MARIA SAUCE

The intriguing flavor of black walnuts is a frequent addition to all kinds of Southern desserts. Black walnuts have a unique taste that makes them well worth the searching it takes to find them. (I keep some in my freezer because I always buy more than I need wherever I find them).

Makes about 2 quarts

*1 cup finely chopped black
   walnuts*
2 tablespoons sweet butter

*1 recipe Great Vanilla Ice Cream
   (page 251)*

If you are using a food processor to chop the nuts, take care that it doesn't turn to walnut butter. Chop the nuts in short pulses, then stir them into the butter which has been melted in a heavy skillet. Stir, over medium heat, toasting the nuts, for about 2 minutes. Add these to the vanilla ice cream when it is almost finished churning. Serve with Walnut and Tia Maria Sauce spooned over each portion. The translucent sauce over the creamy white nut-flecked ice cream is beautiful.

WALNUT AND TIA MARIA SAUCE

Makes about 1 1/2 cups

1 cup broken black walnut meats
2 tablespoons sweet butter

1/4 cup white corn syrup
1/4 cup Tia Maria

Pick over the walnuts for shell fragments, then stir them into the butter, which has been melted in a heavy skillet. Stir over medium heat until they are toasted, about 2 minutes. Blend in the corn syrup and Tia Maria. Serve warm.

🌿 TUILES (''TILES'') FOR ICE CREAM 🌿

Although the French are not famous for their ice cream, they have produced one of the best cookies to accompany it that I've ever tasted. It's a light, uncluttered cookie curved in the shape of the traditional French roof tiles for which it is named. (The French thriftily use up all those egg whites left over from ice-cream making.) The cookies can also be molded over the bottom of a custard cup to make a charming container for a scoop of ice cream. These are sometimes called ice cream "tulips" though they actually curve outward more like a lily.

Makes 10 "tiles" or cups

1/4 pound butter, room
   temperature (1 stick)
1/2 cup sugar

5 egg whites, room temperature
1 teaspoon vanilla extract
1 cup all-purpose flour

Cream the butter and 5 tablespoons sugar until light, fluffy, and completely mixed. Beat in 3 egg whites and the vanilla, then add the flour, sprinkling it fairly evenly over the ingredients in the bowl. Mix just until the flour disappears.

Preheat the oven to 375°F. (350°F. convection). Put 4 dabs of shortening on a cookie sheet and use them to hold a sheet of parchment paper in place.

Beat the remaining 2 egg whites to a firm but not dry meringue. Beat in the sugar. Fold a third of this into the cookie mixture, then fold the cookie mixture back into the remaining beaten egg whites. Stop mixing as soon as it is amalgamated. Spread about ¼ cup batter as thinly as possible into a circle about 6 inches in diameter. Use a narrow cake-icing spatula to do this and keep it parallel with the table top in smoothing out the cookie mixture. You should be able to get 4 cookies to a large cookie sheet. As soon as the cookies are baked they must be formed into "tiles" or cups, otherwise they will harden, become brittle, and break when you try to form them. So, if you are not especially adept at baking, limit yourself to baking only two "tiles" at a time. As with any cookie baking enterprise, you will need 2 cookie sheets to keep alternating in the oven.

Bake the tiles just until the edges start to brown lightly—about 8 minutes. If overdone, they will be impossible to mold quickly enough. Lift a cookie off the sheet using a spatula and quickly drape it around an old-fashioned glass, or any other that is about 3 inches in diameter. To make cups, place the hot cookie over the bottom of a custard cup set upside-down on the counter and, using a tea-towel to protect your hands from the heat, press gently down with your fingers to form 4 flanges. Remove and stand the cookie cups on their rims to harden and dry crisply. If making "tiles," wait until they are cold to stack them. I find they store well in a cracker crisper or a cannister equipped with a dehumidifier knob. Ideally, they should be used the day they're made, but since few of us have time to devote to cookie making on the day of a dinner party, it's good to know that these cookies hold splendidly fresh and crisp for 24 to 36 hours. Unless the weather's humid—in which case don't try to make them.

INDEX

pastry *(cont'd)*
    Italian-style, for tarts, 222–23
    short, for sweet and savory fillings, 224–25
pâté:
    de foie, instant, 34
    simple country, 29–31
    smoked eel, 40
pea(s):
    braised, à la française, 208
    soup, spring, 59–60
peach(es):
    and cream, baked, 244
    Georgia, ice cream with white chocolate
        sauce, 259
    and greengage tart, 244–45
    sherbet with peach puree and bourbon,
        260–61
    shortcake, 243
pearl balls, 28–29
peppercorn, green, steaks, 152–53
peppers, bell:
    roasted, 205–6
    rouille, 16–17
perfect cooked rice, 186–87
perfect fried chicken, 163
Persian rice, 188–89
pesto, salsa al, 174
Philadelphia vanilla ice cream, 253–54
picadillo with rice and beans, 190
pie(s):
    buttermilk, 234
    chocolate bavarian mousse or, 246–47
    crust, good quick, 221–22
    fried half-moon, 232
pilaf, 189
pineapple, grilled fresh, 147–48
pink pappardelle with dried tomatoes,
    171–72
pistachio ice cream/raspberry puree with
    Framboise, 257–58
Pistou, 57
pizza, bialy, 36–37
pizzaiola sauce, 178
plain green salad, 64
poached:
    fish fillets, 106
    fresh salmon, 106–7
    whole fish, 105
pork:
    fillet, charcoal-grilled, 145
    kebabs, grilled, 145
    pearl balls, 28–29
    thirty-minute fillet of, 144–45
    see also ham(s)
potatoes:
    baked bass with, 114–15
    new (parslied gleaners), 211

potato salad:
    Dixie-style, 88
    easy French, 87
    French, 86–87
poultry:
    boned chicken breasts with mushrooms
        and cream sauce, 165–66
    chicken and rice with mushrooms,
        185–86
    chicken breasts, 164–65
    chicken salad Caribe, 98
    chicken salad chez ma tante, 98–99
    chicken salad vindaloo, 98
    iced chicken soup, 58
    jambalaya, 191–192
    perfect fried chicken, 163
    rice salad, 67–69
    Saigon chicken wings, 136–37
    smoky herbed chicken, 146–47
    Sunday lunch chicken salad, 96–98
    tongue and chicken salad, 85
prosciutto, melon or avocado with, 42
pudding, cheese, 236–37
purist burger, 155

quiche, beautiful broccoli, 214
quick no-cook sauce, 170

raspberry(ies):
    cantaloupe ice cream with, 256
    puree/pistachio ice cream with
        Framboise, 257–58
ratatouille, revisionist, 206–7
raw:
    shellfish, 11–12
    vegetable platter *(les crudités),* 13–15
red rice and beans, 194
red snapper Isle des Saintes, 110–11
rémoulade sauce, 82
    moules, 24
revisionist ratatouille, 206–7
rice:
    and chicken with mushrooms,
        185–86
    green chelo, 189
    paella, 182–84
    pearl balls, 28–29
    perfect cooked, 186–87
    Persian, 188–89
    picadillo with beans and, 190
    pilaf, 189
    red, and beans, 194
    salad, 67–69
    shrimp perloo, 118–20
roasted bell peppers, 205–6
romaine, 66
rouille, 16–17

ABOUT THE AUTHOR

MIRIAM UNGERER began her professional career as a journalist and for a time was a fashion editor and writer before deciding that food was an endlessly absorbing subject. She has lived and cooked in Texas, Tennessee, Montana, California, Florida, Pennsylvania and her native South Carolina before investigating the cuisines of France, Germany, Italy, Switzerland, Spain, England, Ireland and Canada. Miriam Ungerer, who's really a South Carolina Lancaster, also has another name: Mrs. Wilfred Sheed. She and her husband live "surrounded by predatory deer" in the woods near the old whaling village of Sag Harbor, on the eastern tip of Long Island.